EXPERIENTIAL MANAGEMENT DEVELOPMENT

EXPERIENTIAL MANAGEMENT DEVELOPMENT

From Learning to Practice

Solomon Hoberman
and
Sidney Mailick

QUORUM BOOKS
New York • Westport, Connecticut • London

Library of Congress Cataloging-in-Publication Data

Hoberman, Solomon.
Experiential management development : from learning to practice / Solomon Hoberman and Sidney Mailick.
p. cm.
Includes bibliographical references and index.
ISBN 0–89930–751–5 (alk. paper)
1. Executives—Training of. I. Mailick, Sidney, 1923–
HD30.4.H62 1992
658.4'07124—dc20 91–24030

British Library Cataloguing in Publication Data is available.

Library of Congress Catalog Card Number: 91–24030
ISBN: 0–89930–751–5

First published in 1992

Quorum Books, One Madison Avenue, New York, NY 10010
An imprint of Greenwood Publishing Group, Inc.

Printed in the United States of America

The paper used in this book complies with the Permanent Paper Standard issued by the National Information Standards Organization (Z39.48–1984).

10 9 8 7 6 5 4 3 2 1

CONTENTS

PREFACE

This book had its origin in discussions we held to review our management development activities over more than twenty-five years. We started with what we have learned and what others have written about management development. We ended by modifying existing learning theory to explain the cause/effect relationships that we identified.

We became more aware in the course of our work that managers behave differently in different venues. Performance in an educational setting does not necessarily result in similar performance in the workplace. In our attempts to make management development more productive, we shifted in the course of time from earlier dependence on passive and synthetic experiential learning to increased emphasis on natural experiential learning. We were led to this differentiation in types of experiential learning and the shift in emphasis by both a closer reading of theory and our own experiences.

No work of theory is unique. The theory in this volume is derived from the labors of many of the giants of learning theory. Their published writings provided our theoretical underpinning, although we diverge from many of their conclusions and models. We are particularly indebted to the seminal work of John Dewey, Kurt Lewin, and Jean Piaget. Other learning theorists who influenced our concepts and models include Albert Bandura, Jerome Bruner, Malcolm Knowles, and David Kolb. Much of our management theory is influenced by the work of Herbert Simon, Warren Bennis, Michel Crozier, Daniel Katz and Robert Kahn, Charles Perrow, and James Thompson.

We put considerable emphasis, in both learning theory and management theory, on the importance of recognizing differences in the way managers learn and transfer learning to their work activities and the roles they play at work. However, no useful theory can be derived from an assumption of uniqueness. While we insist that each manager's unique characteristics and situation must be taken into account to maximize learning and the transfer of learning, we account for this within the framework of a tentative general theory. We have written this volume to introduce this theory, to compare it with other theories, and to indicate how it plays out in practice.

Our focus is on the transfer of learning to the workplace. Children's learning is measured at the educational site. In a real sense their learning and use sites are congruent. The learning and work sites in management development usually are not. This difference and the richer life learning of adults account in large part for the need for different learning approaches.

While we hope that we have simplified and made a contribution to learning theory, our focus is on the practice of management development. In this regard we discuss a number of innovative programs and note how they fit our theoretical model. Two chapters deal with the history of management theory and management development. We make no claim that these are complete in any way or are unbiased samples of the literature. In addition there is a chapter devoted to research in management development. This chapter builds on the outstanding review of the literature by Campbell, Dunnette, Lawler, and Weick (1970).

Throughout the volume we have included examples of management development programs to indicate how practice can be better understood in the light of this theory.

We have attempted to present our theory and practice in a way that will be of use to designers and implementers of management development programs as well as to the managers and the organizations which sponsor and participate in these programs and to students of business and public administration. Consequently we have tried to stay away from the complexities and technical jargon of formal learning theorists and mathematically inspired models while not falling into the oversimplification trap for the sake of popularization.

We point out some of the shortcomings of management development, particularly as it is practiced by institutions of higher learning. We indicate that the structure and staffing which work well for teaching a single discipline, such as chemistry or sociology, may not be adequate for an encompassing field such as management development. Institutions of higher learning are not usually organized or staffed to use natural experiential learning, the approach we think is essential for the transfer of learning to the workplace.

A number of people have helped by reading and commenting on drafts of the chapters, preparing the index, proofreading the copy, and checking the references and the bibliography. Chief among these was Sara Grant, whose review and incisive comments on all twelve chapters were extremely useful and led to improvements in both content and style. Lawrence Plotkin's comments on several chapters were very helpful. Emalyn Bravo's work on the index was most valuable, as was Mahmoud Gaballa's validation of the references and the bibliography. We are indebted to James Dunton for his confidence in us, his patience, and his good advice.

We are grateful for this help and express our thanks. However, we alone are responsible for all the statements, analyses, conclusions, and recommendations.

1

INTRODUCTION

This is a book about learning theory and how this theory can be applied in management development programs to help individuals and organizations improve managerial competencies. It is not the traditional "how to" manual or an abstract text on learning theory. It is a combination of both. Our objective is to give interested persons greater understanding and insight into the possibilities of management development in general and experiential learning approaches in particular.

There are about 2.5 million executives and senior managers in the United States. Their performance has great consequences for the fortunes of their organizations. Their activities, more than the activities of any other group, are characterized by riskier and more significant decision making, and by more crucial boundary spanning. They have great influence on the behavior of all who work in their organizations.

The importance of competent management, even in this technological age, is demonstrated by findings that firms with equal technological capacities can have widely different production curves.

Approaches to improving organizational functioning include revising the organizational structure, changing the composition of the work force, introducing new production techniques, varying the product mix, reducing dependency on the environment by horizontal and vertical integration and merging with other organizations, incentive programs, hiring managers with proven special competencies, and seeking to improve the competence of the managers. Each of these approaches is of value. However, we restrict our analysis to improving management development.

Managers tend, more than other workers, to be interested in improving their performance. Many of their activities for improvement are self-directed. This is as it must be, for in an important sense, all management development must be self-directed. Even if the organization chooses the specific objectives and the programs, the managers' motivation and effort are the keys.

Many approaches are employed to improve the competence of managers. These include recruiting managers who have demonstrated competence, providing incentives for outstanding performance, assigning managers so as to make best use of their capabilities, restructuring managerial roles, and increasing the competence of individual managers through training and education. This latter activity, management development, includes rotating assignments, evaluating performance and providing feedback, contract performance (e.g., management by objectives), on-the-job training, mentoring, and formal training and education in management roles and tasks. Recruitment and incentives, two sides of the same coin, tend to be more costly and more common than management development.

Most companies utilize more than one approach. While not dominant, management development is rarely ignored. The 1989 study of the Society for Human Resource Management found that almost all (96 percent) large firms (5,000 + employees) claim they have management programs. Even a majority (57 percent) of small firms (fewer than 100 employees) support such programs. Although involving only about 0.75 percent of the total employee population, executive training accounts for 12 percent of the total training budget in *Fortune* 500 companies. Middle managers' training is even more common; it represents almost 25 percent of the human resource development budgets for these companies (ASTD 1989).

It is not sufficient to teach managers the principles of good management. Many are proverbs rather than principles (Simon 1947). Those which are not are so very general that they verge on clichés. They do not provide significant guidance for managerial behavior in any specific situation in any real venue. Managers have a great need for the ability to size up a situation, identify the problems and opportunities, determine what should be done, obtain staff support to take the best action indicated, and exercise appropriate controls.

MANAGEMENT DEVELOPMENT

Management development is an organized effort to develop, increase, and improve managerial competencies, either in an individual manager or in a group of managers. Sometimes the objective is to motivate and to help managers conform to proposed new organizational policies. In some cases there are conflicting objectives. Whatever the objectives, management development is a costly, major activity of virtually all American companies.

Management development is not the same as training technical professionals, skilled craft workers, or sales personnel. It does not have a narrow range of competencies and outcomes on which to focus. Professionals in the sciences learn and practice in much the same way in every country. Mathematicians, physicists, and chemists follow similar courses of study with similar content and learning approaches. In management, the learning approach and the learning venue tend to have greater impact on the transfer of learning to the work venue.

The most common delivery method for executives is the seminar. The results are rarely judged on the basis of change in performance but, rather, of the "happiness" of the participants. As managers move up, mentoring, job rotation, and outside seminars tend to replace formal in-house training (Carnevale 1988).

Recent creativity in management development seems to be only repackaging. Some programs consist of exhortations: "be thoughtful, focused and usually understated," "flaunt power," "leverage your opportunities," "work with people who can and will work with you." Whether or not these were once useful guides, they are now of little value. Some programs seek to help managers to tolerate and to function in ambiguous, risky environments and situations.

Obviously it is not easy to achieve significant, lasting changes in a manager's behavior. Routine solutions and habit responses to situations are constants. Relationships with others are maintained in stable equilibrium by many strong forces. Few of these forces are directly influenced by management development. Some of the forces are embedded in the work venue. Some stem from past successes and failures, tolerance for risk and responsibility, and learning style. Some relate to venues away from work.

Programs designed to develop and improve the competencies of public-sector managers seem even less successful than those for managers in the private sector. Chapman and Cleaveland (1973) claim that education for the public service does not satisfy the needs of practitioners. The schools of public administration met this challenge not by making programs more pertinent to practicing administrators but by increasing research activities and the percentage of full-time, Ph.D. faculty members.

Concern with the development of managers was also expressed by schools of business administration. The central topic at the 1983 American Assembly of Collegiate Schools of Business Conference held at Wingspread, Wisconsin, was "lifelong learning for management." A major issue was "how to improve cooperation and interaction between the schools and the business community." This led to a study that made suggestions (Porter and McKibbin 1988). Dissatisfaction with academic programs has led to a trend toward an increased tailoring of the content of management training to meet specific needs of the culture of the system and the nature of its environment (Carnevale 1988).

There are many situations in which management development can do little to improve managers' performance. Although some seem to be endemic to government, they are not unknown in the private sector. These situations result from adopting narrow, short-term organizational objectives and criteria for measuring accomplishments and downplaying the long-term health of the organization. Akio Morita, chairman of the Sony Corporation, noted (*New York Times*, June 6, 1987):

> The big attraction in American business today is the money game, in which profits are made not by manufacturing or selling goods but by guessing whether the dollar will rise or fall. . . . how can you expect your people will be motivated to work when they are traded like merchandise.

More important than this cause is the almost total emphasis on the annual bottom line in the private sector and on reelection in the public sector. Other causes relate to instability in top management and the importation of managers at higher levels for political or short-term reasons (Hoberman 1990).

WHAT THIS BOOK HAS TO OFFER

Many observers believe that management development is not as productive as it should be. In fact, there is a feeling among some that much of management development may be counterproductive for both the individuals participating and their organizations. We believe that our analysis and recommendations point out directions which can lead to more productive management development.

The feeling that there is a need to improve management development, and training in general, is evidenced by the quantity of research in training and development and in the related fields of organization development and career development. A study by Toppins (1989) of research relating to human resource programs showed that 32.2 percent were in training and development, 14.9 percent in organization development, and 11.5 percent in career development. Thus well over 50 percent were concerned with training and education of some kind.

While the proximate objective of management development must be to change the work behavior of managers, the long-term objective must be to motivate and help managers to learn from their experiences in a continuous independent learning process. This book deals with the theory and practice of learning approaches to achieve both objectives.

It is extraordinarily difficult to change human behavior without changing the operative venue. Managers can sit through months of programs directed at changing them in some significant way; enthusiastically agree with the lecturers and discussion leaders; complete exercises using the new knowledge, techniques, and behaviors; and return to their organizations to behave as they did the day they left. At best there may be application of new techniques. We discuss development approaches that are built upon an understanding of the problem, the forces that keep managerial behavior in a stable, dynamic equilibrium and force managers to resist changing their behavior, and the inertia that militates against continued learning.

While it is absurd to assume that a perfect model of management behavior will ever be available, it is reasonable to assume that we can identify and adapt models to fit a given organization under given conditions. Without this assumption, management development would have no content. However, there is no ideal, invariant set of managerial behaviors that can be used as the content of programs to improve management even in well-defined, specific situations. We are not concerned with changing managers' basic thought processes, personalities, and value systems. Our focus is directed toward increasing managerial competence in a specific venue and motivation for lifelong learning.

Since process without content is meaningless, "What should be taught?" is an important question. Our view, which we will elaborate in chapters that follow, is "It depends." This stems, in part, from the belief that in management, as in all practical fields, there is both danger and value in learning and applying theory to everyday life. Thought not anchored to real life produces a jumble of theories, concepts, and models of unknown validity. To adapt Wittgenstein's aphorism, "Don't ask for the meaning of management theory, ask for the use." The greatest danger is when one model is proclaimed "the best" under all circumstances. If a manager is operationally sold on one model (e.g., economic and rational man), he or she tends to explain everything on the basis of it. Managers who are true believers and try to behave according to the true models tend to be rigid and show little real innovation. Some theorists assume that virtually any aspect of management can be learned and used by anyone. For example, Bennis (1989a) states that most people are capable of becoming leaders if they undertake self-discovery and self-understanding. He advances as evidence in support of this hypothesis advice from persons he identifies as leaders. We do not have such high hopes. We believe that acquiring and using competencies is much more situational.

THE MATTER OF LEARNING THEORY

Every practice is based on theory. Nowhere is there more theory than in the learning enterprise. None of the theory is systematically applied in management development. The confusion in the field and the tendency to use theory to support technology, rather than to derive technology from theory, are illustrated by This and Lippert (1979). After describing a number of different schools of theory and listing many learning rules, they conclude that no one learning theory is comprehensive and adequate for all situations (1979). They suggest that practitioners use the theory most applicable for the desired outcome. There is a mainstream hypothesis: that experiential learning is more effective than other approaches for increasing will and competence to learn and use learning.

There are theories positing that changes in learning styles and development are functions of age. Some see these in terms of changes in life outlook, in psychological and philosophical stages, or in sociocultural patterns and values. We see no need to make any of these assumptions. We believe that competencies derive from experience and learning which are integrated in the manager's life-bank. We do not go further than this. We do not relate learning to life stages (e.g., Jung's three stages of life or Erikson's eight stages).

Our major learning concept is the "life-bank." A person's life-bank is the totality of values, assumptions, competencies, habits, and expectations with which the person is born and to which additions are made during a lifetime through learning. This concept is further defined in the text. We assume the following:

- that the conditions under which learning takes place determine how effectively it will be added to the life-bank and used in a specific venue
- that the content of the life-bank is a major factor in determining the ease of learning specific new material
- that experiential learning is more easily integrated as an active element in the life-bank than other learning
- that use of life-bank elements tends to be venue-specific.

It is obvious that the content of a person's life-bank may be a function of age, that the elements in a person's life-bank may be organized according to venue, and that the elements active and used in one venue (purely social gatherings, for example) are not necessarily the same as those in another (for instance, the workplace).

It is not sufficient to know alternatives, to have the will and competence to make decisions, and to work effectively with others in the work venue. It is necessary to have been confronted with the real situation, to have been forced to make choices, to think through the consequences, to make the decision, and to deal with the consequences. This is different from reading and talking about theory or about someone else's experiences. Support for this view comes from the groves of academe (Mintzberg 1990).

We accept that there are different learning styles which have to be taken into consideration. Based on research by Witkin and Goodenough, there is reason to assume a relationship between the culture and the learning styles of people in the culture (Guild and Garger 1985). Kolb (1984) presents some theory and evidence relating learning styles and occupation. It is not clear how these different styles should be factored into a development program. Some theorists advocate adjusting teaching styles to learning styles. Others encourage planned mismatches to help people to stretch themselves (Guild and Garger 1985). The possibility of taking this into account will be discussed.

CHAPTER SUMMARIES

Chapter 2 deals with the perceived importance of management development. It discusses why people and organizations invest and participate in management development, how they invest, what they get for their investment, and the organizations that provide management development services.

Chapter 3 is a brief review of the history and practice of management development.

Chapter 4 discusses the role and tasks of managers.

Chapter 5 presents views of some learning theorists. Our major theoretical innovation, the life-bank, is introduced. There is a brief discussion of the relationship between learning theory and training.

Chapter 6 is a fuller discussion of the role, objectives, and techniques of management development and the problems in implementing change in the work venue.

Chapter 7 is a review of research relating to management development.

Chapter 8 considers the relationships between the learning and work venues as variables affecting learning and its use.

Chapter 9 is the first of three chapters on experiential learning. It includes descriptions and comparisons of synthetic and natural experiential learning.

Chapter 10 is a more detailed description and analysis of natural experiential learning approaches and practices.

Chapter 11 is an extended case study of one design emphasizing natural experiential learning. This is Learning Inducted From Experience (LIFE), a design developed and used by the authors.

Chapter 12 is the summing up of management development issues and opportunities.

CONCEPTS AND DEFINITIONS

Without generally understood concepts, definitions, and models for reference and communication, what happens provides no guide for future thought or action. It need not be assumed that these models and theories are true. What matters is usefulness. Models are useless without concrete representations from experience. It is important for practitioners to remember that no definition is unambiguous, that the usefulness of models and theories is contingent on a host of assumptions, and that language shapes ideas as much as ideas shape language.

We try to clarify what we mean by specific words. In the course of our discussion we refer to concepts and models from the literature that may be unfamiliar, and introduce a number of new concepts and models. The concepts may require special words. We apologize for using special concepts and definitions, but they can simplify explanation and help understanding of our point of view. We try to define them to reduce ambiguity. Some relate to concepts and definitions used by other writers. Sometimes, for reasons that become obvious in the text, our use is not always identical with the uses of others. For the most part, we define the concepts and terms in the context of the discussion.

It is neither possible nor desirable to give every specific model or concept a distinctive name. It seems to us better to use existing words that relate to and describe the new concepts rather than to create new words. Thus you will find a number of new ideas in, we hope, well-fitting old terms. Among these are "life-bank," "venue," "synthetic experiential learning," and "natural experiential learning."

We will not discuss the truth or falsity of any of the concepts or models. These models and concepts are presented as useful tools for analyzing processes and relating different concepts and activities. We do not need to be involved in a theoretical discussion of whether the human brain is programmed in any manner or to any degree, or in biologically grounded models of archetypes. We simply note that, without linking concepts and models, life consists of a set of unique events about which not much can be said. Consequently, some sort of theory or model is needed if we want to talk meaningfully about cause and effect and other relationships among events.

Since it is not always convenient to define each concept and term in the text, and since some terms are mentioned before they are fully discussed, we have prepared a short glossary to reduce misunderstanding. The glossary is placed after Chapter 12.

2

INVESTMENT IN MANAGEMENT DEVELOPMENT

Below the 2.5 million executives and senior managers, there are 5 million managers (American Society for Training and Development 1989). It is this pool of about 7.5 million people who are the participants in management development programs. About 75 percent receive some preentry or qualifying training. About half receive some upgrading or maintenance training during the course of their employment.

According to Carnevale (1988), it is expected that in the future there will be

—more management and more managers.

—nonmanagement jobs increasingly calling for managerial skills.

—more managers because the number of front-line production and service delivery workers will decline relative to the number of managers.

—increased numbers of institutions and thus more managers.

—smaller institutions, the larger the proportion of managers to the rest of the employees. (Carnevale, 1988, p. 21)

As opposed to Carnevale's prediction, there is some indication that larger companies are decreasing the number of management layers in their hierarchies. For example, General Electric "pared 20 or 29 layers from the company hierarchy, from level 1, that of a mailroom supervisor, to level 29, chairman and chief executive" (*New York Times*, February 27, 1990). There is some indication that workers who are not identified as managers will require management skills. In many cases professionals and other workers are performing, and will increasingly perform, some managerial tasks. The increase in the number of those who will assume managerial tasks strongly indicates an increased dependence on management development.

Management development is a costly, risky investment. Although some individuals and organizations invest in management development with total confidence that it will be a good investment, many are aware of the need for estimating costs and benefits and comparing with alternatives. Important considerations in plans to improve management development include: Who invests in management development? Why is there motivation to participate? What is expected? What are investors willing to accept as profitable returns?

In smaller organizations, the chief executive officer is frequently the person responsible for management development. In the large, multinational organizations, the responsible person is most often a senior vice president for human resources or an equivalent high-level executive.

WHO INVESTS IN MANAGEMENT DEVELOPMENT?

Today, in contrast with five or six decades ago, there is little overt opposition in any large organization, private, nonprofit, or public, in industrialized or developing countries, to the general belief that management development is a vital necessity. There is little overt resistance, and there is occasional enthusiasm, among managers for participating in these programs. This is a startling contrast with the situation prior to World War II, when only the military made a significant investment in management development.

While management development is not of the highest priority, it is seen as very desirable by senior management in most companies. Porter and McKibbin (1988), referring to the 1959 Pierson report on the education of American businessmen, note that only 3 percent of companies surveyed in 1930, and only 5 percent in 1946, reported that they had executive training programs. However, by the end of the 1950s one survey indicated that almost 80 percent of companies claimed to engage in management development activities. Lusterman (1977) found that 74 percent of all companies authorized employees, primarily managers and professionals, to take outside courses during working hours.

Persons who participate in management development programs range from students who have never worked, let alone managed anything, to chief executive officers of large multinational companies. Management development is of interest in the public sector as well as in the private sector. Political officials decry the absence of well-trained, competent civil service managers. However, management development programs tend to be forced on political officials rather than originated by them. Reasons for this include unwillingness to make an investment whose benefits are not immediate; possible reduced opportunities for patronage; and concern about the loyalty of the managers. The situation in state and local governments is considerably worse than in the federal government. The Intergovernmental Personnel and Training Act, the only federal effort to improve management at the state and local levels, barely survived one administration.

WHY DO THEY INVEST?

Company executives interviewed by Porter and McKibbin (1988) regarded management development activities as unimportant. The reasons given for this belief included the following:

- glue holding the company together
- important for management to develop their people
- cannot rely on assignments only
- there are fewer differences between managers and managed
- functioning in a more competitive environment
- a need for a more systematic development of managers
- succession
- changed marketplace
- competence to function in new kinds of organizational structures

Some managers expect that management development will help to reduce the uncertainties or alleviate the stresses of the management job. The reason given most often is the over general "to improve competence as a manager." This is also the reason given by companies. It is rarely clear what is meant by this. The purpose of "improved management" is to increase the individual's and the organization's abilities to achieve their objectives, whether it is to make money or to provide better services for less money.

Many emphasize "human relations" to achieve the objectives. However, is there a basic conflict between the means and the objectives? From the hard-nosed management point of view, it is not good business for the "economic man" to offer employees one cent more than is needed to get them to produce at the desired rate. Workers, by the same token, should not do anything more than their employers can force them to do for given working conditions at a given rate of pay. Management skills in this model are demonstrated by being superior to the workers in the conflict. Union official's comments on the human relations model indicate that they see both sides using the "economic" model.

Senior management may have other motives for investing in management development. They include resolving problems relating to political, personality, and structural issues; improving relationships with other organizations; indicating an interest in improved management to people both in the organization and outside; rewarding managers with a sort of paid vacation; and keeping managers sensitive and responsive to change and interested in current thinking and practices. The investment may be seen as worthwhile even if there are no discernible changes in managers' day-to-day behavior.

Some management development is coordinated with succession planning and selecting, motivating, and evaluating managerial performance. Career development is believed to motivate higher levels of performance without any content gain by increasing managers' job satisfaction and identification with the organization. Sometimes it is a prerequisite for movement to more desirable jobs. In the absence of a single well-defined objective, it is not clear how a program should be designed or assessed.

Most agree that programs should be based on an assessment of needs. The evidence from the Porter and McKibbin study (1988) indicates that in 27 percent of the companies surveyed there is no needs assessment, and in an equal percentage the needs are determined without input from the managers who are expected to participate. In only 20 percent of the companies is the determination made by "all levels of line management" without guidance from the human resources staff. Further, not only are the different approaches used in needs analysis of unequal reliability and validity, but they require different competencies in design, implementation, and interpretation. There is little indication in management development literature to determine how valid assessments are made. The techniques described include questionnaire survey, interviews with various levels of management, review of performance appraisals, focus groups, and analysis of the company's performance and future plans.

Programs assume that people act as they do because of anticipated consequences. This assumption received strong support from Skinner's (1971) theory of behaviorism coupled with expectancy theory. It is sufficiently inclusive to provide a basis for advocates for directing motivation to either intrinsic or extrinsic values. However, for extrinsic rewards, there are more direct motivators than management development.

CONTENT OF MANAGEMENT DEVELOPMENT

The history of management in both the public and the private sectors is replete with disputes over the role, goals, tasks, and criteria for evaluating managers' performance. Obviously, unless there is agreement on these, someone will be disappointed.

We discuss the knowledge and skills managers need in Chapter 4, "The Role of the Manager and Management Development." For the moment, we note that there are some differences in the technical curricula that depend on managerial level. Senior managers are more apt to attend workshops in strategic planning; new managers, in employee selection, decision making, and team building (ASTD 1989). For new managers, the objectives are to wean professionals and technical specialists away from their specialties, and to qualify them to supervise and motivate others.

From the academic point of view, Porter and McKibbin (1988) identify five levels of management. After recommending virtually the same technical competencies and interpersonal skills for the first four levels, they jump to the executive level, where they identify the need for acquiring competencies required to scan, assess, and deal with the system's environment as these impact on strategic planning.

The one behavior that seems to be of greatest concern to organizations is "leadership." This is followed by "communication" and "ability to motivate subordinates." Leadership is also the competency desired by managers. In addition, practicing managers want answers to the problems they are facing at the moment. Would-be managers want whatever they are told to help them as managers.

Senior managers see the lower levels of managers as all having substantially the same content needs. They distinguish between the needs of these managers and their own. For example, they tend to reserve "strategic planning" to themselves. At the same time they say that the middle- and lower-level managers need a greater breadth of perspective, a need that the latter do not seem to feel (Porter and McKibbin, 1988). This finding is supported by three research reports in *Training and Development Journal* (January 1985). As a general observation, higher-level managers claim the lower-level managers "need" general learning for which there is no immediate, specific, identifiable use. The lower-level managers request very specific technical learning.

New content areas are always being added. A recent addition is "vision." It was popularized by case studies about leaders who have "vision" in books like Peters's *Thriving on Chaos* (1987) and Doig and Hargrove's *Leadership and Innovation* (1987). As is common with new content, "vision" and its use are not well defined. Some definitions are "the very essence of leadership," " presentation of an alternative future to the status quo," "the ability of leaders always to look at the 'big picture' and not be consumed by details," and the direct reverse, "a leader must be engaged in details, not simply broad strokes." Such differences are not unusual in the definition of new management roles.

While the focus of this volume is not on the content, the content is the reason that people and organizations invest in management development, and the process of development is not independent of the content. We consider the content in Chapter 4, "The Role of the Manager and Management Development," and in Chapter 6, "Learning Theory and Management Development."

MANAGEMENT DEVELOPMENT IS NOT THE ONLY WAY

A major question is "How does management development compare with other approaches for improving managerial performance?" It must be recognized that management development is not always the most efficient and effective means for satisfying perceived needs (Hoberman 1990). Two well-used approaches are to motivate and to recruit better performers. Some others are organizational restructuring of power relationships and managerial roles and tasks; and determining and providing information about selection and promotion criteria and processes, as well as standards and processes for evaluating managerial performance. (For example, changing structure—the definition and distribution of managerial tasks—to fit the proven competencies of managers may be more effective than training managers to fill existing jobs.) There is no hard, decisive evidence in favor of any one approach. Many organizations prefer to purchase rather than to develop managers. Financial benefits are the most common incentives for motivating improved performance and keeping another organization from buying a manager's services. More money may keep a manager "bought," but unless one assumes that a manager's putting in longer hours provides better management, there is no evidence that financial incentives play any role in the quality of managerial performance.

The use of rewards for reinforcement has been the dominant management development approach for a long time. While supported by Skinner's (1948) analysis, it has been strongly attacked by theorists such as Argyris (1962). The arguments include the following:

- The reinforcement approach leads to conditioned responses and not to learning and development.
- Actions that superiors consider to be reinforcements may not be so considered by the subordinates.
- There is no distinction between learning and performance.
- Unless the reinforcement is provided at the appropriate time, usually immediately after the approved performance, the practice may be counterproductive

because the subordinate is distressed at not receiving the reward when it is expected.

- It tends to hinder self-actualization.

Financial rewards are used for reasons other than to improve or recognize performance. They may be incentives to obtain and maintain loyalty to the company and superiors (Hoberman 1990). Reward for personal loyalty is endemic in government. Salaries and promotions in government often are related to campaign performance. Rewards for behavior other than performance tend to decrease all managers' interest in improving their performance and in participating in management development.

Titles are sometimes used to satisfy managers' egos. "Executive" is replacing "manager." As the incremental amount of money paid to a manager becomes less important, the sound of the title becomes of increasing value. New modifiers are introduced. There are now senior, supervising, executive, and senior executive managers and vice presidents. Fanning (1990) reports that at one company a visitor who asked for the chairman was asked, "Which one?" We shall ignore the escalating terminology and use the noun "manager" to denote all persons above the level of supervisor.

There are times when management development is used like patent medicine for whatever ails an organization. Recognition that a desired change cannot be accomplished by management development does not stop executives from seeking to use the approach. In a needs analysis conducted by one of the authors, it became apparent that the most important measure of managerial competence was the manager's ability to anticipate and answer "difficult questions" that members of the board asked about proposals presented by the manager's division. In the circumstance, it was not possible to convince managers to spend more time on "managing," much less on improving their managing. They all wanted to be better professionals and expend their time on professional activities. The organization ignored the report and made a considerable investment in management development—to no avail. This was less painful for all concerned than dealing with the power structure.

Despite all the care in selecting, preparing, and motivating senior management, there is a high degree of failure. It is estimated that between one-third and one-half of persons selected for senior management fail in these positions (Sorcher 1985).

HOW IS THE INVESTMENT MADE?

There are four major sources for management development. Internally developed and conducted programs are the most often employed, in larger organizations, for programs directed at lower- and middle-level managers. In these the training staff is usually responsible for the needs analysis, program design, administration, some instruction, training aids, feedback, and support for line managers serving as teaching faculty.

The second source is university schools of business and public administration. University degree and nondegree programs and faculty members, sometimes hired as consultants, are major outside suppliers. Any analysis and assessment of the return from management development must consider the nature of the products the academy provides.

The large group of associations, general consulting companies, and small specialized training organizations constitute the third source for management development.

The fourth source is the literature. Articles in management-oriented periodicals and books provide models and instructions for effective management and are the most common source of learning for individuals seeking to improve their management competencies. Some books claim to reduce, and sometimes even to eliminate, the need for experience in order to gain managerial competence. While the books may be of some value to experienced managers, there is no evidence that they live up to their promises to persons without any experience.

Training for entry into the managerial ranks tends to be either university-based or informal and on the job. Training for upgrading is equally divided among university programs, formal employer programs, and informal, on-the-job instruction. Executive-level development is most often provided by outside sources, such as universities.

WHAT IS THE RETURN FROM THE INVESTMENT?

There is more concern among human resource professionals than among those who invest in management development to demonstrate the value of management development. In a study of ten years of articles in the *Journal of Training and Development* (Hoberman 1984), two major categories were identified. The first was a concern with the transfer of learning to the work venue. The articles either described techniques to help participants transfer learning or asserted that management development was not effective in helping participants to transfer learning. The second major category was evaluation and cost effectiveness. Articles were of three types: theories and methodologies for evaluating training and development; demonstrations that a specific development program was a profitable activity; and criticisms of current evaluation efforts. In the Porter and McKibbin study (1988) senior management in the private sector did not demonstrate such an overwhelming concern with evaluation.

Nevertheless, it is generally agreed that the payoff should be improved performance. This would involve incorporation of the learning into the manager's life-bank in a form that is transferable to the work venue. For senior management the need goes beyond this. It is improved performance by the organization as a whole. Unfortunately, measuring these outcomes and relating them to management development is beyond the capacity of the trainers and of management as well. The trainers can rarely measure more than participants' satisfaction and knowledge gained. Managers juggle so many variables that it is never clear what led to what. Consequently, at this moment in time, investors must be satisfied with less-than-reliable-and-valid data demonstrating that management development is a profitable investment.

3

THE STATE OF MANAGEMENT DEVELOPMENT

BACKGROUND

It can be assumed that from the time organized, stable relationships went beyond the nuclear family to a more complex society, there have been managers or leaders. With the advent of leaders came concern for their competence. This inevitably led to activities to improve selection and development of leaders.

Peter Drucker (1989) notes that Pope Gregory IX's code of canon law (issued in 1234) was the first real management text and that it has served since then to provide good management for the Roman Catholic Church. However, this was certainly preceded by instruction for the priestly class in ancient Egypt and probably in other early civilizations.

The history of modern, formal management development begins with the education of staff officers in European armies. The senior division of the Royal Military College in Britain was founded in 1799 and became the Staff College in 1858. Every major European country had a well-developed staff and command school by the early nineteenth century. These schools recognized quite early that lectures and discussion did not keep the interest of the military men and would not result in desired command behavior in battle. Consequently they introduced sophisticated field exercises, simulating battle conditions, to test and practice the application of administrative and military theory, and to improve decision making under realistic conditions.

The model of the staff colleges and the increasing complexity of governmental affairs led the French government to found the first national school of administration in 1848. It was designed to teach "principles of administration" to potential and new managers in a classroom setting. "The French emphasized practical education reinforced with 'political economy, statistics, and parliamentary eloquence.' They also encouraged the use of adjunct faculty to supplement the legal instruction with day-to-day application" (Martin 1987). It is interesting to note that while military schools were concerned with human relationships of commanders, the civilian school was not. The emphasis was entirely on technical content and the instrumental aspects of management.

American schools of business administration predate World War I and were among the earliest in the world. As in France, in the earlier periods the emphasis was on technical subjects such as accounting, legal matters, and marketing. Management education was limited almost entirely to content related to the instrumental competencies, with a little human relations thrown in under the heading of industrial psychology.

A department of business administration research and training was established within the London School of Economics in the 1930s. This department and one established about the same time at the University of Manchester were virtually the only programs of higher education for managers in Britain prior to World War II.

The need for new, skilled supervisors in the war production factories during World War II led to the establishment of the Training Within Industry advisory group that developed, publicized, and marketed training and development concepts and programs. The success of this program, with its emphasis on human relations, led to the development of company programs for middle managers in the 1950s. Most of these were isolated courses with no connections to the business and public administration programs in colleges and universities. The first program for higher management was established at Harvard in 1943.

Britain continued to lag behind in recognizing management as a profession and the need for management development until after World War II (Life 1974). Only after the war, when the need for well-trained executives was felt by the British business establishment, was Henley, a special management institution of higher learning, established. Sir Noel Hall, a former Oxford don, was the moving spirit. The primary learning group and approach at Henley was the syndicate, which had been used at the Army Staff College. The focus at Henley, at the beginning, was on preparing professionals in technical areas to become administrators (Life 1974).

Since 1960 not only developed countries but also developing countries, encouraged by organs of the United Nations, have established management development programs in their institutions of higher learning. Some maintain separate institutions for training public managers.

France has taken a leadership role in management development for public agencies. Its national school was completely redesigned and renamed the École Nationale d'Administration. The emphasis on theory, deductive analysis, and legal studies is a mark of French academic programs. The senior managers in the civil service are virtually all graduates of this school, as are many managers in the former French colonies. Many of the graduates of the school in both France and the former colonies have risen to the level of cabinet minister. Michel Rocard, a graduate, was appointed prime minister by President François Mitterrand. While the training is primarily directed toward preparing graduates for the civil service, its graduates dominate in the private sector as well. Graduates have become senior managers and the heads of France's major private companies. The École Nationale d'Administration has had greater influence on the management of both private and public organizations in France than any institution has had in other countries, except possibly the University of Tokyo in Japan.

In the beginning, the developed countries copied from each other, and the developing countries from the developed. It was some time before it was recognized that development needs, content, and methodologies are functions of local conditions. The risk in using an American technique that enforces openness, such as T-groups, in an eastern European socialist country prior to 1990 is well described by Goscinski (1974). Although there is still considerable diffusion, culture-based programs have been developed.

Since about 1940 there have been changes in the content, structure, locus, and, above all, the educational technology used in management development. The recognition that passive learning may not ensure use has led to the development of synthetic experiential learning and increased emphasis on natural experiential learning.

MEANS OTHER THAN TRAINING

Training is neither the earliest nor the most common approach used by organizations to obtain good management. Selection, placement, and incentive programs appeared earlier and are more often employed. The most efficient and effective combination of approaches in any specific situation is a function of many variables. It is worth the effort to spend a few moments on the most important of these.

Selection is based on the estimate of candidates' potential competence to perform a given set of tasks. It is based on the assumption that we can extrapolate from information about past behavior to probable future behavior in a projected set of circumstances.

Many companies prefer to "buy a product with a known track record" rather than to rely on developing their own managerial talent. Vancil (1988) found, in a study covering twenty years starting in the late 1960s, that outsiders who had been hired as candidates to become chief executives at major companies rose from roughly 8 percent to 25 percent of the total of those who ultimately got the top job. To assure continuity, companies often bring in an outsider to be the president who works closely with the chairman, who usually holds the chief executive title. After a short period the chairman retires, as expected, and the former "outsider" becomes the chairman and chief executive. It is not clear whether this is because the chief executives take care that they do not have a successor on deck or because there are no effective development programs. The historical evidence is that dictators frequently have systematically eliminated all potential competitors.

The impact on the executives and lower-level managers who are passed over is rarely discussed. Presumably the organizations involved do not fear their managers' giving less than their best or leaving for other companies. The practice of replacing organizational heads from outside the organization is, of course, usual in every public jurisdiction in the country. Public agencies are the only organizations in which managers generally expect to be passed over in favor of outsiders. The impact of this may account for the nature of management in these systems. Musical-chair management is also a reason given for poor long-term management of many American organizations.

This is not the place to discuss the reliability and validity of means for selecting managers. However, the relationship between selection and management development is of interest.

Education and training are elements in selection used as measures of candidates' preparation to perform a specific managerial role, their potential for growth, and the type of training needed to supplement selection criteria. Similar techniques are employed in development and selection. Among these are the "in basket" and experiential exercises. Assessment center activities for selection and the syndicate approach for management development are derived from a common theoretical base.

Selection does not eliminate the need for training. At best, it reduces the training needed and the time needed to prepare the manager to carry out assigned tasks, and increases the chances that the new manager will use the learning on the job.

In organizations where promotion is believed to be based on performance, there is increased motivation to participate in training that relates to performance (Bryant 1978). The converse is the case in organizations where other criteria, such as loyalty to a cause, are recognized as the primary bases for promotion (Hoberman 1990).

Many companies claim that assignment is a principal means for developing managers (Bryant et al. 1978). However, there seem to be very few formal education or training components in the planned assignments identified by Bryant and colleagues. Managers are usually given new assignments with little introduction to the relevant theory and practice. Companies seem to expect that managers challenged by the new assignment will take full responsibility for their own development.

Incentives are a third alternative to "development." This approach assumes that there is a set of motivators which can spur a manager to "do better." Disregarding the unstated assumption that managers do not perform as well as they can until provided with an incentive—usually financial—and the use of the reward to motivate the manager to stay with the organization, how useful is the incentive to motivate change and retention of a new behavior? This is a concern in management development that is discussed in some detail in a later chapter. While historically financial rewards have been the most widely used incentives for motivating performance, their usefulness has been repeatedly questioned.

In *As You Like It*, act II, scene 3, Shakespeare has Orlando say to Adam:

> O good old man, how well in thee appears
> The constant service of the antique world,
> When service sweat for duty, not for meed.
> Thou art not for the fashion of these times,
> Where none will sweat but for promotion;
> And having that, do choke their services up
> Even with the having.

There are many theories relating to both a general "motivating" function and specific motivators. Vroom's (1964) expectancy theory and March and Simon's (1958) inducement-contribution model are two general functions describing the motivation process. Maslow's (1954) motivational hierarchy and Herzberg's (1966) two factors are models in terms of specific variables.

The various forms of expectancy theory seem to be, at present, the basis for most motivation plans. In these the anticipation of a desired state, which is expected to result from specific behavior patterns, influences the manager to adopt and retain the behavior. Vroom (1964) elaborates this approach, defining four variables: "expectancy," the belief in a specific cause/effect; "valence," the strength of the individual's preference for a specific "effect"; "outcome," the alternative effects that the manager can "cause"; and "instrumentality," possible nonlinear effects that derive from the primary effect acting as a cause.

The March and Simon (1958) inducement-contribution model assumes that a person's contributions to an activity are a function of the perceived inducement to the individual to participate. This is a simpler, more readily understood version of the expectancy function. It fits quite well with current adult learning theory.

While these models are primarily to motivate managers to improve their performance, they also can be used to motivate managers to participate in development and use learning.

SOME DEVELOPMENT ASSUMPTIONS

Management development assumes that managers believe the following:

- They will benefit if they become more competent.
- They have the potential to become more competent.
- Participation will help them become more competent.
- They will be able to demonstrate the competence on the job.

We will discuss these assumptions in a later chapter. For the moment, note that they are not simple assumptions. The most questionable is the last: that if a manager learns a new behavior in a training program, this will result in use of the changed behavior in the work venue.

Lewin's (1951) change process model and Knowles's (1980) adult learning theory, andragogy, remain, with some variations, the basis for much current development theory directed toward increasing transfer of learning to the work venue. Both of these models are discussed in more detail in the following chapters.

THE PROVIDERS AND DESIGNS

The major sources for management development—universities, internal training and development staffs, professional associations, and consulting firms—and the extensive management literature were discussed briefly in Chapter 2.

Internal development management development was the earliest and, with respect to middle management, remains the most common approach. Tutors and advisers who provided special training for rulers and military and religious leaders developed along with increasing complexity and mobility within a society. The literature on advice to rulers and leaders can be found in very early documents. While training the king's clerks was a rationale for the development of colleges, only since the end of World War II have most universities accepted management development as a respectable academic discipline.

University business schools have for many years prepared students as business specialists (e.g., accountants). Only, for the most part, since the 1950s have most business schools been providing education in management theory and practice. Now all offer special management programs for practicing managers.

Programs range in length and concentration from one-day workshops to two full years in residence. The content varies from highly specialized to broadly cultural; from focus on interpersonal relations to emphasis on technical, structural subjects. Educational techniques vary from independent study and the traditional lecture to very elaborate computer-controlled experiential and behavioral science exercises.

The schools have been leaders in research and development of new theoretical concepts to increase understanding of organizational functioning and the role of the manager and to provide clues for dealing with complex organizational issues. While conduct of development programs is the major activity for independent consultants and internal human resource staffs, it is not for universities. Few school-based programs tailor design, content, and delivery to meet an organization's or participant's needs. University workshops frequently are regular courses modified to meet logistic constraints.

There is slow change; some university programs recognize the need to meet the specific needs of organizations. Some recognize that it is desirable to tailor programs to the life-banks of individuals. Carnegie-Mellon University announced that the individual assignments and conferences with faculty will be tailored to the expressed needs of participants. The Columbia Business School offers MBA programs for experienced managers. Some programs offer experienced managers help in dealing with specific problems and opportunities. There tends to be no use of learning theory in the design and conduct of the programs.

The consultants, in general, have led in using innovative educational techniques. Their instructional staffs tend to have greater knowledge and skills in adult education, and greater flexibility to tailor programs to specific client needs. They also are the major content innovators in expressive areas. They are more limited in traditional instrumental areas than the universities.

Associations such as the American Management Association and its foreign counterparts are major providers of management training and education. Their programs tend to be more structured than those of the consulting companies and individuals, but are similar in using many of the same experiential and innovative passive learning techniques and approaches.

The company programs have borrowed content and learning approaches from the universities and the private vendors. A major difference is an emphasis on application of learning.

It is ironic that Porter and McKibbin (1988), speaking for the academic community, find that the major reason why it may be undesirable for organizations to conduct their own programs is that company managers may not have the necessary presentational skills. In another section of their report they level a contrary criticism at academic programs: that it is academics, whose competence is measured by research papers published, who are not qualified as educators.

The most often used individual approach is to help managers learn on the job by a combination of experience and coaching. Mentoring, the subject of some current discussion, is an ancient practice. It probably led to the development of the consultant class in ancient Greece. Aristotle served as tutor to Alexander the Great for the six years prior to Alexander's coming to power and setting off to conquer the world.

Independent study tends to be limited to a reading program. Books on management attempt to provide the manager working alone with a balanced point of view and an armory of theories, models, techniques, and practices to guide behavior, assess performance, and improve decision making. Some independent study materials include exercises and simulations to test knowledge and ability to apply learning.

Machiavelli's *The Prince* (1964) is an early European management primer. *The One Minute Manager* by Blanchard and Johnson (1982) is an example of current popular "theoretical but practical" approaches. *In Search of Excellence* by Peters and Waterman (1986) is an example of the case study, practical approach.

The astronomical number of articles and books published each year is evidence of the interest in improving management. Articles in professional and general magazines, such as the *Harvard Business Review*, present case studies, analyze single issues, describe research, and analyze theories and practices.

University faculties devote their energies to developing theories and models to provide deep insight into the functioning of complex productive systems. Unfortunately, there is usually no reliable and valid evidence to support the theory and research, and little evidence that either has had significant impact on the functioning of the organizations.

CONTENT

Content is the reason for investing in management development. We will only touch on the issue here, as it is the principal subject of later chapters.

There have been many fashionable content areas over the past hundred years. These include scientific management, human relations, leadership, management by objectives, problem solving and decision making, communications, creative thinking, and risk taking. We will illustrate the development and use of content with one popular area.

"Organizational culture" is now a management concern. It is seen as the root cause for people in one organization behaving differently from people in other organizations. "Culture" is defined as the sum total of ways of behaving and thinking that are characteristic of an identifiable population and are passed from generation to generation. Included among cultural determinants are values, technology, relationships, class distinctions, means of communicating, decision-making processes, and organizational symbols and rites.

While systems and organizations are mental constructs that do not carry or possess a "culture," it is clear that people in an organization exhibit and transmit a "culture" to successor generations, and that this "culture" can have significant impact on the organization's continuity and functioning.

Within the same system cultural determinants are stable in subpopulations to different degrees. The attempt in management development has been to get managers to change, and to adopt, retain, and transmit to their role sets specific values for certain of the cultural determinants. These values are expected to lead to changes in behavior on the job. The role set is both the target for change and and crucial for changing and reinforcing change in behavior on the job.

Attempts to change the "culture" of a group of managers must contend with the influence of the managers' role sets and reference groups. Two overlapping development approaches used for coping with a role set are organizational development (OD) and top-down training. In OD a new role set is defined with the "proper" culture. In top-down the change process starts at the top and works down, with the managers at each level responsible for inculcating the change in the next lower level.

Other approaches are also employed. In the selection process, interviews with a candidate's spouse have as an objective determining the influence of the primary reference group, the family. Club memberships and sponsored group activities outside work can limit and control the influence of reference groups. If membership is limited to specific organizations, this can reinforce cultural determinants.

Some theorists attack the entire concept of "management development." They point to the wide range of manager characteristics and the diverse issues and circumstances faced by managers, and reach the conclusion that it is not possible to anticipate managerial needs. The content and the competencies needed are too uncertain and differ too greatly from job to job. This follows from the absence of models that apply to any significant, identifiable population of managers (Perrow 1979). At the other end of the range are authors who claim to have the answer for all managers in all situations.

Inevitably in such a situation the question arises of what we are trying to accomplish in management development. In one set of programs we are trying to develop creative, original thinkers who are willing to take risks (i.e., doing something that is not approved in "the book of rules"). In another set we are making every effort to develop managers who will always "do things the company way."

With respect to the application of learning theory, the situation is more confused and uncertain than with respect to content. There are different approaches with the same theory. Failing to agree on specifics, the debate centers on whether an integrated theoretical framework exists and, if one does, how it relates to practice.

AREAS OF INTEREST AND CRITICISM

A review of the development literature since 1970 reveals that while there are some commonalities among management programs, this seems to result from the limited objectives rather than from agreement on a common model.

Studies of development practices in major U.S. companies consistently report the use of similar approaches to management development. These include the following:

- Selection for promotion is on the basis of performance rather than of seniority or self-development activities.
- On-the-job experience is the principal means used to develop managers. This is supplemented by job rotation, coaching, and formal training.
- The principal educational approaches are lecture and discussion, supplemented by case studies and other passive learning approaches.
- The generally preferred approach, for managers below the top executives, is in-house training programs conducted by company personnel, supplemented by lecturers and consultants.
- University-sponsored development programs are attended primarily by top-level managers. In-house programs for these managers are not deemed appropriate or cost-effective.
- Companies consider self-development and formal training beneficial and support such effort with full or partial tuition reimbursement.

Characteristics that are found less frequently include the following:

- increasing "family" (i.e., within-company) development, and using fewer "stranger" and "horizontal" (i.e., participants on the same level), in favor of "vertical" programs

- assigning managers to special projects to provide opportunities to apply newly acquired skills and to reinforce changed behavior
- utilizing designed job slots for development.

Some practices are talked about but rarely practiced:

- Individual career planning and on-the-job development (more than just experience) are stressed in discussions but not in practice.
- Managers do not receive training to coach or counsel subordinates effectively.
- While managers are held responsible for the development of their subordinates (most firms state that this is an integral part of the manager's job), managers' performance evaluations are not based upon their success in developing subordinates.

Administrative tendencies include the following:

- More than 80 percent of large companies maintain central control of their management development programs (Carnevale 1988).
- Many are standardizing training content with greater emphasis on corporate issues.
- There is increased concern about the quality of training.
- There is a tendency to include under the rubric of "management development" training for the acquisition of specific technical skills.
- There are more professional education programs for trainers.

In some companies management trainers have been raised to the level of senior management.

In a study of private and federal management development, Bryant et al. (1978) generally confirmed these findings and reported that, in the federal service:

- Managers are afforded few opportunities to assign subordinates to positions for development purposes.
- There are few rotation programs.
- Managers who have learned new competencies rarely have the occasion to use them after returning to their jobs.

A study by Ralphs and Stephan (1986) of development practices in *Fortune* 500 companies presented contradictory and confusing findings:

- The greatest need is for training in the use of new technologies.
- Human relations is the major content area.
- Evaluation of management development is the most important issue.

- There is no one clearly dominant, "most often used" management development approach. The order of frequency was internal education, job rotation/multifunction, coaching/mentoring, university-based programs, other external programs, job rotation/multibusiness or product, and special task forces.
- The most important topics in executive development programs are communications and strategic planning, followed by productivity, problem solving and decision making, finance, and employee relations.
- On-the-job coaching/training and in-house seminars are the most common development approaches for middle managers.
- The five most important topics for middle managers, in order of expressed importance, are communications, productivity, problem solving and decision making, employee relations, and team building.
- The five most common OD interventions used are, in order, education and training, coaching and counseling, planning and goal setting, Management By Objectives, and team building.
- Needs analysis techniques, in order of frequency, are informal discussion, interviews, observation, surveys, analysis of records and reports, and group discussion.

Chenault (1987), in her study of management development, notes that despite current learning theory, there are few programs that are longitudinal; developed collaboratively; include individual, personal goals; blend organizational and personal goals; respond to both immediate and long-term needs; use interactive, collegial study groups; or employ adult, learner-centered methodologies. Few have either independent study components or mentors to help connect and integrate content over a one- or two-year period. Few emphasize creative, independent, or critical thinking. Few use experiential learning or seek to prepare executives for lifelong learning. In short, Chenault found, as others have, that few programs use current theory.

Some charge that current academic approaches are counterproductive and do not lead to effective performance on the job. The most common assertion is that generalized learning is not transferred. Others see transfer of learning to the work venue as a problem for all management development. Livingston (1983), Stroul and Schuman (1983), Schneier, Beatty, and Baird (1986), and Kirkpatrick (1986) are representative. Recommendations call for focus on identifying and satisfying specific needs, in some cases the organization's and in others the individual manager's.

Livingston's analysis (1983) is quite specific: "The reason [management education] seems to be a crapshoot is that very little of the learning is directed to providing the practical skills needed to apply the knowledge gained in class to real performance problems on the job" (p. 15).

In response to criticism of academic programs, the American Assembly of Collegiate Schools of Business in 1984 commissioned a research project to respond to such questions as Do business schools train managers? What are the merits of a generalized curriculum versus specific skills training? What do managers learn on the job compared with formal instruction? The results of the study are presented in *Management Education and Development: Drift or Thrust into the 21st Century?* by Porter and McKibbin (1988). The authors, both professors of management and former deans of colleges of business administration, conducted numerous interviews and distributed more than 10,000 questionnaires, primarily to three populations: faculties of business colleges, management development professionals, and managers at all levels in private-sector organizations.

The principal findings from this research include the following:

- The faculties discount their critics. Very self-satisfied, they see little need for change in the content and approaches in the business schools.
- While the corporate respondents are satisfied with the content of the programs, they would like more emphasis on realistic, hands-on education and interpersonal skills.
- Corporate respondents believe that faculty members need more direct contact with the business world.
- A high percentage of managers feels the need for more systematic management development.

An important finding is that while there is corporate support for research by faculty, business by and large does not use the research findings. So much for emphasis on research.

The Porter and McKibbin study (1988) touched on the current emphasis on lifelong learning. Their conclusion is that this emphasis seems to have passed by the schools of business and public administration without much impact. In fact, a major recommendation in the report is that business schools need to become concerned with lifelong learning.

Other recommendations relate to curriculum, diversity among schools, preparation of faculty, and corporate responsibility:

- Give more emphasis to the external environment of organizations (amazing, considering the emphasis in current management theory on an open systems approach).
- Reduce compartmentalization, introduce cross-functional integration (recognition that companies function as holistic organisms, not as college departments).
- Develop stronger "people" skills (not easy in a college classroom).

Porter and McKibbin's (1988) advice to companies includes the following:

- Conduct more effective needs assessments.
- Use strategic planning for meeting management development needs.
- Be more selective and careful in choosing providers of executive education.

Consultants have also been concerned with the attacks on the effectiveness of management development activities. Their responses have been primarily in terms of articles published in the trade magazines.

A major criticism of popular presentations in book form is the reliance on the "one best way to manage" approach. The criticism of the 1988–1989 crop of such books in a special section of the *New York Times Book Review* indicates the level of the books. Among the comments are "Mr. McCormack has nothing remarkable to say, but he does say sensible things in a sensible way. . . . After two books, it seems clear that he is nearing the bottom of his business-advice barrel." "The authors have set themselves the slippery task of . . . how to recognize and deal with business situations 'not treatable with standard textbook solutions'. . . . These guidelines . . . sound much like those we have read in other business how-to books. . . . [They] provide neither helpful hints in making these purportedly crucial decisions nor even good war stories from the corporate trenches." "Ms. Kantor makes it clear that people are the dominant factor and the most important resource in a successful business" (*New York Times Book Review*, October 29, 1989).

O'Rourke (1989) reports:

> "Language of Success" . . . is by no means the dumbest of the [more than a dozen] books I have before me. It's thoughtful; it's full of boring, redundant, tautological thoughts. This more than can be said for . . . "The One Minute Manager Meets the Monkey" . . . the book's argument is, first, don't help others . . . second, be indispensable . . . third, get everybody else to do your work for you. This . . . is the complete and entire secret of how to succeed in business, no matter what all these books say. Not that most of the books say anything. They don't have space . . . they are so grossly padded with inapposite quotations, dull anecdotes and pointless yarn-spinning.

O'Rourke divides the books into three main categories. The first is "If-They-Need-Be-Told-There's-No-Use-Telling-Them." The second is "It's-All-In-The-Title," or the contents page, or, at most, the chapter subheadings. The third category consists of anecdotes by successful businessmen. With respect to content, the comment is "All of the success books, even the nutty ones, are united in obsessions with leadership, communications and managing" (O'Rourke 1989).

CONCLUSIONS

Management development process is a function of the following:

1. the venue (the focal system and the environment in which it is embedded)
2. the desired changes in the venue
3. the competencies of the managers who are expected to serve as change agents
4. the competencies that these managers need to possess to bring about the desired changes
5. the learning program (design and implementation) that will help them acquire these competencies
6. the activities that will motivate and enable them to use the competencies to bring about the desired change
7. the life-bank elements that motivate and lead to lifelong learning.

The change sought from the organizational point of view is not simply change in the behavior of the participating manager but change in the performance and output of the organization. This increases the number of variables affecting the ability of the management development program to deliver the desired change. The additional variables include relationships between the designated change agents and the others not in their role sets, relationships between the short- and long-term organizational objectives, impact of the change on the environment, and the independent changes in the state of the contextual environment.

Most development programs assume one or more of the following:

1. All effective change agents must have the same set of competencies that are independent of both the desired change and the work venue.
2. Passive learning, sometimes supplemented by synthetic experiential learning approaches, is adequate to help managers acquire and use needed competencies.
3. Demonstration of knowledge and ability to use new and increased competencies in the training venue is adequate to ensure transfer of the competencies to the work venue.
4. Lifelong learning is a desirable objective but is either not a management development objective or can be developed in a short-term program.
5. The effectiveness of transfer of learning to the work venue is not significantly affected by the order in which students take courses in a graduate program or in which content is presented in special programs. The only requirement is that the sequence be rational in terms of knowledge acquisition.

We do not accept any of these. Our conclusions are the following:

- Every one of the assumptions is faulty.
- There are other assumptions that are acceptable and can lead to effective management development.

The questions that should be answered include these:

- Are there competencies that good managers have and that managers who are less competent can learn?
- Are there ways to help managers transfer increased and new competencies to the work venue?
- Are some educational approaches more effective?
- Does managers' use of new and increased competencies lead to better performance by the organization as a whole?
- Can management development lead to improved lifelong learning?
- What evidence would help us answer these questions?

The rest of this book is devoted to discussing these and related issues and to suggesting some possible answers.

4

THE ROLE OF THE MANAGER AND MANAGEMENT DEVELOPMENT

INTRODUCTION

The very possibility of planned management development depends on the acceptance of definitions of the role and tasks of the manager, models for managerial behavior, and the relationships between managerial behavior and organizational structure and functioning. These determine the competencies required to perform tasks and the degree to which these competencies are relatively invariant or dependent on local conditions. Consideration of these factors is preliminary to any investigation into management development. It is our view that there is no one managerial role or set of tasks and competencies required for effective management under all conditions. Sometimes the differences are obscured by the use of the same term to denote quite different competencies. "Decision making" is one example. "Leadership" is another. Lawrence and Lorsch (1969) point to the differences in both these competencies, depending on the nature of the work venue of the manager. In terms of just one variable, such as the nature and level of risk involved, the competencies required for effective decision making can vary wildly. In terms of charisma and technical competence, the same is true of leadership. It is also well known that the nature of effective leadership changes with the stage of organizational development.

That managers are expected to perform different tasks, have different competencies, and be able to accept different levels of ambiguity and risk is often recognized in the business world. This tends to be ignored in government, where patronage and political sensitivity are the primary considerations for high-level appointments. The differences naturally lead to different views about the nature and value of management development.

SOME RESEARCH FINDINGS

There are both unsupported normative models of the "good" manager and research efforts to describe what a manager really does. The ideal is a sensitive leader who is a capable administrator, truly consultative and decisive; deals only with what cannot be dealt with below and what does not need to be decided higher up; is innovative, able to take reasonable risk; collegial, loyal to staff, peers, and superiors as well as to the organization; and balances internal and external demands, ethical considerations, business requirements, and personal needs in a manner that satisfies everyone. Porter and McKibbin (1988), looking at the managerial role from the viewpoint of making recommendations for the collegiate curriculum, tend to ignore the type of specialization that occurs in universities. They focus on the broader aspects and highest level of the managerial job, and they identify three groups of variables as most relevant to the field of management. These are economic, demographic, and societal variables. They consider these from the viewpoints of the external and internal environments. The set of economic variables includes change from industrial base to service base, technological change, internationalization, increased entrepreneurism, and change in the nature of work. The demographic variables are population bulges, aging and retirement, and the role of women. Societal variables are values, technology and society, and political structure.

The role of a manager, the tasks to be performed, the competencies required, and, consequently, the content of management development depend on the set of variables and the specific variables within a set that are seen as crucial for effective managerial performance. Without any detailed analysis of the three sets of variables, it is obvious that significantly different managerial competencies are needed for effective management in companies in environments with very different values. We could easily add a dozen additional variables in this category, such as the state of competition, unionization, depression or inflation, quality of the work force, and taxation.

There are two types of research studies relating to the role of the manager. The first is directed to determining what managers do. The data gathering is based on observation and on self-reporting by the managers. The study by Mintzberg (1973) is a good example. The second type of research attempts to identify characteristics and competencies of "effective" managers. The Flannagan study (Campbell et al. 1970) is a sophisticated example. It is based on use of Flannagan's critical incident technique. Critical incidents are managerial incidents that describe "good" and "poor" management. These are defined, and managerial performance is described in terms of them.

Unfortunately there is no significant, generally accepted, usable research on the impact of an organization's culture and environment on managerial performance. The research studies, such as that of Lawrence and Lorsch (1969), provide some hypotheses and evidence indicating that different managerial roles and competencies and organizational structures are needed for organizations to adapt and be successful in different environments. However, as in the case of most research in the social sciences, there are problems with all studies of the managerial role and managerial effectiveness. Specific objections to the research include the following:

- The designs of studies are biased by the a priori identification of the information to be obtained and the use to which the information is to be put.
- The selection of the study population compromises the reliability and validity of the findings when conclusions are extended beyond the test population. In many cases the populations are not managers but students in a simulated managerial situation.
- Studies do not use control groups. Only occasionally are there comparison groups.
- The data-gathering techniques, with the exception of observation such as used by Mintzberg (1973) and similar approaches, tend to be subjective reports of personal experiences and individual opinions.
- There are questions about the personal criteria used in the observational studies. Consequently, the reliability of the data is questioned.
- The only reliable studies tend to be descriptive, with very broad task definitions to permit easier classification.
- Very general conclusions are drawn from what are, at best, simple case studies.

The identification of characteristics of "effective" managers is particularly suspect. There is little to change in the comment made in *Managerial Behavior, Performance, and Effectiveness* (Campbell et al. 1970):

> Much of the business and psychological literature on the topic of managerial effectiveness is based on little more than personal experiences or opinions about traits possessed by "good" managers, what they must do to be effective, or what the products of their effective behavior may be. (p. 15)

Even if we were able to define the role, characteristics, and competencies of individual effective managers, there would be no way to distinguish the effects of different sets of variables. Some of these sets have been described. Others are the culture of the organization, the objectives of the chief executives, and contextual environment. Further, the performance of a manager cannot be evaluated in isolation. Other factors include the performance of other managers, the restrictions and demands imposed on the manager's activities by others, and standards for acceptable performance.

In the design of management development, we must take account of the best available research relating to the role of the manager and characteristics of effective managers. However, we must be prepared to develop our own models based on the needs and objectives of the organizations and the managers who will participate.

With or without support from reliable and valid research findings, it is necessary to use theories of the managerial role and effective managerial behavior to provide a base for development. Only through the use of these theories can we explain cause/effect relationships, gather and analyze information to support program designs, integrate individual insights, and advance and reinforce learning.

SOME MANAGEMENT HISTORY

From the earliest times until the present there has been a tendency to assume that while the jobs of individual managers differ, there are common "management" tasks and universal principles and practices for effective managerial behavior. The need for different competencies in different jobs tended to be overlooked. Unsuccessful managers were not seen as having inappropriate competencies. They were incompetent.

According to George (1972), planning, organizing, and controlling were recognized as key responsibilities of management by the Egyptians as early as 4000 B.C. There may have been an Egyptian book of instructions for managers as early as 2700 B.C. and certainly no later than 2000 B.C. There is reference to management by the Babylonians about 1850 B.C., and by the Chinese by 1100 B.C. The latter identified the elements noted by the Egyptians and added the element of "directing."

These civilizations were not alone in identifying and recommending activities for managers. Before 100 B.C. there were principles enunciated in India and Greece. Xenophon (quoted in George 1972) asserts that in his discussions Socrates advanced the thesis that managers who understand and can use good management principles are capable of managing any enterprise. Moving to characteristics of managers, Aristotle defined the four virtues necessary for effective leadership as courage, fortitude, prudence, and justice.

Governance of great empires such as the Persian and Roman required rules for management. During the medieval period and the Renaissance there were numerous treatises instructing princes on how to gain and retain power and to reign effectively. Machiavelli's *The Prince* is the best-known manual of this type for its universal principles for rulers.

Writing on the theory and practice of administration appeared in the Arab civilization even earlier than in the European. Ibn Khaldun's *Muqaddima*, written in the late fourteenth century, contains, in addition to Arab history and sociology, a discussion of administration in primitive and urban societies and advanced states. The analysis considers such factors as leadership, specialization, differentiation and integration, co-operation and participation, influence of the environment, and organizational growth and decay. It is a far richer and more comprehensive analysis than that in *The Prince*.

There is an interesting difference between the approaches used by Machiavelli and Ibn Khaldun that may have resulted from their differing administrative experiences. For the most part, Machiavelli was a diplomat in the service of his native city. Ibn Khaldun was a paid administrator and judge who, in the course of his lifetime, served several different dynasties both in Spain and in north Africa. Machiavelli presents a theory and supports it with evidence from his own observation. He focuses almost entirely on the role of the ruler. Ibn Khaldun's theory is broader and more objective. He integrates his experiences with the rich commentary of such predecessors as Avicenna and ash-Shahrazuru to arrive at some theoretical concepts. A cautious "traveling expert," he provides very few examples from his own vast experience as an administrator, preferring to select from the comments and experiences of others to develop his models. These, one can assume, support his own behavior.

For obvious reasons, the interest for the first 5,000 years focused on the role of the ruler and public administration. The industrial revolution brought great interest in, and an outpouring of books on, management. From the beginning of the nineteenth century to today there may have been more books published on how to be a "good" manager than on any other "how to" topic.

During the nineteenth century virtually every managerial activity was identified by such theorists and practitioners as James Watt, Robert Owen, James Mill, Charles Babbage, Henry Poor, Daniel McCullum, and William Jevons. By 1881, Joseph Wharton had established a college program devoted to business management (George 1972). The entire corpus of writing on business management prior to the twentieth century, except for such mechanistic and manipulative approaches as those recommended by Machiavelli, focused on the "goal-centered" or "production-centered" activities of the manager. Woodrow Wilson, in addition to being president, is regarded as the "father of American public administration and management" and was author of a number of influential articles. "The Study of Administration" (1941) called attention to the neglect of the role of the executive or "business" side of government by political scientists and to the distinctive roles of elected and appointed top management and permanent civil service managers.

TWENTIETH-CENTURY MODELS

The proliferation in the twentieth century of books and programs devoted to instructing and developing managers is beyond calculation. The early years of the century were dominated by the apostles of scientific management, who continued to focus on the "goal"-oriented tasks of managers. However the "people" tasks were not ignored. Taylor (March and Simon 1958) and Gulick and Urwick (1937) are representative of the private-sector and public-sector theorists.

In the second half of the century, proponents of "scientific management" and the doctrine of "efficient and effective" management have been on the defensive. They are prominent only in technical areas such as operations research. The strongest theoretical (although not the most popular) thrust has been away from postulating clearly defined tasks, principles, and practices for managers and to recommending the development of the ability to employ alternative models and to adapt, learn, and change models based on their use in different circumstances.

It is difficult to use this type of theory, which is ambiguous, defines objectives based on specific circumstances, is tentative, and requires helping participants to acquire a metacompetence (the ability to continue learning from experience and to adapt and change life-bank elements rather than simply adding knowledge and specific skills). The task is made more difficult by participants who seek "answers" to specific problems in management development.

There have been dozens of simplified models of management and sets of principles for effective management. Some theorists pay obeisance to a contingency principle. But, at best, they provide limited, general alternatives and guides for choosing among alternatives. In the absence of acceptable research to the contrary, any set of hypotheses with some face validity can be advocated. When some validity for other systems is recognized, there is an attempt to rationalize differences and to absorb the acceptable elements of the earlier models.

Koontz (1976) identifies six major schools of management theory:

- "management process," in which management is a process for reaching organizational objectives through people working in organized groups

- "experience," which emphasizes study and emulation of successful managerial practices
- "human behavior," which focuses on the relationships among people in the organization and, in particular, the role of the manager as leader
- "social system," which emphasizes the interactions among work groups and between them and their environments
- "decision theory," which concentrates on problem identification and definition, development of alternative courses of action, and decision making
- "mathematical," in which managers define a set of models and processes that are employed to define and analyze managerial problems.

These six categories are, at present, most often collapsed into two. While not all theorists define the two categories in precisely the same way, they generally differentiate between "people"-oriented and "goal"-oriented activities. Examples of these pairs are instrumental and expressive, task and relationship, initiating structure and consideration, production-centered and people-centered, task and social-emotional leader, and task and maintenance specialist. The distinction in each of these pairs is between activities that involve other people and concern for them and those which either do not involve others or involve them primarily to achieve another management end—increased production. For convenience we will use the terms "expressive" and "instrumental."

The instrumental category includes such tasks as scheduling, setting standards, monitoring, assessing, giving direction, planning; obtaining, analyzing and disseminating information; making rules, organizing, establishing procedures, coordinating, budgeting, and evaluating. The expressive category includes leading, coaching, developing staff, developing mutual trust, serving as change agent, resolving conflict, motivating, training, encouraging participation and communication, and considering others. Since the development approaches for these differ, the two categories are usually dealt with in separate programs.

While it is generally assumed that the two categories are independent or only weakly interdependent, there are claims by some theorists and union leaders (Perrow 1979) that the "human relations" approach is just a modern variation of Machiavellian manipulation. They assert that the "real" purpose of seeking "good" relationships is not to benefit the worker but to achieve management objectives more efficiently and effectively. This conflict about objectives is usually ignored in management development in favor of discussing and increasing competence in process.

The development programs focusing on competencies in the instrumental category usually present one best method. Many programs focusing on the expressive role recognize that there are acceptable alternative behaviors. Recognizing that there is a range of values between the lowest and highest values of each variable only infrequently leads to learning how to identify and test the appropriate alternatives in any given situation. Even more rare is any discussion of the interrelationships among three or more variables. We were able to find no real discussion involving matrices of more than three dimensions. Theorists characterize the types of situations in which a specific set of values of the variables (i.e., elements in the matrix) would be most effective (Hersey and Blanchard 1972). Although less rigid than development programs with no alternatives, the number of alternatives is limited and thus the problem of ambiguity and uncertainty is solved.

One effect of the focus on the expressive tasks in the managerial role has been to give much greater emphasis to models of effective management and as a result, in management development, to the manager as leader and as change agent. Bennis (1984) found, in his analysis of the behavior of ninety outstandingly successful leaders, four competencies common to every member: focusing attention through strong commitment to a sense of organizational direction; making ideas real and acceptable to others; communicating effectively through several organizational levels and noise barriers; and being seen as reliable and trustworthy.

Mintzberg (1973), in his research on what managers do, found that "managers' jobs are remarkably alike." He identified ten distinct roles in the categories "interpersonal," "informational," and "decisional." The "interpersonal" category includes figurehead (ceremonial symbol of the unit), leader, and liaison; the "informational," monitor, disseminator, spokesman; the "decisional," entrepreneur, disturbance handler, resource allocator, negotiator. While these categories have some similarities with those proposed by other researchers and theorists, there are obvious differences. Although Mintzberg's categories include both expressive and instrumental roles, there is overwhelming emphasis on the expressive tasks.

The manager as the symbol of the organization has importance beyond the Mintzberg "figurehead." An impressive, highly thought-of manager adds to the effectiveness of the organization in imposing its will on other organizations and in recruiting and retaining good people. It is equally important to establish managers as the " 'symbol' of control and personal causation . . . [to] be used as scapegoats, rewarded when things go well and fired when they go poorly. . . . [It is] a mechanism for dealing with external demands. . . . changing administrators offers a way of altering appearances thereby removing external pressure, without losing much discretion" (Pfeffer and Salancik 1978, p. 263).

While there is some (but far from universal) agreement with the Mintzberg view that all managers perform the same kinds of activities, there is an equally strong feeling that the importance of different tasks within the two (or three) primary categories is not independent of the level of management or the work venue. That is, decision making when there is no feedback from a superior is different from a situation where there may be immediate feedback that may affect the decision maker's future. Further, there are differences in the definition of tasks with the same name and in the competencies required for the same task in different environments.

Research by Jacques (1979) indicates that the time discretion for decision making and task completion varies directly with position in the managerial hierarchy. This might be supporting evidence for role differentiation resulting from decreased pressure to come to closure the higher the manager is in the hierarchy.

In comparisons between middle and top management, the responsibility of top management is seen to be the following:

- to create the vision of what the organization is and where it is going
- to monitor the organizational culture and keep it aligned with the goals and policy of top management
- to define broad organizational goals, the strategic plan for achieving those goals, and each unit's role in achieving the goals
- to determine the structure and distribution of power in the system
- to enact the environment for the system and assign responsibility for relating to it (reserving the most important elements for top management).

In common with all managers, top management is expected to

- obtain subordinate managers' understanding and commitment to system goals and assigned objectives, give them the authority and resources to achieve their objectives, monitor progress, and help to take any necessary corrective actions
- develop and maintain a trust relationship so that there is an appropriate flow of information and responsiveness.

It is middle managers' responsibility to get the policies and decisions of top management implemented. This includes the following:

- interpreting and communicating top management's vision, strategic goals, and so on, so that these will be accepted, and lower-level managers and supervisors will be motivated to carry them out
- obtaining the needed resources
- assigning tasks to unit supervisors and lower-level managers; training, coaching, guiding, and motivating them so that they want, and will, be competent to carry out plans and assignments
- avoiding counterproductive suboptimization

- controlling operations, without undermining the authority of lower-level managers, so that the tasks are carried out as assigned
- serving as boundary spanners to coordinate the activities of their subsystems with collateral subsystems.

The role of the manager, on all levels, as problem solver and decision maker has always been considered important, particularly in American business schools and development programs. The reliance on case studies and "problem" exercises is evidence. This is related to the often identified characteristic of Americans' belief that all problems would be solvable if all the facts were known and we were smart enough. This hypothesis is basic for case studies and experiential exercises, as well as for most techniques in problem solving and decision making.

What many consider to be two major roles of the manager are barely mentioned in the vast didactic literature directed toward increasing managerial competence. These are the boundary-spanning and training roles. From this viewpoint the job of the manager is to represent, negotiate, and deal with salient elements of the task and functional environments for the focal unit, in order to ensure adequate input and acceptance of output and to train subordinates to carry out the required throughput efficiently and effectively. A third managerial role mentioned by Pfeffer and Selancik (1978) involves changing organizational constraints and dependencies.

Other important elements in the boundary-spanning role are to buffer the technical core of the unit from disturbing influences (J. D. Thompson 1967), to serve as a symbol of the unit (Mintzberg 1973), to be the strong leader who can control outside forces, to be the unit's advocate, and to serve as the scapegoat for the unit's failures.

In their discussion of the role of the manager in connection with external control of organizations, Pfeffer and Salancik (1978) describe, in addition to the "symbolic" role already mentioned, two other roles. In the "responsive" role, the manager assesses the environmental context ("scans and enacts," in Weick's [1969] analysis), determines what adaptive action to take to deal with environmental demands, and implements decisions. Pfeffer and Salancik emphasize the manager's role in information gathering and determining which demands to heed and which to reject, rather than only in deciding what to do. The "discretionary" role relates to action to be taken to change the environment's demands.

Many management activities are almost pure ritual (i.e., the acts symbolize a commitment to behavior expected by the manager's role set or "textbook good management" or society). One example is the ritual of receiving and reviewing the output of elaborate management information systems. These develop and contain far more information than is ever used. The ritual symbolizes a commitment to rational decision making. Another is the ritualistic advocacy for extensive employee participation that is rarely allowed to lead to decisions and activities management does not favor.

Management is not a linear process in which activities follow each other in a regular sequence. Several processes go on at the same time. The manager must constantly be assigning priorities, juggling resources, considering different sets of variables and models, and trading off more desirable and less desirable results.

Finally, managers are expected to monitor for nonlinear consequences and assume the risk-taking role for their units. Risk in four areas is emphasized: financial, in terms of acquiring and allocating resources; operational (structure, process, product, and output); openness in relationships with others; and presenting—and, if necessary, implementing—new, not strongly supported policies, activities, and positions.

This review of the literature leads to a complicated mosaic view of management. The demands on managers in complex organizations are in part scheduled and in part random. They sometimes call for reactive and sometimes for proactive actions. They are both disjointed and interdependent, sometimes both at the same time. Actions are sometimes completely programmed and sometimes unprogrammable. The manager is made responsible for organizing the fragments into a meaningful pattern so that subordinates will understand what they are to do and why they are expected to do it.

CONTINGENCY THEORY

This leads us to consider "contingency" in management. "Contingency" or "it depends" has been employed in describing the role of the manager and in the identification of effective managerial behavior. It recognizes that there has been no epiphany—no revelation of universal managerial truth caught, held, and made accessible—for all managers for all time.

Contingency theorists see organizational theory and related theories of the role of the manager as interesting intellectual constructs that are frequently useful for organizing and analyzing data and providing a frame of reference and reasonable cause/effect relationships for decision making. However, they do not believe that these theories contain the lifeblood or the disorder of actual management. The theories of management are constructs treated as if they were real. They are as derivative as the construct "rational man." From the contingency viewpoint there are managerial tasks but virtually only one task common to all managers—directing the performance of others. And, it is noted, there are many alternative appropriate behaviors for directing the performance of others.

Management is seen as requiring balancing of forces and capabilities for stability and flexibility in response to threats and opportunities. To the extent that these are ill-defined forces, the manager works in an uncertain and ambiguous environment. In contingency theories, many models may be employed as substitutes for complex reality. While this tends to reduce the ambiguity and uncertainty of information and to help in evaluating, organizing, and analyzing information in a specific case, it raises the problem of which model to use. Management development can help managers to learn which model to select, to estimate and minimize the risk involved, and to learn from the experience.

The contingency theory of management is related to the distinctive American philosophy of pragmatism rather than to the traditional European rationalist forms. Like pragmatism, it is attacked by management scholastics and managers who seek a grand theory that encompasses all organizational and management theory and unambiguous direction and techniques for managers. Management is seen as not very different from a game of chess. And since computers can beat all but the greatest masters in chess, computers can be built that will be able to manage better than all but the greatest managers. Opponents of contingency theory assert that as the chess programs provide for learning from experience, so "lifelong learning" can be built into the managing programs. What is overlooked is that the rules of chess are fixed. No player can change them to beat an opponent.

THE MANAGEMENT ROLE AND MANAGEMENT DEVELOPMENT

If the primary purpose of management development is to increase the manager's effectiveness, then its nature should be a function of the definition of "effectiveness," the skills required to be an effective manager and the criteria for measuring effectiveness. Unfortunately, there is no more agreement on the definition of and criteria for effectiveness than on the definition of the role of management.

Mintzberg (1973) describes eight sets of skills that are needed by managers and considers ways in which these might be (or cannot be) taught in academic programs. Mintzberg's comments are directed at academic degree programs. They are, for the most part, applicable to management development as well.

1. Peer skills, political skills for dealing with conflict and "infighting," and for negotiating and consulting effectively with peers. Simulation is suggested as the preferred development technique in the absence of "real" development opportunities.
2. Leadership skills to relate effectively to subordinates through motivation, training, and appropriate use of authority and participation. No development techniques are advocated other than "participative" training and experience.

3. Conflict-resolution skills, while included in "peer skills," are seen as broader (e.g., among subordinates). Role-playing is suggested.
4. Information-processing skills required to obtain, analyze, and disseminate information. These are seen as more amenable to academic training.
5. Decision making and problem solving in unstructured, ambiguous situations. These are subjects in many management development programs. However, the nature of the content is seen as "elementary when viewed in the light of the complex ambiguity senior managers face." Current approaches, which are limited to decision making under certainty, risk, and uncertainty, are insufficient. No development approach is recommended.
6. Skill in allocating resources among competing demands. This, it is suggested, may be taught through use of the "in basket" technique.
7. Entrepreneurial skills are defined as the decisional skills related to identification of problems and opportunities and controlled change in the system. (Strangely, the will and analysis needed to take risk in ambiguous situations are not included.) Recommendations for training relate to positive reinforcement for "sensible risk taking and innovation."
8. The master skill "introspection," the ability to learn from experience. This, Mintzberg believes, can only be encouraged and not taught.

Everyone might agree that a reasonable measure of managerial effectiveness is the degree to which a manager's efforts assist the focal system to reach its objectives. However, how does an evaluator compare one set of partially achieved objectives with another, and how does one determine the impact of one manager, even a chief executive officer? There are, usually, many objectives. Which are most important? How do we trade off success in the short term against less-than-total success in the long term? And could we really have been successful in the short term if we are not successful in the long-term? Does this mean that we have to give up measuring short-term results? Do we measure "success" on an absolute basis or compared with what another manager could have done? Or is our standard whether the manager is becoming more effective? What about suboptimization—the situation in which a manager achieves desired results but at a cost to another manager in the same system? Is one criterion the manager's loyalty to superiors, or to the company, or to society? If we leave measuring effectiveness by results, we may get into a deeper morass.

Some authors (Campbell et al. 1970) propose to "define a manager's effectiveness according to his impact on his organization's continued functioning through optimal acquisition and utilization of internal and external resources—an optimizer of present and potential resource allocation." They recommend that "measures of managerial effectiveness should provide a means for observing accurately and recording systematically the full range of a manager's job behaviors" (p. 125). The authors do not discuss these other issues. They do not seem to realize that by their basis for measurement they have redefined "effectiveness."

Managers often tend to measure their own effectiveness by the performance that maximizes the attainment of their personal goals, the degree to which they meet their own personal needs. This can lead to the view that political skills should be the major factor in measuring effectiveness.

Theorists and researchers focus on a mix of results, characteristics, and behaviors, but rarely do two arrive at the same mix as a measure of managerial competence. One theorist favors "achievement," "aggression," "autonomy," and "nurturance"; a second, "achievement," "power," and "affiliation"; a third, "leadership," "sensitivity to problems and aspirations of subordinates," "ability to secure adequate resources," "effective representative to lateral and higher authorities," "getting and disseminating information," and "training subordinates"; a fourth, "personal compliance" and "job knowledge." One model in Campbell et al. (1970) sees managerial effectiveness as a complex function of "ability," "motivation," "opportunity," and "feedback" variables. None of the models provides a guide for measurement.

There are many variables, other than those under the control of the individual manager, that determine the effectiveness of managerial performance. Among these are the structure of the organization, the nature and competence of superiors and subordinates, recognition and rewards, the production system, the environment, and the culture of the organization.

Organizations use three approaches to increase managerial effectiveness: selection, training and development, and motivation. Campbell et al. (1970) found that only one of thirty-three firms studied had a comprehensive program in each of the areas. Most programs emphasized one area at the expense of others. While noting that there had been little significant research on the nature and factors leading to managerial effectiveness, Campbell, Dunnette, Lawler, and Weick (1970) point to the importance of defining in such studies the definition of "effectiveness" and the inclusion of a criterion related to the means employed. If only results are measured, one may anticipate that the means may be corrupt. This can be seen in the 1980s Iran-Contra scandal in the public sector and the Salomon Brothers scandal in the private sector in the 1990s.

It is hypothesized that challenge is a strong intrinsic motivator. While some organizations claim that challenging tasks are assigned for both development and motivational objectives, there is little evidence of the use of planned assignments as intrinsic motivators for improving performance. There is no evidence of systematic follow-up to evaluate the developmental effects of planned assignments.

SUGGESTIONS FOR MANAGERS

From a developmental point of view, management can be considered as consisting of two parallel but related sequences of activities progressing in tandem, with first one and then the other paramount. One is a series of behaviors. The other is a continuous analytic, research, and assessment sequence that both guides and comments on the behaviors and their consequences. If this is understood, these sequences provide the opportunity for continuous learning.

Unfortunately, the opportunity is rarely seized. The time to indulge in the process of learning from experience is never certain. Organizations are established to be action, not learning, systems. While every manager claims subordinates are encouraged to learn from analysis of their experiences, few encourage subordinates to expend time and energy on developing a systematic process to identify and use opportunities for learning, or even for reviewing experience.

Yet if there is not continuous learning and a distinction between failure and incompetence, there can be no continuously well-managed organization. Success tends to inhibit innovation and behavioral changes, and to limit seizing new opportunities or adapting to changes in the environment. Building in a change mechanism is not sufficient. The structure of such a mechanism is based on knowledge of past and potential challenges. In time this becomes outmoded and what was once most effective becomes counterproductive.

Mintzberg's conclusions (1973) with respect to the performance of managers are of interest for management development. In our terms, these include the following:

- Managers are under pressure to perform a large number of brief, varied, and fragmented tasks. There is danger that performance will be superficial.
- There is pressure to assign priority to action over thought, to the present over the future, to well-defined over ambiguous tasks, to specific over general issues, and to verbal over other forms of communication. Managers have an informal, opportunistic approach anchored in the present. There is always a danger that current actions will become long-term strategy.
- Managers are the crucial boundary spanners between their units and superiors and managers of other elements in the focal organization, and systems and individuals in the focal system's environment. They must be effective communicators on the boundary and in both directions.
- Managers' objectives and tasks may be prescribed, forcing them to be reactive. They must become proactive and exercise control by taking the initiative in defining objectives and tasks and in negotiating with superiors and subordinates.

In the final section of his essay "Throwing Care to the Wind," Weick (1969) gives some practical advice to managers:

- Don't panic in the face of disorder; short-term ambivalence may lead to long-term adaptation.
- Never do anything all at once; in interdependent systems a completed action may have irreversible, far-reaching consequences, some of which may not be immediately apparent.
- In interdependent systems the cause of a problem may be far removed from the "triggering" incident. Do not limit the search for causes to proximate events.
- Action, even if chaotic, is preferable to orderly inaction; the experience of action may provide the information and material for improving future activities.
- The most important decisions are rarely obvious: retention decisions may be more important to a system's survival than selection decisions; selection and enactment processes may determine more about an organization's structure than concern with power distribution; the mail clerk who distributes the mail may have more power than the manager; and the person who decides what is known is more important for continued functioning than the one who sets long-term objectives.
- Managers should focus on coordinating processes rather than on people or groups of people. To coordinate, locate the processes of enactment, selection, and retention; identify the causal ties among them; and adjust the causal linkages to force coordination of processes and to maintain managerial control.

We conclude this discussion of the role of the manager and its impact on management development by noting an entirely contrary point of view. Kaufman (1985) advanced the view that organizational survival is in no significant way dependent on rational human behavior but is largely a matter of luck. If Kaufman's conjecture has significant validity, then the most important competencies for chief executives are to have more good luck than bad luck and be able to distinguish one from the other. These are competencies that are not considered by other theorists and those in management development generally.

Some implications for management development from this review of the role of the manager and the evaluation of managerial performance are the following:

- The importance of a competency is a function of assigned tasks and responsibilities, the level of the position, the nature and culture of the organization, and its environment.
- These factors are not constants; they are variables with different rates and conditions for change and complex interrelations. They frequently are not commensurable.

- The organizational variables that can be influenced by managers' performance determine which competencies are important.
- There are few criteria for selection of managers or measures of managerial performance that are generally accepted.
- Evaluation of managerial performance by superiors and subordinates may not be related to a manager's competencies, the needs of the job, or actual performance.
- While some competencies required to perform specific tasks may be acquired or improved by learning (knowledge and skill) from a single course or workshop, others require continuous development over a long period of time.
- Feedback, either from self-assessment or from others, is necessary for learning and making effective use of learning.
- Continued learning from structured, formal or informal activities, from others, and from experience is necessary for continued effectiveness as a manager.
- Management questions that are important enough to ask are rarely answerable by a simple selection from a menu of alternatives.
- The role of chance should never be ignored.

5

SOME LEARNING THEORY

This chapter is devoted to a brief review of learning theory, to which we refer in our discussion of management development, and of the theoretical assumptions we make in our Learning Inducted From Experience (LIFE) approach.

GENERAL THEORY

The literature is replete with theories of learning, adult learning, learning styles, and transfer of learning. All of these relate in some way to management development. The theories are redundant and occasionally contradictory, with little empirical evidence to support any of them. While significant, supporting evidence would be of interest, the issue is, for practical purposes, irrelevant. The concern is "Is the theory useful for management development?" A theory is useful if it helps us to understand relationships. A theory not useful in one situation may be useful in another. Since we will be discussing various theories of adult learning in this chapter, it is useful to spend a moment to discuss the nature and use of theory. We include "models" as theories in the discussion.

That theories and models may not be "true" yet still be useful is a troubling concept to many. However, this doubt should be dispelled by a moment's consideration of the many different maps, none a "true" representation, that provide different bits of useful information about the same geographic area. In general, theory tends to simplify complex relationships by removing from consideration of variables thought to be of lesser concern, in order to permit focusing on the variables of interest.

Simplification serves a number of purposes. It can make it easier to understand cause/effect and other relationships among variables. It can help us increase the accuracy and usefulness of our predictions with respect to the variables being studied. It can provide a frame of reference and a basis for design and implementation of development programs. The simplified relationships can guide us in decision making and assessment.

Beer (1975) emphasizes the Platonic nature of Western culture in its seeing theory as the basis for our concept of reality. This is precisely the danger in the use of theory. Theories may be confused with reality and used as if they were literally true. A theory is a useful invention, but it is a figment of the imagination representing, at best, a partial explanation. Theory should be used cautiously.

Beyond being explanatory, theory should have plausibility and a reasonable degree of testability of usefulness. If not actually testable, it should be possible to obtain agreement on criteria for demonstration of usefulness.

LEARNING THEORY

There are many ways to categorize learning theory. Three general categories are "philosophical," "psychological," and "sociological." The models proposed by the first school tend to be based on speculative, analytical, and logical analysis. The others tend to be based on case studies and statistical analysis of empirical observations. There are a few learning models that are completely in one category. Our learning model uses concepts from all three schools as represented in the work of John Dewey, Kurt Lewin, Jean Piaget, and Malcolm Knowles.

An assumption native to American learning theory, most strongly expressed by John Dewey (1910), is that application is the basis for primary and the most effective learning. Dewey advanced a philosophy of learning rather than an "approach." The philosophy postulated that learning is most effective when it is self-directed, guided by theory and feedback from knowledgeable mentors. Another tenet is that learning must be thought of as a lifelong process rather than as a set of isolated, unconnected occurrences.

Dewey assumed that experience is the organizing principle for all learning and emphasized the importance of learning to learn to engage in a lifelong learning process. He advanced a three-phase learning process. Experience is the starting phase. This is followed by activities to review and generalize the experience. In the third phase, the generalization is tested in practice. This leads to new experiences and a new cycle of learning. Dewey further pointed out that no two cycles are identical because experience changes the objective conditions under which subsequent experiences take place.

Lewin was a founder of the formal experiential learning approach for management development. His basic equation was that behavior is a function, in our terms, of the person's life-bank and the learning venue. In the Lewin (1951) model, learning takes place when experience is analyzed to test and validate theory, and this provides new insight. Learning is gained through observation, feedback, and reflection. A five-element cycle is posited. The elements are abstraction, concrete implication, experience, observation-feedback, and reflection. The last element leads to reinforced learned behavior and to new or higher-level abstraction.

Lewin hypothesized that learning requires going through the entire cycle. From our point of view, the cycle can start at any stage, with some learning (i.e., addition to the life-bank) taking place at each stage. This learning is validated and reinforced by completion of the next stage. The ability to use is usually gained after the "experience" stage. Learning, after initial use, is reinforced by the observation, feedback and reflection stages. Each stage picks up from the preceding one.

An influential training technique, the T-group, was derived from Lewin's theory of learning. T-groups focus on group process, the individual in the group, and relationships with others. The approach emphasizes experience and a feedback process as the basis for learning. Our theory and practice in use of small groups in the preceptorial process, described in Chapter 11, is derived in part from this theory.

Piaget put the same concepts into the form of a dialectic with learning as the synthesis of theory and experience. The preceptorial process makes use of this dialectic.

Most learning approaches that focus on changing behavior can be analyzed in terms of the Lewin (1951) metamodel for change: unfreeze, change, refreeze. The three stages tend to define objectives and assessment points for different types of educational programs. All are directly concerned with "unfreezing," most with "change," and a few with "refreezing."

Thorndike, an early American learning psychologist, defined three similar stages: "readiness" (unfreeze), "exercise" (change), and "effect" (refreeze). The behaviorists' dictum that behavior is determined and reinforced by its consequences tends to attribute the same underlying cause for all three of Lewin's states. Bandura (1969) postulates that input must be coded, organized into a meaningful (existing) framework, and symbolically rehearsed if it is to be retained. He assumes that people are basically reactive organisms.

The use of rewards to change and reinforce behavior, as advanced by Skinner (1948), is based on this learning theory. While the use of rewards had been the dominant management development approach long before Skinner, it was strengthened and reinvigorated by Skinner's analysis. The approach has been strongly attacked by human relations theorists such as Argyris (1962). The arguments include the following:

- The reinforcement approach leads to conditioned responses and not to learning and development.
- Actions that superiors consider to be reinforcements may not be so considered by the subordinate.
- There is no distinction between learning and performance.
- Unless the reinforcement is provided at the appropriate time, usually immediately after the approved performance, the practice may be counterproductive because the subordinate is distressed at not receiving the reward when it is expected.
- It tends to hinder self-actualization.

In our analysis, we assume that people are both proactive and reactive, sometimes both at the same time. Whether they are one or the other depends on the relationships among a number of variables that include the nature and power of the external force, anticipation of consequences, the life-bank, the venue, and the time and nature of the event.

Knowles (1980b) postulates a four-element cycle for adult learning: a concrete experience, analysis of the experience, derivation of explanatory concepts and models, and concrete experience to test the models.

LEARNING STYLES

People learn in many ways. The same person may learn in different ways under different circumstances. Changes in venue, time, content, and other variables may lead to different learning styles. Learning can be the outcome of a conscious effort to learn, a serendipitous consequence of an action taken for another purpose, or an unconscious rearrangement of life-bank elements.

Activities directed toward learning include observing, evaluating, and emulating the behavior of another; receiving, analyzing, integrating, and using information; acting in accordance with a theoretical frame of reference; and analyzing feedback. In the main, people learn by making sense of information, observation, and experiences in a manner that leads them to add to their life-banks.

There is a theory, supported by some empirical evidence, that individuals have relatively stable learning styles (Kolb 1984; Guild and Garger 1985). The learning styles postulated go far beyond the evidence provided. Hypotheses that have been made operational postulate how the learning styles of adults differ from those of young people. Most other theories are of limited practical use in management development.

It seems to be the case that the learning process is a function of the individual's pattern of interactions with the environment. The effective learning style is embedded in the individual's life-bank as metaelements, programmed responses to learning situations. If learning styles were constant for all learning situations, they would be very stable elements in life-banks. It would be extraordinarily difficult to change an individual's learning style in the course of a training program. Our assumption is that this is not the case. We believe, on the basis of our experience and review of the literature, that an individual's learning style may vary with time, the learning and application venues, the nature of the expected learning, and the relations between these and life-bank characteristics. Nevertheless, it is clear that the learning styles should be taken into account. Program design should make it possible to adapt the teaching styles to the learning styles of the participants.

Most theorists assume more detailed analytic models of learning styles than does our life-bank model. Kolb (1984) defines two learning dimensions, abstract/concrete and active/reflective, and four different learning styles. He relates his four learning styles to a person's occupation. While the evidence is not strong, the hypotheses are interesting:

- Abstract conceptualization and active experimentation characterize convergent learners, common among technical and engineering occupations.
- Concrete experience and reflective observation typify divergent learners. Personnel people and perhaps trainers fall into this category.
- Abstract conceptualization and reflective observation are characteristic of assimilation learners, often found in information and research occupations.
- Concrete experience and active experimentation are typical of accommodating executives and managers.

Kolb's analysis indicates that the preferred learning style for managers may result from a desire even greater than that of most adults to apply learning. Kolb also relates learning styles to psychological types, such as introvert/extrovert, as well as to occupational interests.

It is only in recent years that the distinction between adult and young learners has been made. While there have been many contributors to the theory, Knowles (1984a) is the best known. He has integrated many free-floating concepts and hypotheses into an operational model. His term "andragogy" signifies adult learning theory as differentiated from pedagogy.

Pedagogy employs passive learning approaches and radically simplified models to a greater extent than andragogy. Use of pedagogy assumes that the ability to learn and use models can be easily motivated. In terms of our model, pedagogy has an underlying assumption that learners have little in their life-banks to challenge or to be replaced by the content being taught. It is the state of the life-bank, not age, that determines the learning, and thus the teaching, style. If a person's life-bank is rich in the content to be learned and there is a rich, strongly linked relationship between learning and use, andragogy provides better guidance than pedagogy. This is the reason that most adults are not very efficient or effective passive learners. Their life-banks are rich in many content areas. These may contain elements that are related to or are in conflict with the content to be learned. Their life-banks also include metaelements that determine how they relate to others and their expectations for use of the learning.

Assumptions in the Knowles model include the following:

- Adults have rich life-banks. Life-bank content is the underlying resource and the major independent variable for learning activities.
- Adults tend to be self-directed. They want to participate in decisions affecting them.
- Adults have to be motivated by incentives to accept and use new learning.
- Adults tend to be application oriented. (The time lag between learning experience and expected use of learning affects motivation to learn.)

Knowles proposes different roles for the teacher and the learners in use of the pedagogical and andragogical models. In the pedagogical model the roles are omnipotent teacher and submissive students. A facilitator and participants are the roles in the andragogical model. The facilitator is a "leading participant" who helps—does not "drive"—participants to learn what they want to learn. There may be pedagogical and andragogical elements in the same learning experience. The degree of learner participation may vary from very little, in the pedagogical component, to very great, in the andragogical component.

Learning style theorists tend to focus on the role of the teacher: to adjust to the learners' life-banks, motivation, and different learning styles. As we have indicated, we assume that there are other important variables. Among them are the learning and use venues.

LEARNING APPROACHES

Learning approaches can be categorized as passive or experiential. These are not totally clear-cut distinctions, but they are serviceable for our purposes. Passive learning is any learning activity that does not require the participants to gather data, implement decisions in a physical sense, and deal with the consequences. Experiential learning is derived from experiences in taking an action, observing, and learning from the consequences of the action. Learning stems from both the behavior and the analysis of setting objectives, planning to achieve objectives, taking the planned action (behavior), observing and reacting to the consequences of the action, and generalizing from the experience. Experiential learning is also used to reinforce and strengthen competencies.

Passive approaches include discussion, lecture, reading, case analysis, problem assignments, and individual exercises. Passive learning does not generally require operational interaction with others or responding to changing circumstances. Passive approaches are most effective for increasing knowledge and skills that do not involve interaction with others. Exclusive use of passive learning assumes that managers will use the new knowledge and analytic skills in the work venue.

Experiential learning derives from transactions between the learner and the learning venue. Learning takes place primarily in an open system, in the interaction between internal and external vectors and as the resulting vector motivates changes in the person's life-bank. A further assumption is that learning is more effectively integrated when it is acquired and tested in a venue and under circumstances similar to those in which it is to be applied. The greater the similarity, the less need is there for adaptation, modification, and the introduction of new life-bank elements. Understanding abstract concepts, such as "participative management," is usually insufficient to produce significantly changed behavior in the work venue. In experiential theory, experience is the key that opens the door to useful new theory. Without both theory and experience in application in the work venue, there is far less chance that the theory will ever be applied in the work venue.

In Chapter 11 we describe an experiential model for management development. Our basic construct, the "life-bank," is defined as the significant determiner of the conditions under which effective learning can take place, what is learned and how it is learned, and the use to which learning is put. The life-bank is hypothesized to contain metaelements that determine processes for interpreting and structuring experience in order to add the learning to the bank. These metaelements also act as buffers that must be overcome before "new" learning can replace "old" learning.

While experience is a necessary element in the learning process, raw experience does not provide the basis for generalizing cause/effect and other relationships. At best, raw experience is the basis for "common-sense" learning. This is the specific knowledge that action A in situation B led to result C. Only when there are prior concepts and models relating to variables and relevant parameters, or there is prior induction to such models, is it possible to test general models and acquire transferable competencies. The results of action provide the feedback information that is the basis for learning. We do not learn from experience without active hypotheses to connect cause and effect. The fact that a hypothesis proves to be less useful than anticipated is an opportunity for learning.

Experiential learning requires learners to take an action, experience the action and its consequences in real time, analyze what happened, and hypothesize why it happened. This is distinguished from passive learning, in which the learner receives information and responds by describing and discussing a course of action using the information. We distinguish two major categories of experiential learning: synthetic and natural. "Synthetic experiential learning" is defined as learning that takes place when the action is in a venue constructed for the learning experience, a venue different from the one in which it is expected the learning will be used. Synthetic experiential learning utilizes cases, games, exercises, and other experiences that may or may not have a direct relationship to the work venue. The experience tends to be sharply focused in order to provide learning opportunities relating one or more of the three Lewin stages. Synthetic experiential learning is directed toward providing relevant practice, illustrating and giving insight into relationships and use of content, and providing an experience to use cognitive learning in a behavioral context.

"Natural experiential learning" makes use of naturally occurring situations and problems faced by the learner in the venue in which the learning is expected to be used. The experience may be selected to focus on learning or may be unstructured, that is, a special or a normal work assignment.

Few adults risk using in practice untested abstract concepts, assumptions, and models that could have adverse consequences. Persons who are very strongly oriented to the concrete, who tend to base behavior on "common sense"—on learning from experience—are often turned off by abstract concepts and highly theoretical models. Experiential learning is more effective because content and ability to use are tested and practiced in an appropriate venue and integrated into the life-bank.

The critical phases in the learning cycle are refreezing and transfer of learning to the work venue. Natural experiential learning assumes that success in this phase is more easily achieved by experience in the use of learning in real time, with real consequences, and with feedback from the role set.

Another barrier to learning is time. There are two kinds of time: the time between learning and use of learning, and the time spent in acquiring the learning. Adults, whose free time is limited, tend to be impatient. They want training and development to be short-term, learning to be applicable immediately, and significant results to follow at once. Unfortunately, learning and gaining the ability and confidence to use complex new behaviors are rarely achieved in short programs. Further, even if achieved, they frequently do not produce immediate, significant results. A consequence is that learning and motivation to use have to be periodically renewed and reinforced until change is refrozen. This process is integral to natural experiential learning, but it also tends to increase the learning time. The time may be less of a problem because the participants do not leave the work venue for any prolonged period and can apply new learning at any time.

Poor learning experiences in the past may present a barrier to new learning. Dissonance theory postulates a significant reduction in expectations if there was a significant difference (dissonance) between the learner's expectations and the consequences in a similar past experience. A poor learning experience in which either what was learned or the use to which learning could be put was not of any value, can lead to apathy toward participating and using learning. Successful experience in using, particularly in the work venue, can tend to overcome this barrier.

Experiential learning extended over a period of time and involving a number of integrated experiences with directed, incremental impact is less spectacular but usually more effective than learning directed toward achieving a single, comprehensive, multifaceted change. Passive learning tends to be directed toward a single change objective. Feedback during experiential learning permits sequencing learning experiences to maintain motivation because learning is progressive and integrated. In natural experiential learning, persons in the work venue are involved over a significant period of time. They are also engaged in the learning enterprise. There can be continuing feedback and reinforcement until the new behavior becomes the norm. The change is more than in the individual's behavior; it is also in the learning process as this process is subjected to analysis. Possible outputs are individual learning to learn from experience and a more active "learning culture" in the venue.

MOTIVATING LEARNING AND USE

There is usually no self-motivated force directed toward changing behavior and disrupting acceptable relationships in the work venue. Managers must be motivated to participate, learn, and change their behavior. Motivational theories provide some guidance for overcoming barriers to learning and utilizing learning. Lewin's force-field analysis provides an operational process to direct attention to forces driving and restraining change. Experiential learning strengthens motivation to change by providing experience in identifying and evaluating the consequence of using new learning.

There is evidence that a strong motivation for learning is experience in the past, being able to use new learning profitably. This hypothesis, not to be confused with Skinnerian conditioning assumptions, is one of our foundation hypotheses. Learning directed toward changing behavior is most effective when there is dynamic tension between the expected benefits and risks from use of new learning. The Dewey, Lewin, and Piaget models suggest that learning is the result of the resolution of different ways to respond to a conflict situation. Dewey emphasizes the difference between emotion and reason; Lewin, differences between concrete experience and models, and between observation and action. To Piaget, cognitive growth is a result of relating theory to experience and using experience to verify and modify theory.

Lewin (1951) employs a "utility" concept to analyze learners' motivation. That is, motivation to learn is a function of learning's perceived usefulness. This implies that potential participants relate the cost of participation in the learning enterprise to the anticipated benefits of an achievable goal. They assign subjective values to the expected gains and costs (time, prestige, opportunities lost) of attendance; the probability that they will be able to gain the expected competencies or other benefits from attendance; and the probability that they will be able to achieve their ultimate goals through these benefits.

This position is made more precise by current motivational theory. Vroom's expectancy theory (1964) can serve as a means for anticipating the reaction of participants to the development program as a whole as well as to specific elements. In Vroom's formulation, the key variables are the anticipated utility of the possible outcomes of investing to acquire the new behavior, the cost of engaging in the development program to acquire the behavior, and the probability of acquiring the behavior by participating in the program. If the utility resulting from participation is greater than that from alternative investments, positive motivation should result. In terms of expectancy theory, motivators are the direct output of participation in learning, such as acquiring new or greater competencies and the second- and higher-level outputs (the benefits from using the competencies). These are compared with the opportunity cost.

In Lewin's three-phase model for change, the psychological and social states in each of the three phases are so different that it is clear the motivating factors are different. However, the expectancy model is still useful. The first phase, "unfreeze," requires the learners to develop doubts about their current behavior and become motivated to consider changing it. In the second phase, "change," learners have to accept and become competent in a new behavior. The "refreeze" phase calls for the new behavior to become the accepted normal behavior, that is, for individuals to experience reinforcement through confirmation. Motivation to encourage "unfreezing" is different from that required for "change" or "refreezing." This may account for the failure of learning to transfer to the work site when motivation simply focuses on getting participants to agree that the new way is better than the old.

There is no strong experimental evidence to support any of the theories about what motivates a manager to participate, learn, and use learning. Evidence, such as it is, stems from experiments with students and other nonmanagerial groups in quite different situations, subjective comments from managers, and use of related models in economics. All the arguments against the use of the "rational decision" model apply to the motivation models. There is no generally acceptable empirical evidence to provide significant guidance on how to motivate managers to change their behavior in any radical manner. There are always strong forces opposed to any specific change. If the existing situation is in a state of stable equilibrium and there is no threat, any change is risky. Nevertheless, the motivational models provide a frame of reference and a structure useful for organizing, testing, analyzing, and understanding managers' motivation.

FEEDBACK

Feedback is information about the characteristics and impact of an activity, including effectiveness in achieving desired objectives. It is important in all learning approaches, and it is a critical element in the experiential learning process. Feedback is needed in every phase of experiential learning. The learners' self-assessment of their needs (e.g., feedback on current performance, prior to participation in development) tends to motivate learning. The assessment provides information for testing and guiding selection of learning processes and content. It is also the start of the unfreezing process. Feedback during the learning process with respect to change and confirmation (refreezing) is the basis for program modification. At the conclusion of the formal learning process, feedback provides leads for completing the refreezing and the basis for continued, independent learning. Feedback is more effective when it is specific and close in time to the behavior.

Feedback has to be used carefully. Today's observation may be tomorrow's fiction. Feedback is a biased report. Selected observations are presented in a highly subjective, personal manner. Structured reporting forms and standards may either help or restrict observation and usefulness of data. There is a natural tendency to overlook incongruities that arise in use of very general, linear models provided in passive learning and in the combination of folklore and unique experiences that is the source of "common sense."

In all learning processes, including feedback, dissonance presents potential problems as well as opportunities. Dissonance theory postulates that the more strongly held the views and the greater the differences between them, the greater will be the motivating drive for adjustment. To the extent that learning is seen as a force for adjusting differences, there will be motivation to learn. To the extent that learning is seen as a possible source of dissonance, there is no motivation to learn. Feedback from experience that demonstrates low threat and some benefits tends to increase motivation to freeze change. Evidence of greater-than-expected risk or lower-than-expected benefits may have the opposite effect.

Knowles (1987) advocates use of a learning contract. Contract terms are the basis for feedback and evaluating progress. The approach is used in independent study courses and in external degree programs. Knowles emphasizes the role of the contract as a plan for the learner to acquire agreed upon competencies. A typical contract contains learning objectives, resources and strategies to achieve objectives, evidence to measure achievement, how evidence will be judged, and target dates. The contract not only involves participants in planning but also provides focus and standards by structuring the learning and evaluation processes. It is the basis for self-assessment and discussions with a mentor. The contract can be used effectively with both passive and experiential learning approaches.

Some theorists (Kolb 1984) distinguish levels of feedback. At the first level is information about goal attainment. At the second level is information about the usefulness and validity of the criteria selected for first-level feedback, the meaning of the criteria, and their relationships to the goals. At the third level are processes for comparing and acting on incommensurable outputs and corrective alternatives.

The general attraction of specific learning techniques is rarely considered in discussions of learning styles. Enjoyment of games that motivate interest, whether or not related to the content, is an example. The use of games seems to be related to learning style. The play element has a motivating force that goes beyond learning. Huizinga (1955) states:

> The concept [play] seems capable of embracing everything we call "play" in animals, children and grown-ups: games of strength and skill, inventing games, guessing games, games of chance, exhibitions and performances of all kinds. We venture to call the category "play" one of the most fundamental in life. (p. 28)

LEARNING THEORY AND TRAINING

Training is a special kind of education in which learning theory has to be focused more directly on use. Odiorne (1985) and Gagne (1970) are two of the theorists who apply general learning theories to the specialized field of training. Odiorne's ten postulates for training relate more to Knowles's principles than do Gagne's rules.

Odiorne advocates the following:

- Focus on behavior rather than on personality.
- Design for results, not process.
- Relate training to the work venue.
- Use instrumental and behavior content.
- Define training criteria and standards.
- Emphasize experiential learning.
- Use a sequence of objectives to reach the ultimate objectives.
- Use learner self-feedback during the learning process.
- Provide feedback to guide learning.
- Measure training results against goals.

Gagne's (1970) rules were developed primarily for skill training. They emphasize technique and passive learning more than do Odiorne's rules. However, it is interesting to note how they relate to the life-bank concept. Gagne postulates both general guides and specific rules. Among the guides are the following:

- In the teaching/learning process, gain attention, present objectives, recall prior learning, present information, and guide learning.
- Use instructional guides to present information so as to involve and "unfreeze" the student from less effective competencies and views. Guide learning to emphasize key elements for significant change, and use practice to refreeze learned competencies. Use feedback to reinforce effective performance. Continue the active learning process until the participant is competent and the desired behavior is mastered.
- Focus on application through natural and synthetic experiential learning. Deal with barriers to using learning.

Gagne's position is that people learn by combining rules in their life-banks into novel higher-order rules. This leads to Gagne's major assumption (1970) that the ability to solve new problems and acquire new competencies is a consequence of the activity of developing new combinations of life-bank elements.

LIFELONG AND ORGANIZATIONAL LEARNING

Our discussions of adult learning, motivation to learn, and use of learning were based to a considerable extent on the assumption that managers make a rational analysis and choice of whether to participate, incorporate the learning in their life-banks, and use the learning in the work venue. These assumptions presume that people's utility can be converted to one dimension—that is, that the many variables determining "utility" are approximately fungible (the utility function can be mapped in one dimension). In fact, it is more reasonable to assume that "utility" is a function of many independent variables. These variables may not be able to be traded off against each other by any mechanical means or generally applicable set of rules. Nor, even if there is a useful set of rules, can we assume that they are invariant over time. Trade-off can be approximated, to some extent, by the individual learner or a skilled mentor for specific decisions at a particular moment in time. This analysis leads to the oft-repeated hypothesis that the only effective development is the result of independent, individual learning. Unfortunately, this is the most difficult kind of learning. For this reason there has been emphasis in recent years, in recognition that successful education must be lifelong, on helping people to learn how to learn.

There is no evidence that without training and guided experience, many can and will design and implement effective learning plans for themselves. It is a rational assumption that the learning and use venues affect lifelong learning.

In addition to inculcating motivation to make a continuing effort, people must strengthen their life-banks by incorporating more effective metaelements to accomplish the following:

- to seek, process, and integrate new information and competencies into existing schemata for systematically related networks of connected information and competencies
- to develop and master effective schemata for identifying potentially active learning and for identifying and discarding inert learning
- to practice using, testing, and modifying the learning process schemata.

In addition to the effort to develop competence for lifelong learning, there are increasing references in the literature to "organizational" learning and developing an "organizational culture for learning." Though it is not clear what is meant, we tend to agree with Dery's observation (1986):

> The literature on organizational learning would thus appear as an important source of insights for the study of utilization [of knowledge] as an organizational

> phenomenon. Having consulted this literature, however, one is sent back to the stress on individuals, which one sought to avoid in the first place. . . . Learning behavior—on the part of individual members rather than some mysterious collective brain—is organizational learning by virtue of the organizational norms, mental maps, and rules of observation and inference that seek to govern the behavior of individual members. (p. 15)

We note that Dery's analysis supports our assumptions of the relationship between individual learning, including lifelong learning, and the work venue.

SOME ASSUMPTIONS

Based on the hypotheses discussed in this chapter and our own observations during years of designing and conducting training and development programs, we have developed a set of assumptions on which we base our experiential learning approach. We do not claim any priority. We have done what many have done in the past. We borrowed from the giants in the field and tried to extend and integrate their concepts for use in management development.

We have extended Dewey's (1938) principle of continuity to develop and define our primary construct, the individual's life-bank. We postulate, with Dewey, that new learning must not be inconsistent with past learning and experience. This leads us to assume that there is a reactive conservatism in adding to or changing rich life-banks, and to postulate that new learning must be sufficiently motivated and challenging to warrant "unfreezing" and "change." We also assume that forces in individuals have to be proactive in specific challenging situations, to be self-motivated to change. The situational parameters are to a great extent determined by the work venue characteristics and the defined role of the manager.

We modify Lewin's (1951) formula for action as interaction between the individual and the environment with the concepts of venue and life-bank. Similarly, Knowles's (1980) andragogical model is modified to focus on learning styles and, consequently, teaching styles as functions of each individual's life-bank. The concepts "organizational culture" (Bennis 1966) and "organizational learning" (Dery 1986) are tied to and derived from interaction between individual life-banks and the venue. Assumptions related to management development include the following:

- Managers' life-banks contain elements derived from rich education and experience that are both incentives to increase competence as managers and be self-directing persons and disincentives critical of formal learning for development.

- Managers have had a variety of experiences and passed through a number of life phases. These tend to structure their life-banks so that their responses to similar stimuli in different venues cannot be assumed to be similar. However, there tends to be a core of stable metaelements in their life-banks related to the work venue. These include the processes that determine motivation to learn and to establish and maintain relationships.
- More than most people, managers seek to generalize from individual experiences to obtain models that can be incorporated into their life-banks to guide, structure, and give meaning to managerial experience.
- Elements in a manager's life-bank that remain unchallenged for a long time can become self-evident truths which are very hard to dislodge. Successful managers have to be positively motivated to make the effort to seek new learning directed toward changing their behavior.
- Managers unfreeze, change, and refreeze more easily and effectively when the learning venue is very similar to the one in which the learning will be applied.
- Lifelong learning is a function of the individual's life-bank and the learning venue.
- Development is a process of using, adapting, and adding to the life-bank in response to the demands in the use venue.

6

LEARNING THEORY AND MANAGEMENT DEVELOPMENT

ROLE AND GOAL OF MANAGEMENT DEVELOPMENT

Management development is an organized effort to motivate and help managers to change their behavior in a defined manner through education, training, experience, and feedback. Not all of the principal groups involved—the participating managers, their sponsoring organizations (including their direct supervisors), and the providers—have the same objectives. However, all three assume to some extent that the following are true:

- Organizational and managerial performance can be improved by specified changes in managerial behavior.
- The changes in behavior can be determined.
- Managers can be motivated and learn to change their behavior in the desired manner.
- They can gain acceptance and support for the changed behavior from their role sets.

Based on the investment made for management development, it is obvious that sponsors look upon these goals as desirable. Nevertheless, they must see achieving the goals as problematic. There are various reasons for this conclusion:

- Most managers are hired on the basis of their track records as managers.
- Management development is one of the first activities to be cut in periods of financial difficulty.
- Many executives resist having their companies invest the time and effort in management development.

The stakeholders who are most optimistic about the value of management development are the providers. The evaluations of the three groups of stakeholders influence the nature of management development. The sponsors pay the providers and tend to call the tune. Not infrequently they invest for reasons other than belief that management development will increase managerial competencies.

PARTICIPANTS AND VENUES

Under normal conditions, the pressures on managers at work and their response to these pressures are in stable equilibrium. For managers' behavior to change, this equilibrium must be displaced. This is difficult unless there are perceived beneficial consequences for the managers.

Some barriers that change agents must overcome in management development programs are the following:

- The participants have to accept that a change in their behavior is desirable, that is, "unfreezing" is necessary.
- The participants have to accept the new behavior and that the proposed learning will lead to the desired behavior. This can be partially resolved by their participation in determining objectives and means for achieving the objectives.
- Participants have to believe that they are capable of becoming competent in the exercise of the new behavior. This requires its successful use in passive and experiential exercises.
- Participants have to approve of the targeted behavior. If this requires changing basic values, it may not be an appropriate management development objective.
- Feedback has to provide guidance and reinforcement to help managers improve and refreeze the desired behaviors. Managers have to learn to make use of feedback.
- Participants have to have opportunities to adapt the general model to different conditions. This calls for learning to extend learning from limited experience to a wide range of possible experiences.

Generally approved approaches to overcome the difficulties are participation by the managers in definition of objectives and choice of content; alignment of characteristics of the learning and work venues; and changing design as more is learned about the participants and their work venues.

Maintaining significant change in managerial behavior is generally successful only in a supporting venue. The new behavior must be seen as beneficial by the manager, accepted by the manager's role set, and reinforced by senior management. Management takes place in a fairly homogeneous culture. Deviation from the norm is readily discernible and the pressure to conform is great. Only the managers who have participated have been motivated and helped to change. The members of their role sets have not changed and have unchanged expectations. Managers have to learn how to deal with the resistance that can be anticipated. Members of the role set must be motivated to change their behavior to mesh with the managers' new behavior.

Practicing managers rarely have learned how to develop general models based on their experiences or to acquire and test new knowledge. In most systems there is pressure to produce that may involve risk and threat of failure. The effort to resolve these countervailing forces is motivation for management development.

Based on a review of the research literature, Campbell et al. (1970) found "that non-managerial, non-professional personnel in the United States tend to value job security, opportunities for advancement, interesting work, and interesting co-workers most highly" (p. 364). While there is less research on managerial preferences, they found managers favor "a high salary to guarantees of job tenure and fringe benefits" (p. 364–365).

The summary of the research by Campbell et al. indicated the following:

- Managers tend to value esteem, autonomy, and achievement more than security or social relationships to a greater extent than do nonmanagers. "Good" managers tend to value these more than "poor" managers.
- There is little evidence that money is a very effective incentive to improve managerial performance.
- There are laboratory findings, supported by some limited field research, which indicate that giving managers specific, difficult goals tends to increase output to a greater extent than general direction and moderately difficult goals.

Managers are more concerned with improving their performance than are most workers. They seek to acquire information related to their jobs, have a greater sense of competitiveness on the job (the desire to excel), and have a strong feeling of responsibility.

The research noted gives some insight into the unique contents of managers' life-banks. It does not matter much whether these characteristics stem from personalities that led them to become managers or developed after they became managers. The important thing is that managers' life-banks contain both the base for motivating new learning that leads to change and the barriers to change which does not promise beneficial transfer. It is not clear how these characteristics trade off against each other in any specific situation. In fact, sometimes the very same characteristics are seen as leading to diametrically opposed positions. For example, characteristics such as competitiveness and responsibility could lead us to conclude that managers have greater motivation to participate in development. This is frequently not the case. The competitiveness and responsibility could also make them loath to be away from the job for any significant amount of time or to expend time and concentration on reading theoretical literature that cannot be directly applied.

Simon (1957) notes that, in general, people seek decisions which satisfice rather than maximize. It follows that there are life-bank elements which tend to narrow managers' focus in development to solutions to current problems.

The expressive tasks are usually seen as more difficult and ambiguous than the instrumental tasks. Managers generally feel competent to perform instrumental tasks. Thus, while asking for more emphasis on expressive learning, they tend to appreciate learning that increases instrumental competencies. These programs can have specific objectives. And programs are more attractive to managers if directed toward helping them achieve specific managerial objectives.

Because managers are less sure of their competence to handle expressive tasks, they are likely to accept almost anything in the expressive area as useful learning. However, acceptance does not mean use.

Programs for specific organizations tend to be, in part at least, based on a needs analysis. The needs analysis is based, in great part, on a comparison between the characteristics of the organization and the managers' life-banks and the characteristics of effective organizations and managers as defined in the current literature of management theory and practice. Rationally, management development theory mandates that a reliable, valid needs analysis should determine the content. What is frequently ignored is that few needs analyses are either reliable or valid. At best they are based on a comparison between a less-than-reliable estimate of a current situation and a set of questionable hypotheses. Both are selective, radical simplifications of reality. More frequently the analysis serves to support predetermined designs. It can be biased by the process of selecting the operant variables, assumptions about the relationships among them, and the process by which conclusions are drawn from the findings. The conclusions are a set of hypotheses. The needs analysis is not a substitute for determining usefulness of learning in the work venue, which can be determined only by continuously measuring the impact of the transfer of learning.

Even when the needs analysis is a neutral, professional operation, it is never the total basis for program design. More than the needs analysis, the resources and time allotted for a program tend to determine the objectives, content, and educational approach. Organizations and individuals that invest in development wish to obtain the best return from the investment. In practical terms, this may mean limiting the amount of time for development, increasing program content (concern with knowledge learning, not application) and using passive rather than experiential approaches.

Senior management's objectives determine subordinate managers' "needs" and the design of development. Unless top management reinforces the will to take the risk entailed in innovation by demonstrating its own willingness to risk change, management development can accomplish little. At best, it can help to introduce some new techniques. The necessary investment must include more than providing the time and other resources required. It calls for senior managers to be mentors.

We conclude that while there is an expressed desire to motivate and help managers gain generalized competencies, most of the proximate forces tend to reinforce the push for short courses that, it is hoped, will provide immediate answers. This is the case even though there is no evidence that short courses with general answers produce either significant learning or improved performance.

THEORY OF MANAGEMENT DEVELOPMENT

There is no comprehensive theory of management development that provides a model for motivating and helping managers acquire and use specified competencies. Rather than an integration of management and learning theory and practice, management development is a patchwork of bits and pieces of learning theory and guidelines, and management theory and practice. To a greater extent than other learning programs, the learning model implicit in management development is the "unfreeze"-"change"-"refreeze" model associated with Kurt Lewin.

Management theory provides the content. It is the structure on which management practice is based. However, there is no guide to moving from general models to specific application or to transferring learning from one experience to another. Management theory only defines in general terms managers' roles and the competencies managers need. Learning theory is only a general guide for designing the processes to help managers learn. Management practice is concerned with task selection and performance. This defines the nature of the contributions managers are expected to make. Management development seeks to integrate the flow from these three sources. It utilizes management theory and practice to determine program content—the competencies, both expressive and instrumental—needed by specific managers in specific situations. It integrates the content with the most effective learning approaches to motivate and help managers acquire and utilize the competencies effectively in the work venue.

Management development's achievement must be measured by change in managers' behavior and the impact of this change in the work venue. While senior management's objective is change in the work venue that benefits the organization, the individual manager's objective is personal improvement.

Learning theory and practice are directed toward achieving the managers' personal goals. There is little theory and practice relating to improving organizational goals. Only rarely are organizational and personal objectives given equal weight. In university degree programs, the course content and the individual participants are most important. This is equally the case in nonacademic programs in which participants come from a number of organizations. The shift to concern about the organization's objectives is almost complete in programs in which all participants come from the same organization. The impact on the organization becomes the focus. There is also concern with the impact of these changes on the performance of other managers and units.

Two programs that have as objectives both individual and organizational performance improvement are described by Slavenski (1987) and Long (1988). The first includes performance analysis, followed by individual career development discussions and a review of organizational needs. Based on these, individual plans are developed. Long describes a program in which individual objectives are derived from a comparison with characteristics of a model manager, as seen by senior management, and letting the individual managers, with professional assistance, construct their individual development plans.

APPLICATION OF THEORY

The objectives for development set by senior management are only indirectly influenced by current thinking about the role of the manager. Senior managers' perceived needs tend to be derived from an unstructured analysis of their own experiences and those of managers they have observed. This is supplemented by magazine articles and best-sellers describing behavior of "successful" managers and by guidance from the program providers.

The program objectives advanced by top management may not help managers acquire the characteristics of the managers who are rewarded in their companies. The objectives set by most senior management during the past few decades have been related to expressive competencies, such as "improved leadership." In practice, these competencies are rarely rewarded unless there is evidence of a positive effect on profits. Schools of business and public administration and others involved in management development tend to structure their programs to emphasize the managerial tasks that they can teach most effectively. In the schools, these are the instrumental tasks, for which the required competencies are technical skills, not human relations abilities (Porter and McKibbin 1988).

An important task of the development designer is to synthesize learning theory and practice with management and managers' roles. The relative importance attached to the instrumental and expressive roles determines the content of development and, in large part, the learning approach that is used in the development program.

One concern of schools is maintenance of academic standing. When they teach the expressive aspects of management, they seem not to be quite sure whether they are prescribing sound medication or snake oil. They do not seem to be sure whether these competencies should be taught because managers need them to be successful or because some humanist theorists think that they should be taught. A similar case is presented by "charisma." Many books ascribe the success of leaders to "charisma." Business schools are not quite sure how to help managers become charismatic.

Nondegree programs, with participants from many different organizations, tend to use general models. The content varies from specialization in such areas as leadership and problem solving to idiosyncratic mixes of instrumental and expressive learning. The focus in programs for practicing managers is more directly on use in the work venue. This leads to incorporating the specific content, more often than in degree programs, in a more holistic frame of reference. The assumption that use rather than knowledge is the primary objective leads to use of teaching methods focused on use: experiential learning. Most programs conducted by nonacademic organizations and consultants tend to develop and use a variety of synthetic experiential learning techniques. These techniques are used because their effectiveness is supported by learning theory (Knowles 1980b) and they are popular with participants.

Expectancy theory (discussed in Chapter 3), coupled with the Campbell et al. (1970) and Mintzberg (1973) studies of managerial characteristics, provides a guide to motivating managers to participate, unfreeze, change, and refreeze. The theory can be used to estimate the readiness of managers to participate in a specific program and their ability and will to learn and to use the learning in the work venue. It can also provide guidance for motivating transfer of learning to the work venue.

On the job, the outcomes are the consequences of the manager's behavior and, equally important, feedback from members of the manager's role set, which includes superiors, peers, and subordinates. Sometimes feedback is in terms of rewards. Sometimes it is in terms of relationships and cooperation. The analysis of Campbell et al. tends to emphasize intrinsic benefits. These may not always be the most important. However, whether benefits are intrinsic or extrinsic, expectancy tends to be influenced by higher-level managers. This is the major reason why needs analysis hinges to a greater degree on the needs of the superiors than on the needs of the participating managers. It is also the reason why managers agree with this decision. When program participants are given greater say in program objectives and design, they tend to try to anticipate the wishes of their superiors.

While design of the learning process is usually left to the trainers, managers tend to expect that passive learning will be used for knowledge and skills acquisition, and experiential learning for increasing expressive competencies and potential for transfer of learning.

Passive approaches, in both pedagogy and andragogy, are in general used for the efficient acquisition of knowledge. An important difference is that in pedagogy little need is seen for unfreezing participants' beliefs. It is assumed that learners' life-banks have little that will conflict with what is being taught. This is not the case with managers with rich life-banks. A principal purpose of lecture and discussion of new theory and techniques in management development is to emancipate participants' thinking from biases in favor of their current and accepted practices. The passive learning can motivate participants to consider alternatives. This has the potential for unfreezing fixed positions without the threat of the need for change. This stage, which might be considered preparation for unfreezing, can in some cases be completed more efficiently by passive than by experiential learning. However, the passive learning may not provide sufficient motivation for unfreezing.

Many managers enjoy and are motivated to acquire knowledge just to be au courant. They will frequently engage in independent study in the form of reading popular books on management theory and practice just to be able to talk a good game. Unless used and incorporated as an active element in their life-banks, this learning may become counterproductive. It is dredged up to demonstrate knowledge of management and sometimes to deprecate the need for change.

Some passive approaches may, in specific circumstances, be quite effective in completing the unfreezing phase. Some may succeed in the change phase. Virtually none help in refreezing. The case method is frequently seen as being effective in unfreezing and leading to change. A case is described as a management situation that calls for analysis leading to a decision. Typically the participants study and analyze the situation and come to their own decisions. These are then discussed by the group as a whole. The objective is not to come to a consensus but to give participants experience in rational analysis, problem solving and decision making, communicating, and defending their decisions. It is assumed that there is learning from assessing and discussing the analysis and decision making of others. The give-and-take in the discussion has some characteristics of role-playing.

While the case method has the possibility of leading to unfreezing and change, it may also lead to reinforcement of current behavior, particularly if an individual is very persuasive and can defend his or her position and attack those of others effectively. The method was developed as a substitute for experiential learning. It is still extensively employed in some professional schools. Harvard is purported to have more than 4,000 active management-related cases. Most business schools and schools of public administration have their own libraries of cases, as do the independent consultants. The latter frequently develop cases from their clients' experiences. These have the added advantage of being accepted by participants as a continuation of their work activities. However, participants are not doing and reaping the consequences of their decision making.

Shannon (1990) describes a computer program for improving management skills that is programmed to ask a series of questions designed to help a manager to improve performance by tapping and reactivating inactive elements in the manager's life bank. This type of passive program may serve to strengthen refreezing a changed skill.

Learning some competencies calls for a mix of learning approaches. In general this is the case with the competencies we put into the category "judgment." Included in judgment are problem solving and decision making. Passive approaches tend to be superior, most of the time, for learning problem-solving techniques and evaluation of alternatives risks and cost/benefits, to the extent that working with other people is not involved. Experiential learning is seen as superior for improving decision making and competence in risk taking, where others who are involved or the consequences of the action can have significant impact on the decision maker.

An example of misplaced confidence in the effectiveness of passive learning is the attempt to raise ethical standards by courses in ethics. The following is illustrative:

The Chicago Mercantile Exchange has ordered its 2,500 members to enroll in ethics classes—50 two hour classes—by a team of law professors from Kent College, who will present hypothetical situations that Merc members might encounter. This was in response to findings of fraudulent practices uncovered by the FBI. (*New York Times*, April 11, 1990)

We doubt that many of these highly educated people need much education to distinguish right from wrong in their day-to-day operations. We also doubt that many of the teachers of the ethics classes are unfamiliar with the Platonic argument that passive learning is inadequate for changing values. We do not believe that strong personal values can be changed by rational analysis or unrelated experiences.

The two categories of experiential learning, synthetic and natural, and the techniques of each will be discussed in some detail in later chapters. We limit ourselves here to some general comments and comparisons with passive learning. It is clear that managers satisfy, to an even greater extent than other adults, the conditions for andragogical learning—in our terms, motivating persons with rich data-banks to learn and to transfer learning to the work venue. Most managers respond better to experiential learning than to passive learning. However, this tends to be less so with chief executive officers and some high-ranking officials. They tend to be impatient and less receptive to the pace and feedback of experiential learning. They also tend to feel that given the necessary information, they will change their behavior and that their changed behavior will force others to change.

The two most commonly used synthetic experiential approaches are simulations and games. Neither seeks precise duplication of the real work situation. Simulations present a managerial, or managerial-related, problem situation involving a limited number of variables that will be recognizable and challenging to all the participants. Games may not be directly related to management at all. They may be illustrative, or involve the "same kind" of thinking or emotions that are present in management. Synthetic experiential designs tend to have fairly well defined development objectives. These include increasing sensitivity and insight into human behavior; improving ability to work with and influence others; motivating risk analysis and risk taking under specific circumstances; competence in negotiating and conflict resolution; problem solving; decision making; and giving and using feedback.

Synthetic experiential learning has three great strengths: focusing on specific learning directed to areas of identified need and interest; providing experience to practice and test the use of learning unencumbered by any distractions from other responsibilities; and following up the experience with group discussion of the experience and its value for use in the work venue. It uses time efficiently by collapsing time and eliminating variables present in natural experiences.

Briefly, the weakness of synthetic learning is in great part a mirror image of its strengths. The sharp focus and directed experience in a tight time frame are not characteristic of most management. There is experience, but it is not managerial experience. The immediate feedback and discussion tend to be about the exercise and learning experience. Rarely is there analysis of value for transfer to a specific work venue. Further, the competencies required for exercises and games are not always those which are most effective in management.

Where the primary or most difficult problem is seen as the need to unfreeze existing life-bank elements, there is a tendency to favor emotional approaches. The "shock' development approaches employ synthetic experiential learning to achieve unfreezing. Common objectives of these approaches are to increase self-confidence, acceptance of team activities, and willingness to take risk. Some aim at developing personality types that will provide greater support for top management and the dominant culture of the organization. Where they seek to produce change as well as unfreezing, these approaches tend to focus on the total personality of the participant rather than on the managerial role. Two popular types are the "human potential" and "New Age" programs. Their content and techniques range from physical "shooting the rapids" and mountain climbing to EST and spiritualism. In approaches such as EST, participants are subjected to a planned sequence of abuse, trauma, boredom, and discomfort. These approaches assume that participants' concepts of the real world and their relations to it, in particular managerial assumptions, can be unfrozen and left open to radical change by unusual mental and physical challenge, forms of shock therapy, and, in some cases, confidence in the existence of a higher being.

For a while, the most popular approach for unfreezing was "sensitivity training," in which participants engage in both unstructured and partially structured forms of group interaction and psychoanalysis. The National Training Laboratories was the central force in this movement. Criticism of the approach focused on the design's perceived overemphasis on limited competencies in the expressive role and its failure to integrate these with the instrumental role and other expressive competencies.

Where the design objective is primarily to induce change, rational arguments and passive learning approaches are frequently the first choice. Problems with the existing behavior are discussed. The superiority of the proposed new behavior or technique is described and demonstrated through discussion and analysis of alternatives. When passive learning is not expected to suffice, some tend to use experiential learning to reinforce the change achieved by passive learning. The model introduced in passive learning is tried out in experiences involving experiential learning.

Refreezing is generally seen as the most difficult stage to accomplish in management development. In addition to continuing management development for this stage, three other approaches for refreezing are used:

1. Change the incentive system to motivate managers to change and to continue the changed behavior by making a significant, well-defined difference in the managers' expectancy between continued use and disuse of the new behavior.

2. Change the organizational structure (task assignments and processes) to make it obvious that failure to continue the new behavior will be counterproductive for many in the organization, including key members of the manager's role set.
3. Change significant characteristics of the culture of the work venue to make the new managerial behaviors expected and "natural." This may involve directed planned change in related work groups to give all compatible, interrelated objectives.

While the needs analysis may clarify to some extent what the objectives and content of the program should be, and help program designers to determine appropriate learning approaches, it is not known how prepared managers are to use the learning.

It is fairly well accepted that there are different learning styles. There are a number of different classifications of these (Guild and Garger 1985). Kolb (1984) proposes four learning styles that, although stable, are not seen as frozen. They are subject to change in the course of life experience. Kolb describes the styles in terms of two learning dimensions: abstract/concrete and active/reflective. The factors that determine the preferred style include psychological type (introvert/extrovert), educational specialization (social/physical science), professional career (social/science based), and current job. Kolb notes that the demands imposed by the venue "exert a somewhat stronger, but more situation-specific influence on the learning style" than do the basic personality orientation and education.

Of particular interest to us is that Kolb conducted some research with respect to managers' learning styles. He found that different learning styles exist and are partially explained by the managers' undergraduate specialization. He concluded that managers' preferred learning styles result from a concern to apply ideas and tend to be abstract and active. This reinforces the arguments for use of passive learning for unfreezing and providing knowledge leading to change, and use of experiential learning for reinforcing change and refreezing.

Mouton and Blake (1984) are among the few management development practitioners who deal with the problem presented by learning styles. They combine learner-centered education and instructor-centered education (andragogy and pedagogy) to achieve the advantages of both types of education in the process they call "synergogy." This has three primary elements:

- Programmed learning designs and instruments are employed to "enable the learner to learn without a teacher."
- An emphasis on team rather than individual performance is expected to increase individual involvement.

- Learning approaches and instruments are designed to encourage participants to share knowledge and thought processes.
- "Learning designs and learning instruments . . . allow members to methodically share knowledge, explore each other's reasoning, and examine implication for understanding." (pp. 60–61)

Many program designs combine formal passive and experiential approaches. Some combine organizational development with structured passive approaches. Frizell and Gellermann (1988) describe a program in which management development and organizational development were joined. Use of learning to effect change and a peer group to monitor and help refreeze change were built into the program.

Learning theory and managerial experience both lead to the conclusion that to be effective, change resulting from management development must be acceptable and supported in the work venue. Yet no two work venues are the same. Just as development can fail by not considering and adapting to the characteristics of the participants, so it can fail for want of considering the characteristics of the work venue. However, it may be possible to adapt models from other work venues. Wall and Ondrasik (1988) show how. By tying the modifications to ongoing performance evaluations, they developed a sequence of incremental modifications of an American design for supervisory training to produce a design useful in Third World economies.

Academic institutions teach what faculties want to teach. They tend to emphasize the instrumental tasks and competencies we define as knowledge and skills. Much of academic management education consists of definitions, analytic models, and manipulation of generalized variables (symbols representing real things and activities) and axioms (relationship and cause/effect assumptions). In the work venue, managers are faced not with symbols and axioms but with concrete situations and people. These vary, but usually not in the same way as the variables in models. It is expected that managers will be able to transfer the symbolic learning to use in the work venue.

Discounting providers' predilections, the content of programs is determined by research studies of the role and tasks of managers. Even the needs analysis is based on the definition of the expected role, tasks, and competencies of the manager. Sometimes the research is quite general, involving the activities of managers in many organizations. Studies by Mintzberg (1973) and Sutton and McQuigg-Martinez (1990) are typical. Sometimes they are specific to one organization. We believe that even when limited to a single organization, the studies are only guides of limited value. Tasks performed by managers not only change significantly from organization to organization and from manager to manager in the same organization (Sutton and McQuigg-Martinetz 1990), they also change for the same manager as the situation changes. This research supports a contingency definition of the managerial role.

In the contingency definition, there is no fixed set of primary managerial tasks or competencies, nor any certain solutions for any class of management problems. To be effective, a manager needs an arsenal of competencies and must be able to engage in continuous analysis and to learn from experience. Management development must focus on helping managers learn to add to their life-banks from a variety of sources. The most important source is structured observation and analysis of their experiences. They must learn to relate experiences (cause/effect relationships) to the armory of models in their life-banks, to select and adapt the ones that are most appropriate for the specific situation. They must learn to develop, test, and use the models that help them make sense of their experiences.

Long (1988) describes a program in which there was strong organizational pressure for changes in the role and competencies of managers. There was no agreement on what the changes should be. Top management recognized that unless the organization's goals and strategies were well defined, time spent on needs analysis and management development would be counterproductive. Consequently, before designing the development program, top management spent a year defining organizational objectives, studying the alternative strategies for achieving these, and identifying, evaluating, and selecting models of managerial styles and competencies needed to implement the strategies. The program was designed to motivate managers to acquire the style and competencies of the models. The models were presented and discussed with all executives in a week-long seminar attended by top management. Executives were motivated and helped to compare their own styles with those of the models. After there was agreement on a specific model, the executives designed their own development plans (Long 1988). While Long does not point them out in his article, there are several applications of theory: top-level support; uniform objectives with individual application, strong unfreezing motivation; individual determination of the degree and manner in which to change behavior to a predetermined model; and feedback from performance to direct change and help refreezing.

Claims that the world economy is changing so profoundly that there will be radically new occupations requiring different competencies have led to the educational objective of helping learners to acquire general competencies which will be adaptable to all circumstances, including those not foreseeable. The solution of choice at the moment is liberal arts content plus training in problem solving. Although primarily a pedagogical objective and learning process for schoolchildren, this solution has also been prescribed for managers.

This seems, on the surface, to be similar to the contingency position, but in specifics this is not the case. The emphasis on introducing a sample of all human knowledge as the base for creative change is very different from introducing alternative approaches. Contingency does not assume that management problems and challenges will involve change so radical that it makes current managerial competencies useless. Changes will occur, but most will be incremental. The contingency assumption is that we do not know in advance which management approach or technique will be most useful. This leads to the concept of an armory of techniques and approaches, and learning to select from alternatives. Liberal arts does not provide an armory; it provides general knowledge that may be not an all-purpose but a no-purpose tool. There is no evidence that liberal arts learning is of value for managers as managers. Its value is personal enrichment and possible social use. These may be helpful in some personal relations. Management development should add to a manager's armory the desire and competence to continue learning from experience and independent study.

A still popular content area is "human relations," which embraces a multitude of abilities, including leadership. The focus tends to be on participation and concern for subordinates. There are sharp differences among both theoreticians and practitioners about the soundness of the approach. According to Simon (1973), a major principle of the human relations school is that making work rewarding and enjoyable is a higher objective than increasing efficiency and effectiveness. Many "human relations" advocates would claim that these are not conflicting objectives but that making work rewarding tends to increase efficiency and effectiveness. It is not evident that top management accepts the reasoning of the "human relations" school or that labor leaders accept Simon's analysis.

PROGRAM DESIGN

There are a number of stages or steps in the design of management development programs, and they draw on different aspects of learning theory. We identify six steps. Although we describe these in sequence, and for the most part they are carried out in this sequence, they need not be. Each step assesses and builds on feedback from the preceding step. It is important to use the feedback. In a well-implemented program, there may be movement back and forth between the steps.

First, based on the needs analysis, a tentative program is designed. Second, the tentative design is discussed with senior management and the managers who are expected to participate in the program. The objectives are to verify assumptions and to reach consensus with respect to progress objectives and program design. This also starts the unfreezing phase by obtaining agreement on the need for specific change and motivating the will to change.

In the third stage, managers are helped to acquire and begin to use new competencies that are expected to lead to changed behavior. This continues the unfreeze phase and introduces the change phase. In the fourth stage, change is continued and refreezing is emphasized. The objective is to provide practice leading to increased competency and confidence in the value of the new behavior. The learner is given opportunities to act, observe, and assess results. Feedback is made the basis for learning. Whether feedback is positive or negative, there are opportunities for independent learning leading to new insights. This is the most difficult stage. It is essential to complete change and to initiate refreezing. It may be necessary to go back to the first stage, to reconsider objectives, to the third stage, to assess and revise the content and learning approaches.

The fifth stage focuses on individual learning. Participants are expected to use the learning routinely in the work venue. The experiences are systematically analyzed to clarify the cause/effect relationships; assess and improve development design, managers' performance, and other variables; and to move on to a higher level of learning. This stage also completes refreezing. It is the change phase for lifelong learning.

The sixth stage goes beyond the specific content and competencies of the development program. It involves the manager's own periodic review of process and results to determine new needs and opportunities and to increase self-directed learning from experience. The objective is to refreeze the lifelong learning process as a life-bank metaelement.

Some programs consist only of the third stage. Where the program designer assumes universal management needs, the program is designed to meet those needs. This obviates the necessity for the first two stages. In most university programs the last three stages also are omitted. Few programs include the fifth step and virtually none include the sixth.

The fifth and sixth stages are primarily the participants', and to some extent the organization's, responsibility. However, these stages should not be ignored by the trainers if an objective is to help participants to incorporate motivation and methodology for independent lifelong learning as metaelements in their life-banks.

ANALYSIS

Some issues that plague program designers and other stakeholders that should be considered are the following:

- Who should determine content and learning approach?
- To what extent should learning theory determine the design and conduct of programs?

- Is helping managers learn how to learn from experience essential for management development?
- Who is responsible for motivating managers to learn?
- Is transfer of learning to the work venue a development or a management responsibility?
- How important is the lifelong learning objective?
- Should management development be focused on or limited to helping participants gain immediately needed competencies?

To what degree should managers participate in planning development? Knowles and other theorists assert that motivation to learn is a function of participation in program design. Some program designers have moved beyond having managers participate in program design and implementation to making each manager responsible for his or her own program design and implementation (Mouton and Blake 1984).

There is a limit to the individual manager's participation in the design and implementation of the training programs. The guidance of the trainer cannot be done away with even in individually designed programs. No needs analysis is neutral, and the designer's signature remains on every program. It is not possible to eliminate the teacher, facilitator, mentor, preceptor, or whatever you call the person who plays the guiding and, in the last analysis, assessing roles. Even if the manager does not attend a formal program but depends on reading the literature, the trainers do not disappear; they are the authors whose work the manager reads.

Nevertheless, what content will be transferred is determined principally by the participants and their sponsoring organizations. Nowhere is this more apparent than in the effort to improve managers' leadership. Leadership is, as has been noted, a management development objective strongly emphasized by client organizations and managers. It is, however, only one managerial competency. It is strongly situational and tends to be gained and strengthened by successful experience. A leader in a wilderness exercise may not be a leader in a bookkeeping department. A leader in a placid environment may not be effective when the environment becomes turbulent. Probably more money is spent on books about leadership than on books on any other management roles. There is no evidence that people who know all about leadership are effective leaders.

There is little evidence that much of the learning theory used in management development has been tested for effectiveness. More to the point, perhaps, there is little evidence of the conscious, significant use of learning theory in design and implementation of programs. Knowles's andragogical theory is referred to more often in articles about management development than any other learning theory, but there is little evidence confirming its use to a significant degree.

To a great extent training and development have not changed from instructor-dominated activity in which the participants are relatively passive learners, to experiential learning in which managers are learner-participants. In practice, the experiential learning activities remain instructor-planned experiences. Case studies and synthetic experiential exercises alike tend to bear the weight of the conclusions it is expected the participants will reach.

Research by Faris (1983) indicates that although professional trainers have adequate knowledge of learning theory, there is little evidence that the theories and approved practices are actually used. Faris studied the application of eight generally accepted steps for designing and conducting training programs. He found that the greatest divergence from the recommended practice was in middle-management programs. The steps in Faris's study included specify requirements; develop training objectives; develop and test training; evaluate program output; assess and modify training program; develop accountability. Top-management programs were not included in the study. But since application of learning theory varied innversely with the hierarchical level of participants, it may be assumed that the least learning theory was used at the executive level. This agrees with the observed tendency of chief executives to prefer short, passive learning with emphasis on content.

The need to use learning in the work venue is a continuing motif in management development and is related to three operational themes: How does the learning process affect transfer? How is the transfer best accomplished? Who is responsible for developing the will and capability to transfer learning to the work venue? Bennett (1956) emphasizes the importance of selecting participants with the will to use learning and of assigning mentors to provide feedback. He points to the need for practice in use. Livingston (1971), criticizing academic management development, repeatedly advances the theses that experience is a necessary condition for developing managers; that experience must come before formal learning of content; and that the whole thrust of management education should be on use in the work venue: "Preoccupation with problem solving and decision making in formal management education programs tends to distort management growth because it over develops an individual's analytical ability, but leaves his ability to take action and to get things done underdeveloped" (Livingston 1971, p. 82). He goes on to point out the importance of problem finding and to recommend guided experience (i.e., experiential learning) in identifying problems and issues in real business situations and dealing with these together with other stakeholders as the key to becoming an effective manager.

Academics responding to the Livingston article (*Harvard Business Re-*

view, March–April 1971) attacked his position and pointed out the importance of selection, and the value of passive learning for knowledge acquisition and of the use of case material to simulate experience. They emphasized the need for theory before experience and the responsibility of the participants to transfer learning to the work venue.

Mintzberg (1973) discusses preparation of managers from the viewpoint of schools of business and public administration. An academic in the tradition of Livingston (1971), he finds school programs wanting. In particular he finds that "Cognitive study [which is the schools' stock in trade] is useful but generally sterile. Learning is most effective when the student actually performs the skill in as realistic a situation as possible and then analyzes his performance explicitly" (p. 188). Further, methods successful in teaching instrumental disciplines do not carry over to teaching expressive abilities. The skills and abilities that Mintzberg thinks necessary but not "taught" adequately are developing and maintaining effective peer relationships, leadership, conflict resolution, and obtaining, processing, and disseminating information. He also states that the opportunities to improve management judgment are inadequate. Competencies under this heading would include decision making under ambiguity, resource allocation, search for problems and opportunities, and self-analysis.

Revans (1974) notes that "The skill-contending school (i.e., teaching by talk or discussion) may teach us contention; it does not teach us action. Since management is an action-oriented trade, the conscientious management professor must needs ask himself how to make good the deficiency" (p. 132). Revans advocates increasing managerial competence by supplementing learning from books, discussion, and synthetic experiential approaches with planned identification, analysis, and solution of current and projected operational problems and evaluation of the results. In the Inter-University Program for Advanced Management, after participants were introduced to current theory and practice of management and some application of "basic cognitive ideas," they were assigned on a full-time basis to a field project that lasted up to one year, in order to give them experience in applying and modifying the concepts, techniques, and approaches learned in the first part of the program. Throughout the field experience there were discussions with academic staff and professional managers.

Sampson (1953), focusing on the motivation provided by the opportunity for immediate use, advocated using the work venue problems faced by executives as the basis for development activities. However, he does not indicate how one can have the right experience on tap to use for every manager and for every learning module or educational objective. Priority between learning theory and experience is a "chicken and egg" situation. Some theory is needed to focus observation, structure analysis, and give meaning to experience. Some experience is needed to develop and give meaning to theory. Which part of the learning cycle to emphasize and give priority may be a matter of the individual learning style and other life-bank characteristics.

Hornstein (1984) states:

> Data and experience have shown that [management development] has one almost overwhelming flaw; it attempts to create organization change in a workshop setting away from the job. Separated from their co-workers, individual managers are exposed to educational experiences aimed at changing knowledge, attitudes and behaviors related to their job performance. But when the workshop ends and managers return to their own work places where old practices and policies prevail, they find it extremely difficult to put their new skills and knowledge into practice. (p. 52)

This finding casts doubt on the value of all training not tied to the work venue.

Should programs be concentrated or extended over a long period? Concentrated programs, jam-packed with content and given over a limited period, are seen as giving participants and organizations a good return for their investment. Participants obtain a great deal of knowledge. If the knowledge is seen as an active addition to the life-bank that is available for use, it is of greater value. However, being away from the job, full time, for two or more weeks may present a reentry problem. Also, concentration of learning introduces a possible barrier to change and use. Few learn any new, complex task in a single learning experience of a week or two. Without practice and repeated reinforcement, few acquire the competence and will to get role-set support.

The trainers' responsibility to link learning and application is not easy. Trainers can influence only what takes place in the learning venue. They assume that managers have the will to use learning and will be able to use the learning in the work venue. This may be less the case in management development than in any other work-related training. Unless transfer is dealt with satisfactorily, the result of management development may be dissatisfaction for all concerned.

Should the focus be on the individual or the system? Learning and transfer of learning must be by individuals. However, the learning (new behavior) must be played out and have beneficial impact in the system. The same managerial behavior can have widely different impacts in different organizations and different situations. Thus behavior and performance on the job are related but not synonymous. While most needs analyses focus on performance, most training focuses on behavior. Unit performance and its impact on the total system are the most objective measures of managerial performance. If this is the case, then learning theory applied in management development must be modified to focus on the system's objectives. Since there are many subsystems and systems in which an individual performs, the selection of the focal system becomes of crucial importance in the design and evaluation of management development.

To what extent do considerations of the work venue play a part? This is the heart of the arguments of academic critics. Rational-empirical evidence supporting change is usually not sufficient to motivate adults to change their behavior in any significant way. There are always strong counterforces that dictate no change, including tradition, fear of risk, and uncertainty. It may be that changed role-set norms can more readily lead to changing the norms of the individual manager than changed managerial norms can lead to changed norms in the individual's role set.

Management development programs assume the irrelevancy of many organizational cultural characteristics in selection of content, educational approach and methodology, and training techniques. This assumption in present when needs analysis is the basis for rational design of management development. Evidence of implicit cultural assumptions is provided by the paucity of articles found in a review of ten years of the *Training and Development Journal* that raises questions such as Whose need? The individual's, the work group's, the system's, society's? There is little discussion of priorities, stakeholders, and issues in determining needs.

FINAL REMARKS

The extensive outpouring of popular management books indicates that there is a felt need for a body of managerial content on which to base learning objectives and processes for application of learning. However, we do not believe that the current crop fills the need. What would be useful are popular explanations of such concepts as frames of reference and rules for connecting organizational events and managerial behavior, and models for explaining cause/effect and guiding thought processes. The professional learning and management literature contains some of these. The professional literature should be part of every trainer's stock in trade. The participants' life-banks are for the most part unknown. It is up to the trainer to uncover and build on the contents of the life-banks in the course of the program.

Learning theory and consideration of the work venue and the tasks of the manager have led us to some principles for management development. Among these are the following:

- Development objectives and approaches must be based on managers' life-banks and their work venues.

- Managers must have input into program design.
- Education and training alone cannot motivate managers to change their behavior significantly. There must be positive external supports and incentives for the change. These may be structural, reward system, or group change processes.
- Management development objectives, content, processes, and learning are most effective when they are individualized and aligned with the individual learning style and other life-bank elements.
- Learning is more effective and useful when development focuses on concrete competencies.
- Passive and experiential learning are useful for achieving different learning objectives. They should be employed selectively.
- Learned competencies and values do not remain refrozen for any extended period in the face of the inability to gain acceptance by the manager's role set.
- The competencies most easily acquired and retained are those which managers can apply.

There are disincentives for managers to voluntarily take time away from their jobs for training. "Econometric studies have consistently shown that only 15 percent of the variation in income among Americans can be accounted for by formal education. The remaining 85 percent is accounted for by learning in the workplace" (Carnevale 1986, p. 24). Assuming that this observation holds true for managers and that differences in salaries are roughly related to performance appreciated by top management, it would follow that learning on the job is about six times more effective in determining managerial behavior than is formal training. If what is appreciated by top management is more effective managerial performance, this supports the expressed desires of managers to satisfy the needs of their superiors and to be able to apply learning in the work venue.

Management development cannot produce every change that senior management may want. It is rarely effective in changing an organization's culture. This is the case even when top management announces changes in its goals and spells out how the culture must change to achieve the new goals. Dechant (1988) describes a not unusual case in which the organization's "systems and processes had to be changed to carry out and reinforce the culture changes required." She reports that top management's pronouncements and the development activities succeeded in unfreezing and helping managers learn the content of the desired changes. It did not achieve refreezing. Strong incentives were required to get managers and the rest of the work force to maintain change. In other cases, major structural change may be required.

There is little more than some case evidence that the competencies acquired in development programs are retained for any extended period.

There is a tendency to forget that refreezing is not a one-shot effort. A necessary condition is continuous use and feedback for reinforcement.

Academic programs do not seem to change to meet the needs of their clients, the students and the organizations that are expected to employ their graduates. The emphasis in accreditation is not on how well graduates are prepared to accept and perform managerial responsibilities; it is on academic research, whether or not usable, and on training academics. Thus the schools of public administration have virtually done away with advanced programs to train practitioners by recommending discontinuance of the Doctor of Public Administration degree. This leaves only the academic Ph.D. degree. Research to demonstrate the need for change to produce practitioners rather than researchers tends to be ignored.

In 1982 the schools of business administration took some cognizance of their critics who claimed that the universities' MBA programs were not preparing managers or providing managers with the basis for lifelong learning, and that management development programs for practicing managers were inadequate. However, a need was felt to strengthen relationships between the schools and the business community. The Future of Management Education Development Committee was appointed. Other than the sponsorship of the study by Porter and McKibbin (1988), there have been no significant results from the committee's deliberations. Our reading of the report indicates that the study produced two major findings: the schools are not doing the education and management development jobs that companies and our economy need, and the research being produced is not read by the business leaders for whom much of it is intended. Nevertheless, the colleges seem to see the results of the study as not requiring any significant change in program structure or content.

Human resource professionals and trainers have to learn to develop and exploit effective feedback during the course of a program and to be prepared to make changes in both content and approach. They must have the will to change planned programs even when these have been based on a careful needs analysis and the use of models that once were successful.

The possibility of professional obsolescence exists among human resource professionals to a greater degree than among managers and other professionals. Not only must they be concerned with reconsidering techniques and approaches that research indicates are no longer efficient and effective, they must be concerned with the obsolescence of assumptions about organizational culture, management characteristics and managerial performance, and differences among organizations and individuals.

Management development theory has moved from career development to career management for managers in recognition that learning must be continuous and lifelong. This has the consequence that the personal career management plan may be the key to improving management. Andragogy (as well as pedagogy) applied in management development means that managers will not learn what they do not believe is useful. This reinforces the assumptions that adults must be responsible for developing and implementing the plans for their own improvement. Trainers have to serve as counselors, consultants, providers of feedback, preceptors, and facilitators. They will not be the ones who unilaterally determine the curriculum and decide how the participants should learn and what they should use in the work venue.

7

ASSESSMENT OF MANAGEMENT DEVELOPMENT

INTRODUCTION

There has been a fair number of studies of management development. Have there been enough? Have the research and evaluation been appropriately designed and implemented? Are the findings reliable and valid? Have the findings been of use? These are only a few of the questions that have been asked about research and evaluation. They are best answered by a review of the literature and a discussion of our own experiences over the thirty years we have been engaged in management development.

Some studies are described as "research." Others are called "evaluations." And a third group is labeled "evaluation research." In a technical sense one can differentiate between "evaluation" and "research." Evaluation is a judgment process directed toward improving operational (and occasionally strategic) decision making. Research is a learning activity in which data are gathered and analyzed to test hypotheses and produce new knowledge. Virtually all reported studies are evaluations of specific management development programs. For convenience we will distinguish between research and evaluation only to the extent that evaluation is designed to test the one hypothesis that the action taken has not led to improved operations.

Evaluation includes descriptive and analytic processes. Performed rigorously, it calls for specific defined procedures; explicit criteria; reliable, valid sampling and data gathering; use of analytic techniques justified by the conditions imposed on the data gathering; and interpretation of findings based on the analysis and limited by conditions imposed by the study.

There is little, if any, evaluation of either executive or management training that meets these criteria. There tends to be more evaluation of management training than of executive training. Where there *is* an evaluation, it is a measure of the "happiness" of participants or their supervisors with participation, not necessarily with output (Carnevale 1989). Rarely are evaluations more than an informal process involving casual data gathering, ambiguous objectives, intuitive criteria and standards, subjective judgments, and broad generalizations. Most research tends to be summative rather than formative. That is, the focus tends to be on the final output of the management development process rather than on the contributions of the elements, such as content, learning approach, and participants' characteristics. There is no research that distinguishes between effects of design and implementation.

Despite this negative view of management development evaluation and research, we believe that much can be learned about the state and possible future of management development by a closer look at these activities.

RESEARCH OBJECTIVES

As noted, the overwhelming objective of the evaluation effort is to measure the final output of management development activities. The objective is to prove that the activity is worthwhile. This is unfortunate. As implied by Suchman (1967), unless one can validly generalize environments and conditions one cannot infer from the acceptability of a program in one time and place that a similar program in another time and place will be acceptable.

The givens of management development are that it is desirable to improve the performance of managers, that this is possible through management development, that the manager will be able to gain support for the changed behavior in the work venue, and that the change will be beneficial to the organization. As a result, much of the research seeks to evaluate the return on development, the cost/benefit relationship.

There are additional reasons why restricting research to evaluation is undesirable. Evaluative research does not seek new knowledge to improve management development. At best, it tests the usefulness of existing knowledge. It tends to ignore process, fails to distinguish between the impacts of design and of implementation, and focuses attention on the immediate outcome.

While there is recognition for the importance of evaluation of maintenance of changed behavior (refreezing), there are no reported longitudinal studies. There is less recognition of the need for formative studies. There is need for timely, ongoing feedback and analysis of participants' learning and performance, to help participants to refreeze new behaviors and trainers to adjust and reinforce program elements.

In a review of evaluation literature, Roback (1989) found few references to programs in which the design considered "evaluation" of usefulness of content or impact on job performance. There are even fewer references to the impact of the needs assessment and program implementation. A major reason (although Roback does not note it) is our almost fanatical concern with the bottom line and the tendency to ignore the contributions of individual elements and sequences of elements that influence the measured output.

Trainers focus on demonstrating a favorable cost/benefit ratio for management development. They tend to ignore the fact that organizations invest in management development for reasons other than improving output. We believe that it may be more important to test and improve the theory and practices than to assess success. There should be more investment in research relating to the comparative values of different educational technologies and approaches.

Major study objectives are measuring the transfer of learning to participants' active life-banks and use of learning in the work venue. Analysis is usually restricted to two factors. The first and primary one is the competence and will of the learner to use the learning. Second is maintenance of the changed behavior. There is a tendency to ignore intervening variables. In management development, transfer is only one element of reentry. The ability of the manager to gain acceptance for the use of learning may have little relationship to the design and implementation of management development. It has greater relationship to the state and characteristics of the work venue and of the manager's role set.

Failure to take factors such as these into account raises a very serious obstacle to evaluating holistic effectiveness of program design and implementation by any absolute standards.

In his review of training and development, Carnevale (1986) emphasizes the importance of research relating to learning in the workplace:

> The learning process in the workplace remains a black box. The state of the theoretical and practical art of leveraging earnings and productivity through training and development is relatively primitive. While we have devoted billions to research and dissemination of best practices in formal education, workplace training remains the silent partner in the nation's learning enterprise. (pp. 25–26)

The objectives of management development evaluation and research should be sharpened and broadened, and new research designs developed. Improving the design and implementation of management development depends on this.

REVIEW OF THE LITERATURE

Georgenson (1982) estimated that only about 10 percent of the $100 billion that is expended annually on training in industry leads to changed behavior on the job. There is no indication that there has been any significant change in this percentage since then. Since a good part of the training is for directly applied skills on which returns are probably greater than 10 percent, the return from management development may be even less. This is of concern to consumers, both organizations and individuals and providers, including organizations' human resource staffs, universities, and independent program suppliers.

The authors reviewed ten years of articles in *Training and Development Journal* (1977 to 1987) for those dealing with research and evaluation. Most turned out to be reports of "successful" programs and recipes for improving management development based on a single case analysis. While the expressed aim in many was to measure the link between classroom learning and work experience, there was little reliable and valid evidence that significant learning was transferred. There is more evidence for the value of carefully selecting candidates for management positions, rotating managers through various management jobs, evaluating managerial performance and providing good feedback, and growth through challenging assignments. Evaluations tended to be subjective. The only objective criterion was knowledge gained. The evaluations were summative, with little attempt to determine the contributions of individual design elements. The primary criterion was participants' satisfaction. In the programs reported, content tended to be heavily skewed to human relations.

Campbell et al. (1970) reviewed the research literature for the post-World War II period to 1970. Virtually the only acceptable research they found was descriptive studies that identified the content, techniques, and processes in management development. The total emphasis on passive approaches that was found would not be true today.The evaluation of methodology could not be lower. They found that it lacked rigor and consisted almost entirely of case studies illustrating a specific technique or approach. Although they ended on a cautiously optimistic note implying that development can change attitudes, the evidence presented did not indicate any transfer of learning to the job.

Baldwin and Ford (1988) reviewed research relating to transfer of learning in the broad field of training, including management development, to provide a summary of transfer research and to suggest directions for future research. They considered studies involving three input variables: training design, trainee characteristics, and work venue. The output variables studied were learning/retention and generalization and maintenance of learning on the job. They did not discuss interactions among the three input variables or the possible impact of the output variables on them. They did note the absence of reported studies of interventions to change the work venue. Their overall critique of the research agrees with the comment of Campbell et al (1970): "We know a few things but not very much."

In response to the question "What percentage of the skills learned in a course are lost without follow-up coaching?" the average estimate by managers was 69 percent. The happiness quotient, determined by having participants fill out a questionnaire at the end of a program, is the evaluation technique almost certain to yield a positive result and is used most often (Ralphs and Stephan, 1986). It is also suggested that professional trainers know how, and want to do, a better job of evaluation, but that they are not supported by higher management. In addition to the obvious objections to the "happiness sheet," such as lack of objectivity, we know that transmitting new, seemingly useful knowledge, teaching specific techniques, and providing definite answers are very satisfying to participants. This type of content always gets very high happiness ratings. There is no significant evidence that much learning is transferred to the work venue.

In a review of the research literature with respect to learning competency skills, work habits, and transfer, Fitzgerald (1985) found the common thread running through all the studies to be that the most effective place to learn transferable work competencies is the work venue.

Using a five-point scale Ralphs and Stephan (1986), in a survey of evaluation practices in the *Fortune* 500 asked, "How often are the following evaluation methods [for development programs] used in your company?" Using a five-point scale—5, almost always; 1, almost never—the alternatives and answers are the following:

	5 Only	**4 and 5**
A. Evaluation by learner filled out at end of course	73%	86%
B. Evaluation filled out by instructor at end of the course	12%	23%
C. Evaluation by boss, peers, or subordinates	8%	23%
D. Follow-up evaluation by participants	7%	16%

E. Follow-up questionnaire by participants	5%	14%
F. Use of pre-tests or posttests	6%	15%
G. Use of business records	5%	12%

A study of forty-one researchers dealing with summative evaluations of training and development programs reported in the literature between 1980 and 1983 concluded that summative evaluations are not conducted effectively. More attention needs to be given to components of evaluation, and training specialists need greater competence in evaluation (Parker 1986).

There are studies of the relationships between participants' characteristics and success. Baldwin and Ford's (1988) review found that managers with a greater need to achieve and greater belief in the value of training are more apt to use what they learn. Also, managers are more apt to use learning when they are permitted to set goals and their change in behavior is supported by their role sets. (This tends to support the generally agreed-upon hypothesis that a major obstacle to retention of effective changed behavior in the work venue is the perception of the members of the manager's role set that their interests may be threatened by the change.)

Evidence presented by Noe and Schmitt (1986) supports a related "utility" hypothesis. Responses of participants, their immediate supervisors, and program staff members in this study indicated that change in behavior in the work venue, as a result of participating in the program studied, was a function of level of job and relationship to career planning.

Several researchers have attempted to determine whether differences between public-sector and private-sector management lead to differences in the content of management development. Gold (1982) compared objectives of five successful public sector organizations and five from the private sector. He found that the single most fundamental difference was the emphasis in the private sector, and the absence in the public sector, of the profit objective. A second related difference was the inability of public managers to articulate a "clear consistent mission." Despite these differences, Gold found that the same set of "proverbs" was taught to managers in both sectors. There was no evidence that they were applied in practice in either sector. The proverbs were the usual ones in academic programs, such as "Delegate authority and responsibility to the lowest possible level."

The Federal Executive Program has not been able to establish a program that will ensure a competent career executive corps (Wynia 1972). Hoberman (1990), in an analysis of management development in two United Nations organizations, questions whether executive development can have much impact on performance in a highly politicized environment. This may be the situation in governmental agencies.

There is more criticism of academic management development than of programs of other providers. Livingston (1983) points to the paucity of usable research. As noted, he states a reason that management education is problematic "is that very little of the learning is directed at providing the practical skills needed to apply the knowledge gained in class to real performance problems on the job." There are many criticisms of academic management development programs. Their conclusion is that development is not based on solid needs assessments or subject to careful evaluation.

There is no significant evidence that graduate schools of business and public administration produce capable managers. In fact, there is no evidence that any programs for a self-selected, heterogeneous group produce significant changes on the job. There are many critics, in addition to Livingston, who claim that the schools have failed. Two major studies of graduate programs made prior to the current wave of criticism were quite critical of the schools and made numerous recommendations on how to improve the situation. The only recommendations adopted were to increase research capabilities and full-time faculties. There seems to have been some improvement in technical education but no major changes on focusing education, in either degree or nondegree programs, on the transfer of learning to the work venue.

The deans of graduate schools of business in both the United States and other countries have been interested in answering their critics and concerned about both the effectiveness and the future of management education and development. Two colloquiums were jointly sponsored by the American Association of Colleges of Business (AACB) and the European Foundation for Management and Development. These led to a conference in Paris in June 1980. The participants focused on two major issues: the manager's future educational and developmental needs and action steps to meet those needs. AACB sponsored a subsequent conference in March 1982 at the Wingspread (Wisconsin) conference center of the Johnson Foundation. Although the major topic was "Lifelong Learning for Managers," note was taken of the numerous articles critical of business education. The conferees felt that there was insufficient information to respond to the criticism or to determine the degree to which the schools were meeting the needs of business and the types of changes called for. This led to the Future of Management Education and Development Project conducted by Porter and McKibbin (1988).

Porter and McKibbin (1988) did not ignore the many criticisms of the schools of business. However, they found that criticism was useless as a basis for making recommendations. The recommendations would be either so narrow and detailed as to apply only a few specific situations or so broad and simplistic as to be meaningless as guides for change. Consequently they settled for gathering information and discussing what they considered to be the key issues.

An interesting implication of Porter and McKibbin's study seems to be that university programs are impervious to change. They found that while corporate managers generally approved of the content areas, they wanted to see more "realistic, practical, hands-on" education with greater emphasis on human relationships, such as leadership, development of subordinates, and interpersonal relations skills. Despite the need felt by company executives, few of the deans of schools of business administration who responded to the questionnaire felt any need to provide hands-on experience for their students. The findings imply that few faculty members have had sufficient managerial experience to be able to provide insight and information from their own experience—experience that would, to a limited extent, make up for the failure to provide experiential learning for their students. This supports critics who claim that university programs are twice removed from reality.

There are as many critics of evaluation and research as there are of management development. Baldwin and Ford (1988) identified two major problems with the research: insufficient theory to guide the research and no adequate criterion measures of transfer. Without these, findings cannot be cumulative. They decried the wide use of self-reporting. They reviewed seven survey studies directed to correlating transfer of learning with work climate, leadership climate, and supervisory support. They found that the criterion problem is not dealt with satisfactorily and that correlation findings do not permit inferring causality.

There is as much loose analysis in negative articles as in the "success stories." Skinner (1971), starting from the assumption that management development has not paid off, advances five reasons for this:

1. Training groups are too large. It is not possible to motivate large groups to change their behavior in any significant manner.
2. Management theory is inconsistent. This develops dissonance in participants, who then refuse any message.
3. The status of trainers is frequently lower than that of the participants. This tends to encourage participants to depreciate the content of programs.
4. Invalid management models are rarely unfrozen.
5. Significant behavioral change cannot be achieved in the usual inadequately planned, short-time programs.

However, for every reason that Skinner gives for failure of development, the negation of that reason can be advanced with as much justification. Thus, with respect to the fifth reason, length of program,

Sampson (1953) points out that removing an executive from the job for any extended period ensures that learning will not be put to use. This follows from the hypotheses that reentry is more difficult the longer the manager has been away from the job and that learning is not retained as an active element in the life-bank unless it is put to use almost immediately. Thus, the longer the program, the greater the chance for failure.

The most optimistic review of the research literature we found (Burke and Day 1986) had the following muddled conclusions:

> The results for the content area of human relations training, however, revealed this type of training to be on the average very effective and likely to produce some improvement in managerial performance regardless of the situation. It should be noted that only three studies were involved in this analysis and thus the power of this analysis is suspect. . . . Self-awareness training, which typically uses some form of laboratory education/sensitivity training, was also shown to be fairly effective, on the average, in changing managerial behavior on the job. [However] the criterion measures typically used for evaluating self-awareness training were of questionable utility . . . [and] may not necessarily reflect changes in actual job performance. (p. 241)

There also seems to be some confusion in Burke and Day's (1986) findings with respect to general management training. In one place the authors conclude that "Because there have been few well-designed studies within this area, no definite conclusions can be reached as to the effectiveness of general management functions training. In contrast to the results based on learning criteria and subjective behavior, general management training was shown to be very effective, on the average, in improving performance as measured by objective results" (p. 86). Their analysis of the impact of training methodology again produced mixed results. There are additional problems with the selection of case studies. Studies of managers are lumped with studies of supervisors, ROTC leaders, volunteer leaders, and others as if there are no differences with respect to cause/effect relationships in these different populations. But Burke and Day are not alone. None of the reviews of research literature takes into account the very different types of programs, populations, and research designs in the studies reported.

In a study of management development in private-sector and public-sector organizations with a reputation for having outstanding programs, Bryant et al. (1978) reported

> . . . an increased concern expressed by some companies about the "quality" of out-of-company training. Several firms had developed "approved" lists of university programs, and only approved participation in these programs. No specific criteria was [sic] revealed for the evaluation of programs other than the

reliance placed upon the opinions of company personnel who had previously attended the courses. . . . In addition to individual performance evaluation, both industry and government have instituted measures to evaluate their formal management development programs. Evaluation factors are primarily concerned with the utilization of resources, the plans developed to carry out the program, and an assessment of the extent to which program objectives have been achieved.

One final research finding: Verlander's position (1988) is typical of many trainers. While agreeing that research to date shows the need to make programs more "developmental, without any objective evidence, he nevertheless claims that there have been many effective developmental programs."

DESIGN

Design of a study, whether evaluative or research, defines the objectives; indicates the general approach to be used; states the assumptions made; and describes the treatment (the development program, the population, and the methods for selecting the population), the methodology for gathering the data, the techniques for determining the reliability and validity of the data and for analyzing the data, and the criteria and standards for accepting or rejecting a hypothesis. There is no one "correct" design. Design is usually determined more by available resources and other constraints than by "correct" theory. However, there are some principles.

Most evaluation and research designs use a simplified system model of management development. In its most sophisticated form, the anticipated output of management development is the learning that is transferred to the manager's life-bank in an active mode. The input factors considered are elements identified in the needs analysis of the manager's life-bank and the work venue. The throughput includes the program's content and occasionally its learning technology. The implementation is rarely considered. The outputs usually considered are participants' satisfaction and knowledge gained. Both are usually measured at the end of the program. This limited design stems as much from lack of interest on the part of suppliers and consumers as from the difficulty of the research problem and the level of research competence. In more sophisticated research, other output relationships are hypothesized, including how and why changes will take place, and relationships among various input, throughput, and output variables.

Differences in management development design have considerable impact on the design of research. An obvious case is differences between designs with short-term and long-term objectives. Long-term objectives tend to present many more complex research problems because the number of intervening variables increases rapidly as application and assessment are delayed. Management development and evaluation of these programs are two different complex processes. While each has its own cause/effect sequences, they are interdependent. The research findings can hardly be valid unless the research processes and hypotheses are taken into account in the design and implementation of the management development, and the latter are taken into account in the design and implementation of the evaluation plan. There is no indication in the literature of reported evaluations that there is any consideration of how these two sequences relate to each other.

Evaluation design should be developed with and tied into program planning (Brinkerhoff 1988). This statement proposes that at every stage, from needs analysis (goal setting) through program design and implementation to measuring the change in individual participants and total systems, related programmatic and evaluation designs should be prepared at the same time.

This approach permits the impact of each stage to be estimated separately and for changes in design for later stages to be based on information obtained from the evaluation of earlier stages. While this approach is very attractive and perhaps even necessary, there are problems. Tying program design and evaluation tightly together from the beginning tends to restrict modification of the program design. The articulation between research and design is weakened if significant changes are made in program design during the course of a program. The dangers of letting evaluation processes and standards impact on a program can be seen by the impact of standardized tests on school curricula.

Some hypotheses important for the design of programs—for example, adult learning theory—are not currently testable by reliable and valid, empirical, probabilistic techniques. Thus their continued use requires caution. Unfortunately, research findings do not indicate how caution should be exercised. Many research findings that seem to be useful were obtained for nonwork groups and for workers other than managers. Thus, most research on the advantages of experiential education has been in connection with preparing young people for employment and is only peripherally related to management development (Fitzgerald 1985).

The objective of rigorous experimental design may be unattainable. Operational management development programs can never satisfy the experimental design criteria for randomly selected test and control groups drawn from the same general population. The inability to satisfy the randomness criterion raises significant questions with respect to the use of traditional statistical tests of significance. This is ignored in the research reports.

There are several less rigorous approaches that may be useful but that seem not to be used. They include the following:

- the quasi experiment in which a cross-sectional study is made after the fact, comparing the performance of program participants with their performance prior to participation and with the change in performance over the same period of a matched group of managers, from the same general population, who did not participate in the program
- comparative analysis, comparing the changes in performance of managers who participated in two different programs but who otherwise were subject to comparable systemic and environmental conditions
- the explanatory study to refine and to a degree substantiate a theoretical model (rather than to test the statistical significance of a specific development hypothesis) by comparing the outputs of programs based on the same theory but in which specific key elements are given different quantitative emphasis (e.g., with the same total time, varying the time spent on lectures and experiential exercises)
- assessing the influence of the various elements that make up a program, using both subjective and objective data.

These approaches assume that development is useful and seek to determine how to make it more focused and useful. They do not state preconditions for the measure of performance, or the process to measure change in performance, or the quantitative measure of a program's output, or how to distinguish between the results produced by specific input or throughput variables. They assume that the information will be relatively unbiased and provide leads for hypotheses and guides useful for program improvement. This is not to advocate research without an explicit statement of the theory underlying the design. Not to have an underlying theory would make the activity meaningless.

> All observation involves theorizing, and . . . perception is impossible without conceptual processes. . . . Nietzsche's label for this philosophical doctrine [that the contents of observation should be free from conceptual contamination] is not, I think, unjust; he called it "the dogma of immaculate perception". . . . Observation is already the work of understanding. . . . An observation is made; it is the product of an active choice, not of a passive exposure. (Kaplan 1964, p. 29)

The focus on success and case studies means that other important hypotheses go untested. There is no reported research on possible counterproductive effects of management development. For example: much of management training gives participants what A. N. Whitehead referred to as "inert ideas". According to Whitehead, this is unutilized and untested learning. These are ideas that we have called "inactive life-bank elements." As Whitehead noted, these ideas are not only useless but harmful. This is an important hypothesis that has never, to our knowledge, been tested.

More useful designs for research than the attempt to measure total transfer on the basis of the entire development effort are, from the professional point of view, those which focus on the elements of the development process and estimate the degree to which each element contributes to a specific output. The elements most often considered are the following:

- *content*, the expected cognitive learning measured by transfer of learning to the participant's active life-bank and profitable use in the work venue
- *educational technology*, the educational processes and techniques employed to help the participant learn and transfer learning, measured by learning demonstrated during and at the end of the formal program and by effective transfer of learning
- *reinforcement*, refreezing, measured by continued use of learning and the ability to adapt the learning to new situations in the work venue.

Assessment should be designed as a feedback process to provide information helpful for design and implementation and for developing testable hypotheses, as well as evidence of the usefulness of a particular training process in practice. There is danger of contaminated findings when research is sold to a client as a means to provide evidence of the value of management development. The criterion may not be achievement of learning objectives but greater acceptance of organizational goals and procedures, loyalty to top management, salary increases, or promotions. These may be desirable objectives, but they are not objectives attainable by management development.

A fundamental design issue is which output variables should be measured. Should the variables relate to organizational characteristics, performance of the individual manager, the manager's career success, or the participants' views of the program's effectiveness? Should the change in the values of the variables be measured before or after return to the work venue, a short time after return or over a period of years? A major area for research, perhaps the most important from the practical point of view, is transfer of training. Transfer skills are metaelements in a person's life-bank. Some transfer competencies are generalizing from specific instances (developing general rules), adapting general rules to specific situations, cue recognition, association, and discrimination. These are probably not general but discipline- and venue-specific. Use of learning gained in training in the work venue is not easily quantified and measured. In its place other factors are almost always measured. Some substitute career success, using as the criterion for career success the rate of salary increases. Others use the highest salary at the end of one year; the rate of promotion as a manager; the highest managerial level attained; or combinations of these to obtain an overall index of recognition. Factors that have nothing to do with either performance or management development but that play key roles in salary and position changes are ignored.

Suchman (1968) stresses the dynamic nature of most action and service programs and argues for an evaluative research design which becomes an inherent part of the service program. To provide for this form of continuous evaluation, one must formulate the evaluative research hypotheses in terms of contingencies and developments that may occur during the course of the program and that may require the collection of new or additional data. In natural experiential programs there is less need to anticipate what can possibly happen.

TECHNIQUES

Suchman (1968, p. 31) lists six steps as essential for the process of evaluation:

- identification of goals to be evaluated
- analysis of the problems the activity must confront
- description and standardization of the activity
- measurement of the nature and degree of change that takes place
- determination of whether the observed change is due to the activity or to some other cause
- estimation of the durability of the effects.

Suchman goes on to note:

> Three main conditions of the experimental method as they apply to evaluative research [are]: (1) sampling equivalent experimental and control groups; (2) isolation and control of the stimulus; (3) definition and measurement of criteria of effect. . . . This problem of the validity of criteria of effectiveness is crucial to evaluative research. These criteria represent the observable operational indices for measuring the attainment of program objectives. (1968, p. 110)

Trainers agree that the primary objective of organizational sponsorship for training and management development is to improve organizational functioning. However, a review by the authors of more than ten years of articles relating to assessment of training and management development in various publications, including the *Training and Development Journal* and the *Public Personnel Review*, turned up no evidence of significant organizational impact. Of the three categories of criteria, learning, use of learning in the work venue, and positive impact on organizational functioning, learning was by far the most commonly used. It was virtually the only criterion for management development. Learning was assessed primarily by statements from participants and written tests. These findings are consistent with those from the earlier study of the literature by Campbell et al. (1970).

Further evidence of the practice is provided by a survey of 1,200 members of the American Society for Training and Development reported by Grider et al. (1988). This found that most trainers use evaluation methods they think are less effective. They consider a measure of change in behavior on the job to be the best measure of training effectiveness. This is closely followed by a measure of the impact on the organization's output and by comparison with established competency criteria. Far lower on the scale are responses from participants and their supervisors to the request for evaluation of the training and estimates of the impact of the training. "Asked why they didn't employ the evaluation methods they considered most effective, the trainers polled commonly cited time constraints, expense and lack of expertise in measuring behavior, results, and competency" (Grider et al. 1988, p. 110).

When management development design is not focused and tested in action, there is a tendency to use fuzzy concepts to maintain deep-rooted, current beliefs and practices by clothing them in arcane concepts and theory. "The specific procedures for formulating significant program objectives, for deciding upon the criteria by which the achievement of these goals will be judged, and for developing reliable and valid measures of these criteria constitute the basic methodological problems in evaluative research" (Suchman 1968). There are no generally acceptable procedures for determining needs and programs to satisfy these needs.

As noted, some management development objectives have nothing to do with learning new competencies and behaviors. Some are seen by top management as a paid vacation for deserving subordinates and by some as a symbolic gesture to indicate interest in improving management and preparing current managers for higher assignments. The common "happiness" rating is a satisfactory measure of goal achievement for these top managers.

Techniques used to gather data determine findings as much as any element in research design. Designs that involve interviews and observation of people at work can rarely take into account the extent to which what is seen or heard is influenced by the interviewer or observer and the research objectives. In structured interviews, the investigator predetermines the range and nature of the responses by the specific questions and the sequence in which they are asked. In observations, there is no way of determining the representativeness of the sample and anything other than the immediate impact of the behavior. Further, the frames of reference of the actor and the observer are rarely the same.

Most management development research consists of measurements of the experimental group made after participation. This is the weakest evaluative research design. Two somewhat stronger designs are used on occasion. These are "one-group, pretest, posttest" and "posttest" comparison of two groups, one of which participated and the other did not. In the latter design, there is sometimes a pretest for one or both groups. There is no use, as far as we could determine, of well-known classic designs that include randomly selected experimental and control groups of managers from the same general population with reliable, valid pretests and posttests for both groups. There is a paucity of longitudinal studies to supplement short-term findings.

Some very competent practitioners decry attempts to evaluate management development. They say, in effect, that there are no effective techniques. Some point out that the multiplicity of objectives which have different values for different stakeholders makes it impossible to relate resources and activities to any one objective. Others refer to an issue already discussed, the claim that development effects are, and should be, long-range and cannot be measured reliably and validly in the short term. Still others note that the effects are general in nature and subject to too many intervening variables, few of which can be identified and defined unambiguously, to permit testing any meaningful cause/effect hypotheses. And still others say that it is too difficult to distinguish among the effects of design, implementation, and evaluation itself. In the absence of well-defined test and control conditions, it is not possible to make any statistically reliable studies. Neither sponsors nor practitioners are enthusiastic evaluators. They are interested in the program activities.

The critics derive support from the theory of evaluation. The theory as presented by Suchman (1968) tends to agree that it is questionable whether the three Suchman conditions can be satisfied in any research on management development.

Many management development programs have a heterogeneous set of participants. In the effort to make sure that there is something for everyone, trainers scatter all kinds of information and provide exercises with different processes and learning objectives. Parry and Robinson (1979) label this the "Johnny Appleseed" approach. They found, as did the other researchers noted, that most organizations are content to use the "happiness" quotient for evaluation rather than impact on the organization. However, with this type of mishmash, no valid research could have been designed.

Some researchers and trainers advocate collaborative approaches for increasing the value of evaluation activities. They propose that the stakeholders at some stage jointly determine the criteria, standards, and processes for evaluating. One technique using this approach, which does reduce the problems of defining objectives and standards, is the learning contract. It is employed in university independent study programs and some management development. The participant and instructor together determine what the learning processes and outcome will be, the criteria and measures at specific points in the process, and grading.

McEvoy and Buller (1990) postulate five reasons why organizations invest in management development. Evaluation for return on investment is quite different for each. Further, the reasons are not mutually exclusive; several may be operative for the same program. Possible reasons for sponsoring a specific program are the following:

- Attendance is a reward for managers who have performed well, rather than an attempt to improve their performance. This applies to many programs that are off site.
- Attendance is a symbol or a rite of having arrived at a new, usually higher, management level.
- There is need to inculcate participants with important aspects of organizational culture rather than the specific management content.
- It is felt that managers should exhibit a specific behavior that is not directly related to performance.
- The activity itself, rather than its impact, is considered to be the objective.

Obviously, in such cases few organizations will be willing to invest to any significant extent in measuring changes in organizational performance.

CONCLUSIONS

After review of the research literature, we conclude the following:

- There is overemphasis on reporting "success."
- The usefulness of the research is limited. Case studies are of little value except as illustrations of approaches used in one set of circumstances.
- The use of holistic criteria cannot help program designers to know the cause/effect relationships between variables.

There is no research that demonstrates a highly significant relationship between development efforts and participants' subsequent performance. This does not prove that there is no relationship. It may be evidence that it is a highly mediated relationship. Our evidence of the many variables which can have impact leads us to believe that this may indeed be the case. A major problem stems from the criterion that is usually advanced as the most valid, "managerial performance." Evaluation of a manager's performance may have little to do with the actual performance of the manager. A study by Wong and Dortch (1986) indicated that there is a need to define input, throughput, and output variables and theoretical and operational relationships between these. Output criteria (e.g., those used for rewards) are, at best, intermediate and personal rather than strategic and systemic. This tends to encourage short-term sightlines, extensive suboptimization, and adherence to the social and cultural norms of the organization.

One reason for this shortcoming pointed out in the reviews of research is that valid research is not possible in the absence of clear, operationally defined input variables (e.g., learning principles).

We have relied heavily on reviews of research studies. It should be recognized that conclusions from secondary sources have to be taken with a large grain of salt. There are serious problems. One is that the reviewer has selected the research papers and has determined the aspects of these to study and report on. However, in the research report to which we refer, the authors selected what they believed to be as good research as there is available. The second kind of problem arises from use of meta-analysis, a technique for consolidating the findings of different research to arrive at a more reliable conclusion. In this analysis there is a tendency to play down the effects of differences in the studies of objectives, definitions, populations, design, data gathering, and analytic techniques.

A criticism of the research literature is that there is not enough information about either the design of the studies or the design and implementation of the management development programs studied to make the reports of value to practitioners. Few provide sufficient information on methodology for confidence that the research satisfies the conditions for using the statistical techniques employed.

An important issue is the usefulness of the research. There is little evidence that feedback from the research influences program input or throughput. To be useful for professionals, research findings should be cumulative and validated by replication. Neither criterion can be met in the absence of generally accepted development hypotheses, objectives, definitions, and criteria.

Although in a very general sense there is agreement on the meaning of evaluation (a measure of the degree to which the development experience has led the participants to change their behavior in a predetermined manner), there is no agreement on how to demonstrate a causal relationship. There is no agreement on how to account for intervening variables. The design—to identify and define behaviors that determine managerial effectiveness and to compare the manager's behavior before (based on the needs analysis) and after participation—is neither easy to execute nor productive. Measuring organizational change resulting from development is even more difficult. Our ability to identify and measure the variables that affect throughput and output of complex social systems is even less than for individuals.

A barrier to research is management's tendency to want to get on to development, even if it is less than perfect. There is the feeling that to be concerned with analyzing and perfecting programs may mean that programs never get off the ground.

However, the absence of statistically useful findings does not argue for eliminating assessment efforts. Recognizing all the flaws, there nonetheless are usable findings. The outputs from some development designs are easier to control and estimate. The contract approach is one such design.

Process evaluation, a form of operations research, may be the most useful research for management development. Learning objectives are directly translated into process stages in terms of behavioral and organizational consequences. Fewer controls and less monitoring are necessary. Less expenditure of resources is required. Feedback leading to modification of the program is more rapid. Further, achievement of the objectives of participants, organization, and trainer are considered at the same time and trade-offs are possible. In natural experiential approaches, the act of designing assessment for program elements focuses consideration on objectives and criteria for accomplishment.

Conscious assessment during implementation sharpens observation and review of relationships between design and implementation. Continuing review of input, development activities (throughput), and output helps to clarify concepts, improve technology, and identify possible alternative designs. Also, program activities can provide information about intervening variables, and the number and impact of intervening variables are reduced.

Building an evaluation or research component into the development plan is valuable, even if it is never completely implemented. It forces identification and consideration of the assumptions and uncertainties underlying the development plan and can lead to consideration of new goals, objectives, and activities.

While we recognize the difficulties and cost of research and evaluation and do not believe that research can be the primary activity for development professionals, we feel that research is a necessary element of management development. Prior to any research, there should be an assessment of researchability. Some hypotheses are not testable in the development context. The inability to determine statistically significant values does not decrease the usefulness of going through the process of designing research; less than statistical significance can be a useful guide for future activities. Research can be meaningful, useful, and cost-effective if practicing professionals are pragmatic about the nature and limits of the research, and use the process of designing the research to sharpen program design and use the findings as an incentive, not a substitute, for thought.

8

THE VENUE

There are three venues that affect learning and the use of learning. In a very real sense, this book is primarily concerned with the "learning venue," in which planned new learning takes place and is incorporated into the learner's life-bank. The second is the "work venue," in which it is anticipated the new learning will be used and which we believe must be the primary learning venue for managers. The third is the "individual venue," in which the individual lives apart from work and learning venues. While we will only touch on this venue, it plays a key role in determining and maintaining values, beliefs, relationships, and other factors that set limits on potential changes in an individual's behavior.

In this chapter, we will be concerned primarily with relationships between learning and the work venue. We define the work venue to have two components. One is the work system or the organization in which the participant is a manager. The second, the "environment," is defined variously by different theorists. We define it to include all systems, individuals, and other forces that impact on the manager's behavior but are not elements of the manager's work system. The environment has more impact than is generally recognized on the managerial role, on the competencies managers need to function effectively, and on management development.

The principle of interaction enunciated by Dewey (1938) hypothesizes that learning is a function of the transactions between the person's life-bank and the learning venue. This hypothesis implies that no two persons learn (add to their life-banks) the same things from a learning experience. We extend the hypothesis to note that there are two venues in which learning takes place, a planned, usually formal learning venue and the work venue, in which informal and unplanned learning may take place. Sometimes, as in natural experiential learning, the two coincide.

Closed productive systems cannot continue to exist. They need both input from and acceptance of output by the environment. However, systems that can control input from and output to their environments can function in great measure as if they were closed. This is an objective of many systems.

Three factors that have the greatest influence on the functioning of large organizations are its culture, the internal power distribution, and the forces in the external environment. The culture underpins an organization's structure and functioning. Power provides the driving energy and direction of the group efforts. To the extent that a system is open, forces in the external environment determine what the organization's input and output must be to survive, whether the organization will survive, and at what level it will continue to function. The characteristics of systems vary greatly. However, to the extent that a system is closed, its culture tends to be fixated on achieving greater closure. Its structure tends, to a greater extent than open systems, to be oligarchical. The "enacted" work venue tends to have fewer variables with narrower ranges. This tends to limit alternatives and distracters and to increase the influence of the work system on learning. Management development tends to be technical and to employ passive learning and such experiential approaches as coaching and mentoring.

Development courts failure when the states of the work system and the environment and their relationships are not considered in the design and implementation of the program. Development content, learning approaches, and change techniques must be acceptable and effective for helping managers to function effectively in both components of the work venue.

We are concerned with the work systems and the environments not only because they determine the behavior of managers but also because they determine objectives of development, the nature of the appropriate content and behavior changes, and how to help participants unfreeze, learn and change, refreeze, and use learning in the work venue. We follow Weick (1969) in considering the relevant environment as the "enacted'' environment: ''The human creates the environment to which the system then adapts. The human actor does not react to an environment, he 'enacts' it. It is this enacted environment, and nothing else, that is worked upon by the processes of organizing'' (p. 64). This defining or, in Weich's term, ''enacting'' of the environment is a crucial managerial function. We use the concept to include the work system itself as enacted from the individual manager's point of view. This makes helping managers gain the ability to enact the appropriate work venue an important development objective.

The enacted work venue is not the same for all managers in the same organization. This is in part the result of their having different roles and responsibilities. To a greater extent it may be the consequence of having different life-banks, unique combinations of knowledge, experience, values, perceptions, interpretations, and expectations. People differ in ways that are very difficult to anticipate. While performance is dependent on motivation and competence, both of these are dependent on the characteristics of the two components of the work venue and their interrelationships. Identical managerial behaviors in dealing with the same issues, in the same work venue, do not necessarily lead to the same result.

THE WORK SYSTEM

Organizations are mental constructs, models of human-machine systems that function as if they were simultaneously open and closed systems in time and space. Managers, primarily concerned with the productivity of their units, seek to function independently of both time and the system's external environment. But they cannot do so without damage to the system as a whole. Nevertheless, we will consider the impact of working in a closed system separately from consideration of the impact of the system's environment in order to emphasize the role and development aspects that derive from internal forces. However, we will not lose sight of the environment, which determines to a great extent what happens in the system.

A great number of variables have been defined in organizational theory (Katz and Kahn 1978; J. D. Thompson 1967) to describe the functioning of productive systems. We will consider four to indicate the impact of work system variables on the managerial role and effective alternatives for management development. The variables we will consider are culture, people, structure, and technology.

''Culture'' may be the key variable in analysis of systems. Systems are mental constructs that do not possess or transmit a culture. The members of an organization, in their interactions with each other and in their relationships, as members of the organization, with people outside of the organization, exhibit the culture of the organization. We define "culture" in general terms as what distinguishes the people in one organization from those in another. It includes the sum total of similar ways of thinking, reacting to stimuli, and other characteristics exhibited by a significant subset of the members of the organization that tend to be transmitted from one generation of members to the next.

The cultural characteristics exhibited by the people in an organization are not a sudden or even a generational development; they are values, assumptions, approved behavior patterns, and other characteristics passed from generation to generation. To extend the concept of the term, the culture is the life-bank of an organization. It may have even more stability than an individual's life-bank. An organization's policies, plans, and activities evolve out of, and are integral elements of, its life-bank. Managers must, in development activities, be able to place their organizations in a temporal sequence, that is, to know how its life-bank was developed, how it can be expected to evolve, and the roles they must play to be effective managers. Without this knowledge and understanding, the manager is fixed in the present, unable to learn how to influence the functioning and development of the organization.

In organizations headed by the founder, or in which top management is only one or two generations from the founding generation, there is usually considerable influence of the founder on the culture. This tends to be particularly strong with respect to goals, roles, interpersonal relationships, reward structure, technology, and prohibitions. The influence frequently extends to management staffing practices and management development.

"Organizational culture" includes well-established and generally accepted elements, both assumed but not formally enunciated and formal policies and practices committed to writing, such as the following:

- the process for enacting the work venue, determining its leading elements, state, and ability to affect people in the system
- the consensus on the nature of, and need to advance, the primary organizational goals
- the rationale for norms, and acceptable variations from the norms, for decision making, acceptable risk, authority and responsibilities, disagreement, participation, feedback, and verifiability
- acceptable use of time and other scarce resources
- assumptions about people's motivation and their ability and will to change, participate in decision making, and accept responsibility
- expected interpersonal relations
- boundary-spanning activities.

Some cultural determinants are more stable than others. The more stable cultural determinants include values, thought patterns, habits, skills, relationship patterns, beliefs about the organization, and assumptions about the environment.

All the elements of an organizations's culture may not be obvious to the people in the organization. However, whether or not they are conscious of the culture, it guides and controls their behavior. The culture, which establishes, enforces, and is reinforced by a system's structure, determines to a great extent the parameters for effective management development.

Cultural factors underpin the structure of an organization. Defined and undefined roles, tasks, and official relationships are the exposed structure. Factors such as friendship and interpersonal and interunit tension are the unexposed structure. Conflicting stresses in the structure induce dynamic tension. Limited, constructive tensions tend to increase ability to achieve and maintain an effective power distribution, define and focus efforts on goals, and develop adaptability and stability for growth and survival. When the tension is slack or unsupportably high, flexible adaptability to the environment tends to disappear. In these situations of satisfaction and great internal conflict, the culture provides justification for resistance to fundamental change. Management development tends to focus on helping managers be agents of stability rather than of change.

Young organizations tend to be more open to their environments, to have a culture more accepting of risk and change, and to be less bureaucratic in structure. As large, productive systems age, they tend to have hierarchical, bureaucratic structures.

A culture in which each manager's power and responsibility are limited but absolute within a well-defined area tends to favor a structure following the power distribution. These structures are as constricting as bureaucracies in which power follows the fixed structure. Organizations with well-defined units and power distributions tend to have defined communications channels and coordination by rule and/or accepted informal agreements.

Stable culture and structure and fixed processes tend to mechanize and reduce spontaneity and flexibility in organizations. However, life in complex systems would be complicated to the point of anarchy if there were not a generally accepted culture and defined structure and practices to ensure continuing cooperation and coordination among subsystems and agreed-upon solutions to similar and overlapping problems. In such systems, it is rarely possible to effect any significant change in one unit without some resistance in other parts of the system. Nowhere is this more obvious than in government. This resistance tends to limit an individual's ability to transfer learning to the work venue.

It is a reasonably well accepted management assumption that the technology and structure of a system determine interdependencies and strongly influence relationships among people in the system. Some deduce from this the corollary that the principal way to change behaviors is to change the technology and the structure of the system. If this is assumed, management development and incentives can play only supporting roles to gain acceptance for and competence in instituting and maintaining systemic change. Even if this corollary is not accepted, management development design cannot ignore the roles of technology and structure in determining managerial behavior.

Systems generally have both a general culture characteristic of the entire system and, imposed on this culture, cultures characteristic of identifiable subpopulations. The latter frequently have different, sometimes diametrically opposing, objectives and characteristics. Examples of such differing subcultures are those of managers and workers, staff and line executives, corporate and company managers, sales and production managers, and finance and marketing managers. These managerial groups tend to have different basic assumptions with respect to strategic and operational objectives, and expected norms of behavior. These cultural characteristics tend to be related to the subpopulation. Most individuals transferred from one department to another tend to pick up the new culture after a short time. Design of management development for specialists has to recognize the legitimacy of these differences regardless of whether the managers are expected to return to their special units or to move to another area.

When a great number of managers come from the same subculture of the national population (e.g., white, middle-class, college-educated males), they tend to impose, without much thought or effort, their values, rules, and rites as integral elements in the culture. While middle managers tend to use top managers as models, it is rare that the values of top management are also those of lower-level managers. Coincidence in values between levels of management is less likely when there are rapid changes in organizational objectives and in top management personnel. This is seen most clearly in government when there is a radical change in political goals. The conflict stemming from the differences in cultural values can, unless dealt with rapidly and effectively, become ingrained below the surface. To some extent the effort to change the values of middle management rapidly, to conform to new top management values, accounts for attempts of political agency heads to put their appointees into all management positions. It is also related to political attacks on "the bureaucracy." Management development in these situations is directed to changing values and reducing conflict.

Recognition of the impact on the system's functioning of conflict between the values and objectives of policymakers and the personal values and objectives of managers below the top level has led some private-sector organizations to introduce New Age training programs to shock managers to change their values. More generally, however, approaches other than management development are employed to move managers' positions closer to those of their superiors. These include individual career development discussions between manager and superior. In these discussions system career succession plans and selection criteria are compared with the manager's behavior and the manager is counseled (Slavenski 1987).

There are other reasons for being concerned with culture and the system in addition to the impact of culture on attempts to change the behavior of individuals. Some development programs are directed toward changing the culture of an entire organization and toward training managers to become change agents to lead to the "new" culture (Mailick, Hoberman, and Wall 1988).

Within an organization needs vary greatly, in terms of the desires and expectations of the manager's role set as an entity, and of individual members of the set. There are significant differences in the behavior expected from a manager by the chief executive, the immediate supervisor, peers, subordinate managers, and others. Consequently most effective behavior, however this is defined, is always a matter of trade-offs. There are differences in the sight span of the actors. In the public sector the sight span of elected officials is frequently not beyond the issues relating to and the time of the next campaign. That of senior civil servants may be longer. Buyouts, consolidations, and other organizational uncertainties in the private sector introduce significant differences in the sight spans of managers at different levels. It is difficult to deal with these issues in management development.

While management style may change with the individual filling a position, the expectations of the persons reporting to the manager in that position may not. Their expectations may in time influence the style of the manager to a greater extent than the manager's behavior influences theirs. The role of the manager, however it is described, is to gain the cooperation of subordinates and to motivate and control their activities to achieve a specified set of objectives. The forms of "guidance" may be paternalistic, autocratic, participative, or inspirational, but it is always to achieve objectives communicated by the superior manager. Effective management styles in one situation are not necessarily effective in another. In each case there has to be an assessment of the situation taking into account the relevant set of variables. Not least among these are the role set's point of view and the technology and processes for the unit's throughput.

In recent years, there has been some emphasis on the impact on the managerial role of internal communications and input-output relationships between organizational units. The difficulty in helping managers to increase their competencies in designing and using communications and delivery systems effectively is that effective designs are specific, not general. The designs depend on the nature of the joining between units. This is apparent by considering the two extremes:

- Between richly joined units, where the key variables in one system are directly and substantially influenced by changes in variables in the other, careful, continuous, unambiguous communications are needed.
- Between poorly joined units, where the variables in one are only weakly or occasionally affected by changes in variables in the other, no such care is needed.

Common culture, defined structure, and accepted practices are some of the parameters that tend to ensure that the relationships among people at work are in stable equilibrium. Stability is also supported by the efforts of managers to maximize their utilities. Change can take place only when they change their views with respect to utility for change. To motivate them to adopt a new behavior or to accept a new behavior that might tend to displace a satisfactory equilibrium, it is necessary to convince them that it will be to their advantage and that this potential gain clearly outweighs the risk of any possible loss. It is difficult to achieve this degree of confidence in most managers by using passive learning approaches.

Thomas Szasz's (1961) hypothesis that there is a "human need to follow rules"—that is, to conform to the accepted group behavior—tends to explain the strength of organization culture. This tendency is quite apart from efforts to maximize utility and the desire to please superiors. It also serves to explain why participants get into the spirit of a synthetic experiential exercise but fail to follow through in real life.

THE ENVIRONMENT

Of equal, and sometimes greater, importance than the closed-system activities for organizational growth is the influence of the environment. We find it useful to structure the environment as consisting of three types of elements: task, functional, and contextual. We define the environment of the system to be more than the systems and individuals (and their power, activities, beliefs, values, relationships, and structures) that can impact the input and the acceptance of the output of the focal system. The "task environment" consists of the elements with which the focal system has direct, one-to-one relationships. The "functional environment" consists of those elements in the focal system's space which have significant impact on the focal system through a sequence of elements culminating in an element of the task environment. To these identifiable sources of environmental influence, we add the "contextual environment," which consists of everything not in the system that affects input or output of the focal system but is not identifiable as either a task or a functional element. The contextual environment includes the total national and international cultures in which the focal system is embedded,the social, political, and economic forces and conditions that have, or could have, impact on the focal system.

This environment is much more than the enacted environment. While only the enacted environment influences managerial behavior, this more inclusive environment determines the system's fate. It is the environment that defines the conditions for an organization to continue to function and grow. An important role of management is to continuously scan the environment to identify elements that have or could have significant impact on the functioning of the system. The purpose of scanning is to enact the environment to which managers should react. Management development is important for becoming competent in this activity.

The problem of enacting the appropriate environment is complicated. There is no one unambiguous organizational environment. There are many environments. Each manager enacts a different environment. It is enacted in terms of the specific classification of relevant factors in the individual manager's life-bank. A development objective is to help managers learn to enact an appropriate environment. This is rarely possible using only passive learning approaches.

Lawrence and Lorsch (1969) indicate that in American companies the relevant factors relate almost entirely to the task environment. The factors in their study and the studies they reviewed include the rates of change in demand and supply, the level of competition, the speed of feedback, the nature of opportunity and risk, and whether the task environment is favorable or unfavorable. Other writers, particularly those who compare American and Japanese management (Fowler 1989), focus on the contextual environment. Development content and approaches cannot be identical for programs based on different concepts of the environment.

The importance of the contextual environment is most obvious for the operations of global enterprises. The international organizations find it necessary to adjust to host societies by changing operating rules and concepts of leadership, interpersonal relations, conflict resolution, time, competition, and team functioning (Rhinesmith et al. 1989). Managers moving from advanced Western societies to older, non-Western or socialist and former socialist societies become very aware of differences in management assumptions. American managers are attuned to a society that emphasizes the value of privacy, individual responsibility, and competition. In other countries the emphasis is on close group relationships, group and team responsibility, and group goals. Team cooperation and participation are intrinsic to many cultures and do not have to be taught. Nepotism is expected. Loyalty is to the group, not to the work supervisor.

Managers going from one organization to another within the same country usually are not able to continue to use the same enacted map of the contextual environment without change and reorientation to help them function effectively. A common example is the movement from the private sector to the public. Discussing this issue, James Kouzes (1987) states: There are fundamental differences in the dominant management principles in the private and public sectors. In the private management the driving force is through hierarchical influence and control over subordinates and policy. Authority is clearly defined and power flows from the top down. The bottom line measures success. In the public sector, in democracies, officials derive legitimacy and authority from the consent of the governed. Every elected official is responsible to numerous, frequently competing, conflicting constituencies. It is necessary for all opinions to be heard for effective governance. Shared powers require discussion, negotiations, compromise, and consensus building for effective policy determination and implementation. Decision making is obviously less efficient and requires different competencies than in the private sector.

The state of the environment can have significant impact on the state of the focal system and the needs of its managers. Emery and Trist (1969) define the states of the external environment in a manner that gives some indication of the difficulty faced in management development when the participants come from organizations whose environments are in different states or the program designers are not sensitive to and knowledgeable about the environment. They postulate four states:

- placid-randomized—There is no concentration of resources or connections among elements of the task environment and the timing and nature of demands on the focal system; the contextual environment is stable.
- placid-clustered—There is a generally predictable pattern (in a statistical sense) but no significantly competitive pattern in the availability and distribution of resources and the connections among elements of the task environment and the timing and nature of demands on the focal system.
- disturbed-reactive—The task and functional environments tend to be interdependent with the focal system and competitive and reactive to its activities rather than placid or unconcerned.
- turbulent—The availability of resources, the relationships with the task, functional environments, and the states of the contextual environment are highly variable, uncertain, and potentially very disturbing to the focal system.

The environment usually presents far greater ambiguity and uncertainty than the elements of the system itself. This stems from an inability to identify and define the relevant variables. Even when relationships can be identified in terms of their values, their relative and absolute rates of change, and their interrelations, it is difficult to determine their import for internal variables of the focal system and the specific manager.

Boundary spanning is a principal managerial role. Most managers span the boundaries between units in the focal system. Some span between the focal system and elements in the environment. The competencies required for these different spanning functions are not the same. The chief executive is the principal boundary-spanning manager. Competence in this activity is the major consideration in the selection of a chief executive. Some observers feel that this is so crucial that it is important to ensure "that executives can be replaced easily when environmental conditions require new skills or a new symbol" (Pfeffer and Salancik 1978). The reasoning that leads to this conclusion is based on the hypothesis that the chief executive should be the primary "risk absorber" in an organization.

Organizations that are more open to their environments tend to have many more managers who are boundary spanners with the environment. These boundary-spanning managers have to have greater decision-making authority in relations affecting input and output. A consequence of this greater authority is that these managers tend to have great influence with other internal decision makers (Lawrence and Lorsch 1969). For a system to function effectively, the centrifugal force exerted by the environment needs to be balanced by structural and procedural equivalents of an equally strong centripetal force: stronger communication, coordinating, and conflict-resolving roles and processes. Systems that are very open to their environments require a different emphasis on managerial competencies than do those which are less open. Managers who are risk-taking boundary spanners may be more responsive to natural experiential learning.

The more dependent a system is on its task environment, the less freedom its managers have to change their behavior without considering acceptance of the change by their counterparts in the task environment, and the greater the importance of the boundary-spanning function. A major role of these managers is to buffer the technical core of the focal system from direct, outside pressures. A complex, dynamic task environment with many different elements calls for a greater number of boundary-spanning managers with a wider range of competencies. Development for these managers has to identify work venue priorities relating to technical and managerial competencies. The thrust has to be to develop the competencies that will be useful for reducing the uncertainties coming from the environment.

When there are changes in the environment, people in a system tend to experience a rapid rise in internal tensions. There is a felt need for review of goals, technologies, and staffing. Conflict may develop. Unless additional resources, new technologies, and other ameliorating forces become available, tensions may escalate. The equilibrium system model for efficiently functioning systems (Katz and Kahn 1978) may no longer be applicable (Gleick 1987).

The managerial approaches are in large part determined by what the top management thinks will be most effective for achieving the system's and their own objectives in a given environment. In a highly competitive environment the organizational structure will favor managers selected and trained to do combat with competitors (Lawrence and Lorsch 1969).

The importance of responding effectively to the environment was a major reason advanced for investing in management development by chief executive officers interviewed in the Porter and McKibbin study (1988). In particular they expected improved response to a faster pace of change and greater competition in the marketplace, and the ability to deal with more sophisticated customers and suppliers. There was a feeling that managers in the organizations may not have had the experiences to permit relying on their expertise.

MANAGEMENT DEVELOPMENT AND THE WORK VENUE

Sometimes management development is designed to resolve difficulties related to the state of the work system. The state of the work system is determined by the coincidence between the system's life-bank and resources and its needs for survival and growth as determined by its continuing operations and its problems and opportunities. If there is little coincidence, the state of the system tends to become "turbulent": things are loosed from their moorings. Relationships and cause/effect assumptions become uncertain. People worry that the unexpected may happen, and everything and everyone become suspect. To the extent that there is good coincidence, the system tends to be "stable": the expected is the norm. Past solutions continue to be useful, and relationships continue. Management development may be too late to help in quieting turbulence. Natural experiential approaches that test the usefulness of alternative models to find those which are most useful in an evolving situation may be the only approach which has a chance to produce positive results.

In the Porter and McKibbin study (1988), company executives stated that management development was expected to provide the glue holding the company together: to homogenize management culture; to help managers deal with a new type of work force (i.e., to be able to lead and inspire rather than simply to order); to teach managers how to function in different organizational structures (e.g., matrix and flat structures); and to develop flexibility to adjust to the faster pace of change. However, it was felt that content should depend on the specific managerial responsibilities. Porter and McKibbin ignored the fact that the organizational structure the executives employed in their organizations was largely hierarchical. This told more about the expected behavior of the managers than the statements inspired by reading and attending executive development seminars.

Technical advances may change the roles played by middle-level managers. Some technologies increase the ability of top management to control in greater detail than they do now. It has been noted by Goleman (1988) that when companies install management information systems to increase the flow of information to higher levels, lower-level managers tend to control the flow to reduce the ability of higher management to evaluate and control their activities. A not uncommon tactic is to overload the system. The managers are reacting not unnaturally to a technology that reduces their independence and subjects them to greater control. Management development that seeks to get the managers to agree to this may be blowing against the wind. It is anticipated that some new technologies will permit a structure in which workers perform tasks now performed by managers. While there may be more people performing managerial tasks, some middle-level managers may be eliminated and some downgraded. Management development will have to take into account the fact that the resistance of supervisors and middle managers will increase as they perceive that their greater efficiency will decrease the need for their services.

The time span to achieve objectives, usually set by top management, has impact on internal functioning and on relationships with people in the task environment. Nowhere is this more obvious than in the public sector. It explains elected officials' understandable general lack of interest in management development for civil servants. Increasing managerial competence through management development is not a short-term objective. Elected officials have only a short time span to demonstrate their competence. In the short term, it may be the best strategy to bring in managers who do not have to be motivated to accept new objectives and approaches, and seek to maximize the system's status, reputation, and perceived value as soon as possible with respect to the population on which they are most dependent for reelection.

Management development must be concerned with "organizational learning" as well as individual learning. When managers change their behavior, the organization must change in some manner. This requires that organizations have the ability to acquire active knowledge (to learn in terms of an organizational life-bank) and to use the learning to change in some manner. However, it is not clear what it means to say that an organization "learns" or has a life-bank. Even if we ignore the problem of meaning, there is little theory on how organizations learn and less on how organizations "use" learning to change. An organizational life-bank must contain a set of rules and processes to identify, capture, classify, store, and retrieve relevant learning from the life-banks of its members. There must be a process through which individuals can contribute to and draw on the organizational life-bank. Something is present that is more than a management information system.

Our earlier conclusion (Dery, 1986) that, at most, an organization's life-bank is a composite of its members' life-banks is not completely satisfactory. We cannot ignore the impact of much that we defined as "culture": organizational history as contained in records, and processes and relationships that are continued from generation to generation without any new analysis or evaluation. The transmitted fragments of experiences of predecessors that persist through generations of managers are elements of the organization's life-bank. Dery is correct that this can be observed only as it influences the life-banks of individual managers. The contents of the organization's life-bank are both more and less than the sum total of the contents of the life-banks of the individuals in the organization: more, in the sense that some elements of individual life-banks complement each other and produce more than their sum; less, in that not all the relevant contents of individual life-banks are "organizational" elements. Many organizational life-bank elements are passed from generation to generation in the organization in no conscious or overt manner. In our model there is a significant critical mass of material in the organization's life-bank that guides individual performance. New organizations and organizations in a state of violent change do not have the advantage or disadvantage of having such guides for their members. In such cases natural experiential learning tends to be of limited value with respect to comparisons with and integration into past performance. It may be of greater value if viewed as an experimental process.

THE LEARNING VENUE

We have assumed that there is a close relationship between the locus of learning and the use of learning. Schein (1986) relates this to the organizational culture. He states that learning outside of the work venue fails because it is not supported by the organizational culture while that gained in the work venue succeeds because it is supported. We agree that learning in the work venue is crucial, but it is not the entire story.

We have emphasized in this chapter the importance of the work venue in determining what participants learn and use in the work venue. This gives the learning venue a neutral value. It may not help in the transfer of learning, but it is not a negative force. We now ask if this can be assumed.

According to Menell (1976)

> Well-planned facilities have a direct effect on the attitudes of the people to whom a program is presented. . . . For optimum results, the students should have a sense of well-being and be in a receptive frame of mind. . . . Their environment . . . play[s] an important part in supporting these attitudes. (pp. 7–12)

Many management development centers have facilities comparable with those of the best resort hotels. It is not surprising that some participants see the experience as a vacation of sorts, no matter the objectives of either sponsor or supplier. In university programs in which an undergraduate atmosphere is set up, participants may revert to their undergraduate learning pattern: learning to accumulate knowledge for its own sake, not for use. In some cases the learning venue, by its risk-free, protective, interesting, and opulent nature, may be counterproductive in terms of behavior on return to the work venue.

It may be a valid assumption that the greater the differences between the learning venue and the work venue, the more difficult the effective transfer of learning. Even if the negative relationship is not perfect, it must be a matter of concern to program sponsors and suppliers, particularly for resort-type and New Age programs.

THE INDIVIDUAL VENUE

Top management has always attempted to control the personal venues of subordinates. It has for the most part given up on controlling the individual venues of workers, but not those of managers. In many organizations, top management remains strong with respect to control of the individual environments of managers—if not always through overt direction, then covertly through paid memberships in specific types of clubs, location of the workplace, and company dining rooms. These controls are seen by participants as perks even when the controls are recognized. The activities are planned elements in maintaining the organizational culture and management development. They tend to strengthen relationships, improve interunit communications, and encourage conformity.

The efforts to control the individual venues may lead to increasing importance of training and development. Moving a company headquarters from a city to a suburban or rural area has the effect of reducing the openness of the system and giving top management greater control over individual venues. It also can lead to new barriers to growth by decreasing the innovation and responsiveness required to keep systems productive and competitive. This may account for increases in management development to substitute for the greater, more invigorating challenges in the urban society.

New Age and "ethics" programs recognize the importance of the individual venue for learning and, consciously or not, are involved in the transfer of learning to the individual venue as well as to the work venue. This has been the basis of some of the challenges to programs directed toward changing personal values.

CONCLUSIONS

The effectiveness and efficiency of an organization are not entirely determined by the activities of people in the organization.

> Organizations exist in interdependent environments and require the interlocking of activities to survive. Control over this interlocking or structuring of activities is never in the hands of a single actor such as a manager. Books about how to manage . . . are ill-advised because they give the impression that there is some set of rules or procedures that will guarantee success. The essence of the concept of interdependence means that this cannot be the case. (Pfeffer and Salancik 1978, p. 267)

This observation goes beyond books. It goes to the heart of management development to prescribe a limit to its effectiveness. The hypothesis is that the work venue may make it impossible to design management development such that a change in behavior of a single manager or a small group of managers can exert sufficient influence to have great, continuing impact on the functioning of a large, complex system.

The state of the environment and the relationship between the functioning of the focal system and the environment always determine effective managerial behavior (and not the reverse). Development courts failure when it does not consider both design and implementation with regard to the states of the work system and the system's environment. The content, learning approaches, and change mechanisms and techniques must be acceptable and effective in what exists, even if the objective is to change what exists.

We have indicated some ways in which management and management development are influenced by the work venue. Some others should be noted.

Pfeffer and Salancik (1978) identify four techniques that managers should learn for dealing with the environment: scanning, loosening dependencies, managing conflicting demands and constraints, and designing an effective boundary-spanning position. We extend these approaches to the total work venue, thus including the individual's work system. "Scanning" becomes the process of enacting an appropriate work venue. Difficulties faced in scanning include determining what to scan and what to do with the data. Scanning assumes an enacted work venue. Many managers find it unprofitable to expend resources to enact an extensive work venue that may lead them on the one hand to immobility and on the other to respond to unimportant changes in the venue.

The purpose of "loosening dependencies" on the environment is to reduce control by the task environment and increase decision-making discretion within the focal system. In terms of the work system it is decentralization. This permits adjustment by smaller units without reducing the effectiveness of the total system (unless there is significant suboptimization as a result of the greater local decision-making powers). In both the environment and the work system, loosening dependencies may call for extensive management development and organizational development.

"Dealing with conflicting demands" is related to "loosening of dependencies." In terms of the environment, both are served by diversification and growth. In terms of the work system, dealing with conflicting demands is a major objective of many management development modules. The problem is how effective passive learning is for dealing with the real conflicting demands within an organization.

"Designing effective boundary-spanning positions" is structural, but once the structure is decided, selection and management development have important roles to play.

Not all managers occupy positions that enable them to play equally effective roles in efforts to improve the performance of a system. Consequently the selection of managers to participate in management development may be a more decisive factor than either the competence of the participants or the quality of the development program. If interplay with the environment is the function that is most decisive for the system, then boundary-spanning managers are key. If production, costs, and other internal variables are most decisive, then these managers are key. In either case, it is the on-the-job role and environment that govern selection. With poor selection, management development may have little positive or negative impact.

Just as individuals are prepared to change by unfreezing, so it may be necessary to unfreeze the organization to prepare the people in it to accept and reinforce the individual changed behaviors. It may be necessary to slow down or speed up the changed individual behaviors to bring the timing into synchronization with the readiness of others in the work venue to accept the changed behaviors. Unfortunately, it is rarely possible to predict how ready people in an organization are to accept and reinforce changed behavior. Just as motivators are required to encourage managers to learn and use new behaviors, so it may be necessary to provide motivators for the managers' role sets to accept changed behavior. This could lead to a basic hypothesis that all management development should help managers to become change agents.

Just as cultural differences have to be considered between systems in different contextual environments, so the cultural differences within the same system have to be considered. There are obvious booby traps in assumptions about communications and other linkages between subsystems that have different sets of values, objectives, technologies, speech patterns, and dependencies. There are significant intrasystem differences between production and sales subsystems. In implementing management development, there are similar differences among program participants and between them and program designers and implementers. Just as cultural differences between patient and therapist are accepted as key factors in psychotherapy, so do cultural differences have to be accepted in management development.

There is general agreement with our assumption that the work system and environment have impact on the role that a manager is expected to play and can play. We have introduced the possible influence of three venues—work, individual, and learning—on learning and use of learning. As a consequence of these considerations, we have raised questions about relating the content and expected use of learning to the learning venue.

There are assumptions but insufficient research into the relationships among the venues, learning approaches, and transfer of learning to provide a solid basis for the design of management development. From one point of view, we can do little if "every organization has its own particular pattern of assumptions about the world" (Schein 1986, p. 31). From another point of view, some typing may be useful to provide a frame to "observe, apprehend and . . . to explore" (Deal 1986, p. 32). We suggest that a proper mix of learning approaches will provide the basis for our learning. We further offer the hypothesis that the mix will be most effective if the major learning technology is natural experiential learning. We turn in the next three chapters to experiential learning.

9

EXPERIENTIAL LEARNING

INTRODUCTION

There is increased emphasis on experiential learning (Carnevale 1989). The rationale is that passive learning approaches which mimic experiential learning are only mental exercises involving the manipulation of symbols. One critic of academic management development states, "The case method, lectures, discussions and theories of various kinds have been around for some time. They are helpful exercises for mind stretching. But how much of that instruction ever finds its way back to the office." (Livingston, 1983, p. 15).

Preference for experiential learning approaches is expressed by both corporate executives and educational theorists. Both believe that experiential learning, by motivating active participation, leads to transferring learning to the work venue more effectively.

EXPERIENTIAL LEARNING

We believe that because experiential learning is more effective than passive learning for integrating new learning with existing life-bank elements as active elements in the learners' life-banks, the learning is more readily transferred to the work venue. Properly designed experiential learning is a helical process. In passive learning, the participants acquire knowledge more easily. But the knowledge tends to be inert, not integrated with existing life-bank elements and not available for use. Few learners have the will and capacity, on their own, to make knowledge from passive learning transfer to the work venue. In experiential learning each experience is an occasion to review, test, and improve the general model induced from earlier learning and experiences. It is the occasion to move to a higher level in the helix by creating a new model and substituting the new model for the old in the life-bank.

We introduced the concepts "synthetic" and "natural" experiential learning to distinguish between approaches in which different learnings are employed. Natural experiential learning uses the work venue with naturally occurring demands, relationships, uncertainties, and processes. Synthetic experiential learning employs special models and constructs to substitute for experience in the work venue in order to permit focusing on specific learning objectives. There is a wide range of synthetic experiential approaches—from group analysis of case studies, close to passive learning, to the use of exercises based on naturally occurring experience in the work venue. Different venues provide different learning opportunities for incorporating active elements into the learner's life-bank. Synthetic and natural experiential learning call for different techniques for incorporating and keeping the learning "active."

Experiential learning approaches, both synthetic and natural, assume that experiences shape responses to change as well as the competence to determine the nature of the change needed. These approaches challenge the participants to select, identify, and design the process to satisfy needs. They provide experience to help unfreeze, change, and refreeze elements in participants' life-banks.

Most experiential approaches replace the teacher with a facilitator. The facilitator does not assume the teacher's unquestionable, expert authority or maintain total control over the learning process and content. He or she introduces experiential learning activities, monitors performance, and encourages feedback and self-analysis. The facilitator serves as a guide, mentor, and consultant. The role is to facilitate open discussion, keep things moving, summarize for reinforcement, introduce new issues and concerns, encourage experimentation and risk taking, and guide the learning process.

Experiential learning is sometimes supported by learning contracts. In the contract the roles, objectives, and commitments of faculty and participants are spelled out. The contract serves to increase participation and motivation.

Experiential approaches frequently are directed toward solving the reentry and utilization problems. It is assumed that these problems are more easily solved when participants do the following:

- apply learning in problem identification, rational analysis, development of alternatives, and decision making in a reactive venue
- have experience in relating to people in both cooperative and difficult circumstances
- experience management as a group activity and learn how success upon reentry depends upon the acceptance and support of their role sets
- play different roles in exercises, learning how behavior must change as management positions, roles, and tasks change.

In addition, natural experiential learning assumes that some learning is learning venue-specific and transfer is more effective when learning and use venues are identical.

Both synthetic and natural approaches involve participants actively. In synthetic experiential learning, experiences tend to be planned. Learning is structured by defining in some detail the issue, the environment, and the relevant variables. This is never the case in natural experiences. Major natural experiential learning tasks are for participants to identify and define the focal issues and the relevant variables, and to enact the environment.

We discuss synthetic experiential learning in the rest of this chapter. Natural experiential learning is discussed in Chapters 10 and 11.

SYNTHETIC EXPERIENTIAL LEARNING

Synthetic experiential techniques encourage risk taking by providing virtually immediate gratification for being right and turning being wrong into a positive learning experience. Time and space can be compressed. A year and more can be reduced to an hour and less. A dozen plants scattered around the world can be brought into one room. Many variables can be eliminated to permit focusing attention on the variables perceived to be crucial for the specific learning. Action can be completed. Feedback can be immediate. Teams of participants can work on the same exercise and compare results. For many of these reasons, expectancy theory provides strong theoretical underpinning for synthetic experiential approaches. The experiences and feedback give participants confidence in being able to use the learning to achieve a desirable objective.

Assumptions on which synthetic experiential approaches are based include the following:

- Participants' competencies in gathering and organizing data, analyzing new situations, and solving unfamiliar problems tend to increase by working on assignments and problems related to the work venue in a novel, unfamiliar setting.

- Acceptance of and practice in taking risks in a nonthreatening environment increase the will and competence to take risks in the work venue.
- Giving managers the time and incentives to develop and evaluate alternatives will increase their will to do the same in the work venue.
- Being self-directed in exercises leads to being self-directed on the job.
- Experience as a team member in an exercise translates into being a good team member in the work venue and improving team leadership capabilities.
- Use of learned behavior and positive reinforcement in an exercise increases motivation to use the behavior in the work venue.
- Unfreezing and learning to change a deeply rooted assumption or approach in an exercise increases openness to unfreezing and appropriate change in the work venue.

There are various practices used to make synthetic experiences come closer to experience in the work venue:

- identifying and defining management roles and tasks that relate to the learning objectives and content
- determining which competencies should be changed
- involving senior management and participants in setting learning objectives
- identifying situations in which specific competencies are important for satisfactory performance
- selecting appropriate content and designing exercises in which use of learning can be assessed and discussed.

Some see synthetic experiential situations as superior, although temporary, learning systems. They argue that learning is more efficient because, while relevant conditions of the natural system are present, there are no continuing job demands and pressures and significant stimulation from the game aspects. Walle, arguing against this position, notes, "The effect of the temporary system as such may in some cases be counteracted by the members' insistence on applying the 'mechanistic' rules inherent in their notions of competence" (1968). He further notes that problems which participants "are not willing to regard as relevant for managers are thereby less likely to be subject to learning". He goes on to state that what members in these groups learn and apply are criteria to be accepted by the other members as competence.

To be effective, synthetic experiential learning should do the following:

- be accepted as a valid learning experience
- have a valid relationship to one or more of the "trilogy"—the unfreeze, change, and refreeze elements of the change model

- involve participants in activities in which it is clear they are applying or developing the basis for useful theory, technique, or practice
- have clear, easily understood and applicable rules and conditions
- require follow-up discussion and analysis to clarify and reinforce the learning
- be directly related to problems, issues, conditions, and relationships in the work venue
- not play into and reinforce participants' weaknesses
- permit immediate feedback and analysis
- compress time and space in an acceptable and useful manner
- tie into other managerial tasks.

Synthetic experiential approaches can be classified in three dimensions—according to the level of experiential participation, the control imposed on process and outcome, and the relationship to management theory and practice. Management case studies are low in experiential participation, high in controls imposed on process and outcome, and high in terms of relationships to management theory and practice. Games tend to be high in terms of experiential participation, of varying levels in terms of controls, and low in terms of relationships to management theory and practice. Spontaneous role-playing tends to be high in terms of experiential participation, low in terms of controls, and on varying levels with respect to management theory and practice. Simulations that include elements of case studies, role-playing, and games run the gamut in all three dimensions.

Some synthetic experiential approaches are employed in selecting managers as well as in development. The "in basket" was developed to be used in selection, and the decision tree in training. In both, the intent is to approximate a work sample: in training, for analysis, learning, and reinforcement; in selection, for diagnosis and assessment.

Examples of Synthetic Experiential Techniques

Synthetic exercises vary from activities involving a single, well-defined situation to complex computer simulations. In some, dozens of problems, issues, opportunities, and other variables are presented. Participants are required to set priorities, assign resources, develop and implement plans, and evaluate the consequences of the actions taken. Some are further complicated by a continuing flow of useful, distracting, useless, and possibly misleading information.

While in the past the case study was generally seen as a form of synthetic experiential learning, it no longer is. It is seen by many as passive learning that has some experiential learning elements. Case studies in the form of examples and illustrations appear early in formal management education. They still are the primary experiential component of university programs. They are used to test and reinforce specific knowledge and technical competencies and to provide practice in analyzing management situations. They can be focused on specific learning objectives effectively. Cases can be divided into phases so that the process can be stopped at any point to make sure that participants are going in the right direction and to consolidate learning before going on to a subsequent phase. The approach is flexible enough to be used for independent and group learning, and as exercises to test and reinforce learning. Solutions can be discussed by a group as a group exercise.

In addition to providing experience in analysis of data, development of alternatives, and cognitive decision making, earlier practitioners saw the case study as a means for providing experience in working in a group. Those who use the method for this purpose include a discussion and analysis of group dynamics and participation in arriving at decisions (Pigors and Pigors 1961). This uses the case analysis as the occasion for synthetic experiential learning in group participation in decision making. The case study is experiential learning for some technical competencies, such as financial analysis, in which technicians work alone and discuss their conclusions with others.

Some variations of the case approach increase its experiential learning characteristics. Some use existing organizational situations in which the action has not been completed to allow participants to compare their solutions with those of the responsible managers. The values and shortcomings of case studies are generally those of other passive learning approaches. If properly designed, they can have significant values similar to some synthetic experiential learning approaches.

Games are an extremely versatile tool. They are competitive simulations with formal rules. Most frequently the relationship to real managerial tasks is symbolic and metaphoric. Some provide job-related activities in a competitive frame. The competition tends to increase interest and provide the basis for feedback by comparing performances. The simple and highly abstract characteristics of games permit their use in many different situations to achieve quite different educational objectives. The leader can direct the discussion in a planned direction.

The use of games in training is supported on a theoretical basis by Huizinga (1955). On the basis of sophisticated historical and social analysis, Huizinga presents a strong argument that the instinct for play and the response to competition are among the most fundamental elements of human culture. In fact, he goes beyond humans to discuss play in other higher forms of animal life. He also notes that games people play have been long recognized as among the most important factors shaping and describing a culture. The great popularity of games among participants in management development, even games that are quite abstract and bear no obvious relationship to managerial tasks, is not only indicative of the deep-rooted play incentive in humans. It is indicative of how American managers are conditioned.

Well-designed games are usually interesting and enjoyable. They are used as ice breakers, to "wake people up"; to bring them into a "creative mood"; to induce a spirit of competition; to reduce tensions and help participants to enjoy themselves; and to bring people together in a cooperative spirit. However, they are most useful in the unfreezing process.

Gaming can also be used in the change stage and to provide occasions to practice newly gained competencies. Some games give participants a deeper understanding than any other form of activity of the interrelationship between hostility and friendship in everyday relations. They can be used to increase the competitive and gaming spirit in managers, leading to increased productivity and openness to risk taking. Trainers use games to increase participation, making for more dynamic and satisfactory experiences.

While there is some anecdotal evidence that games produce measurable changes in the short term, there is none that they have lasting impact. It is hypothesized that the nature and duration of impact increase when followed up by or used in tandem with other experiential learning and as the content and processes match elements in participants' work venue.

Many simulations are adaptations of the game to situations that are closer to the natural organizational psychosocial and structural environment. To make application of learning more "real," ambiguity is frequently introduced and not all the information is made available at one time. The game element is maintained by the overt introduction of competition, either in terms of competing teams or of competing against a standard. The elaboration possible is unlimited in terms of problem complexity; introduction of new relevant, irrelevant, and ambiguous information; changes in objectives; use of computers and videotaping and other equipment; the number of teams; the nature of the competition; sequencing of events; and number and nature of issues and goals. However, with each elaboration a key advantage of simulation over natural approaches is lost as the ability to relate outcome to specific cause is decreased and made more ambiguous.

Effective simulations are the following:

- selective descriptions of real situations structured to provide experience of a specific kind—for instance, working in a team to develop a position on a labor relations issue
- relevant to participants' work venue

- situations that involve decision making and expose participants to the consequences of the decision
- structured to permit rapid assessment of participants' performance
- interactions with others in situations that involve work venue-type relationships
- structured so that individual and group behaviors can be compared.

Some more sophisticated exercises are branch-type. In these simulations, all alternative decisions are anticipated at a number of intermediate points and participants are given additional information at these points as well as at others during the course of the simulation. The information depends on their activities and decisions up to the specific point.

Many simulations are not games. They do not have game elements, such as competition and uncertainty. Some illustrate practical processes that participants are expected to carry out. Others are developed from theoretical models that participants apply to obtain greater understanding of cause/effect relationships.

Role-playing is an activity simulation. It is a post-World War II development that was used early on to give participants experience in one-on-one interpersonal relations in an environment which encouraged experimentation with alternative ways to react to a stressful situation. Learning takes place in both the experience and the analysis of the interactions and their consequences. Spontaneous role-playing is sometimes introduced when a course of behavior is suggested in a discussion. The role-playing can test the suggested behavior.

Formal role-playing tends to be a simplified simulation in which the focus is on acting. Discussion can come before or after the role is played. Role-playing has many characteristics of a game. There is a tendency in role-playing to let the play element, not the learning, be the focus. When the play behavior is counter to the learning objective, there is the possibility that it may be counterproductive and actually reinforce inappropriate behavior.

Laboratory training, developed in the 1950s, has been one of the most influential approaches. It and derivative approaches are based on the hypothesis that giving participants specific types of new experiences, usually stressful, can lead to useful personal insights, concepts, and theory. Major objectives of this training include helping participants gain greater self-insight, understanding of factors that influence individual and group relationships and functioning, and interpersonal skills. Experiences are designed to give participants firsthand confirmation of the validity of an approach or concept and practice in its use.

Two major development approaches stem from laboratory training: the many types of "direct action" approaches and Organizational Development. Most tend to be at the extreme "human relations" end of the range of synthetic approaches. Some, such as organizational development, are natural experiential learning. The direct action approaches include the controversial New Age programs. New Age programs focus on changing attitudes, interpersonal skills, and, in some cases, beliefs and fundamental values. Unfreezing and change, as well as knowledge and insight, are obtained through experience and observation of others in both structured and unstructured situations. The activities are followed by discussions to clarify and reinforce learning. Sometimes the experience involves an emotional shock to accelerate unfreezing. Group and individual skill practice sessions are conducted to reinforce change and lead to refreezing. Exercises are directed toward increasing ability to assess the impact of behavior and to generalize and learn from the experiences. Objectives with family groups include helping participants to work together better as teams, reduce suboptimization, and accept organizational goals, policies, and values. Techniques employed by different New Age programs include meditation, relaxation, self-hypnosis, inducements to trancelike states, guided visualization of events, teachings of mystics such as Gurdjieff, encounter groups, and EST. In each of these approaches, an experience unrelated to the job is expected to lead to unfreezing deeply held beliefs and changed behavior in the work venue.

The rationales advanced for use of these approaches, in addition to general effectiveness for unfreezing, include the following:

- greater speed in unfreezing strong, basic beliefs and fears
- greater creativity of participants
- greater willingness of participants to take risks.

Some New Age advocates claim that more traditional learning is usually superficial and at best incremental. In either case the learning cannot lead to any radical change. These approaches also have some elements of brainwashing.

Improving "risk taking" has become an important goal in much management development. Many define "risk taking" as "taking an action when the outcome is not unknown" (e.g., Moore and Gergen 1985). We prefer "taking action when the outcome is uncertain and the expectation of loss, as a result of taking the action, is not insignificant." Willingness to take reasonable risk is seen as an important managerial characteristic. Without getting into the issue of what constitutes "reasonable risk" or the personal/systemic/cultural factors that influence risk taking, we note that the most popular training approaches to decrease the unwillingness to take what superior management considers "reasonable risk" are the "adventure" and related approaches. The theoretical basis for these approaches is the assumption that if participants can be motivated to take a risk in response to a physical challenge they do not believe they can meet, the discovery that they can meet the challenge "translates into their whole attitude about how they approach life, how they approach work, how they approach managing." (Gall, 1987).

Many of these approaches are derived from Outward Bound, which was developed as a prep school program in Scotland by Kurt Hahn (Druian, Owens, and Owen 1980). This is a wilderness program directed toward building self-confidence and personal responsibility, and finding meaning through group and individual encounters with unfamiliar situations in unfamiliar environments under conditions of psychological and physical stress. There is also some relationship to laboratory training.

Problem-solving/decision-making workshops are at the extreme analytic end of the synthetic experiential range. Activities are directed toward helping participants acquire and practice processes and techniques for identifying, defining, and solving problems that can be employed in any managerial situation. The analytic content is usually enriched by the inclusion of some form of brainstorming to increase group participation, provide a change of pace, and introduce a means for increasing the number and richness of alternatives at every stage of the problem-solving process.

The theoretical work of Gagne (1970) provides a model for many of the decision-making and problem-solving approaches to development. Rules that Gagne postulates lead to effective transfer of learning to the work venue include the following:

1. Identify the problem (problem sensitivity).
2. Establish questions (defining the problem).
3. Reason, deduce, and hypothesize (analysis and theoretical solution).
4. Observe, test, and experiment (natural experience).
5. Evaluate the results (analysis of experience).
6. Draw conclusions (revise hypothesis and reinforce).

This analysis assumes that problem-solving skills are metaelements that help people to integrate new and reactivated competencies more efficiently into their life-banks as active elements.

Kepner and Tregoe's (1960) simulation exercises are typical of approaches that emphasize practicing analytic skills for problem solving and decision making. These are primarily passive but can include some synthetic experiential learning. One technique is to use role-playing in the resolution of problem situations involving dynamic tension. Problems are sometimes related to work venue activities.

Computer simulations are used extensively for learning instrumental competencies. The simulations consist of a set of arbitrary rules structured to evoke responses to stimuli in such a manner as to test, instruct, and provide practice for participants in a specific management task or technique. Although of considerable value in advancing learning in instrumental areas, computer simulations have the shortcomings of all simulations to an exaggerated degree. There is less flexibility because faculty cannot easily change the program. In real managerial situations involving others, problems and issues do not come with well-defined stimulus-response relationships. Real-life management only rarely permits focusing all energies on a single situation. There are always interruptions, surprises, and unexpected trade-offs. There is the press of everyday routine and the sometimes personal demands of members of the role set.

A prototype of a technique involving responding to and observing the consequences of the decision made in a classroom situation is reported in *ETS Developments* (1989). A computer controls sound and video stored on videodisc. The viewer is asked to respond by making a selection from alternatives at a specific point in dramatizations of classroom management problems. The consequences of the choice are simulated in the screen. Although the Educational Testing Service developed the technique for testing, it is clear that it could be adapted as a synthetic experiential technique for independent study.

The Henley "syndicate" program provides development for middle-level managers and professional specialists who are potential managers. Both groups are assumed to have rich life-banks on which to draw during training. The focus is on helping competent specialists to become good general managers. The various exercises and syndicates provide experience in working in a group, dealing with great volumes of relatively ambiguous and imprecise information, and producing, presenting, and defending reasoned, completed position papers (Mailick 1974). It is an extended synthetic experiential learning. Participants are divided into small groups. A staff member who serves as a group consultant and observer is assigned to each group. Development is postulated to follow from increased insight and sensitivity to the values, views, and behavior of others; understanding of the connection between individual and team behavior; and the state of the environment. Unfreezing and change are assumed to follow from feedback and self-analysis. In addition to unfreezing as a consequence of gaining increased knowledge, it is assumed that the experience will lead to refreezing behaviors acquired from increased competence and will to use the knowledge.

Criticisms of the Henley approach include the following:

- Competition among groups tends to induce undesirable behavioral practices among participants.

- More than developmental learning, there is a tendency to seek out methods to "beat the system."
- The assigned staff person often enters into the competition.
- As in many other approaches, there tends to be greater emphasis on maintaining the purity of the approach rather than on adaptation to improve the development of the participants.

Evaluation of Synthetic Experiential Learning

Models that are the basis for both management theory and synthetic experiential learning are rationalizations. They are useful inventions to fill in the gaps in our knowledge and simplify cause/effect relationships. The exercises are designed to demonstrate the usefulness of the models. Use in exercises does not provide the unbiased test conditions essential for assessing a model's usefulness in the work venue. They are not proven relationships in the real, complex situation. Use of the models in both management theory and management development tends to reinforce the assumption that they are "reality." This can lead to significant error in the work venue. There is a wide gap between the neat models of theory used in case studies and simulations, and the inchoate world of reality and the processes by which a potentiality becomes an actuality.

Some adverse results from the use of sophisticated synthetic experiential learning are noted in the use of simulation in the training of airplane pilots (Fisher 1989). Simulation in the training of airplane pilots is one of the earliest uses of sophisticated computer-type programs. Simulation is used in the military for the same reasons as in management development: it is safer, less costly, more intensive, and more rapid than learning from natural experience. For the development of some skills, synthetic experience is the only realistic way to learn, for example, aerial combat. In management development each of these reasons is a consideration in addition to the ability to compress the real time for a sequence of events.

Adverse effects have been noted in the military:

- Participants are led to distrust their normal approaches that worked in the past.
- Proposed new models are distrusted if their use in the simulation does not result in the "book" answer.
- To get good grades, pilots try to "beat" the problem, which may lead to failure on the job.
- Participants learn to respond to the variables on which the simulation is based rather than to those in the actual situation.

- Participants discount the space-time differentials between successive events based on the simulation rather than on the real situation.
- Participants respond to planted cues instead of seeking and identifying cues.

Fisher notes, "Some researchers believe that the closer a trainer mimics reality, the more disturbing the disparities become" (1989). These adverse results, albeit in less obvious form and probably less dangerous, may occur in all extensive synthetic experiential learning.

Responding to the criticisms of synthetic learning, advocates readily admit simplification but point to its necessity. Without simplification, it would be impossible to create an entire organization and to give the participants the range and density of experience needed in the limited time available for formal development. Opposed to oversimplification there is the danger of overelaboration, which would make the experience so specific and so complicated as to destroy its generalizing educational value. Further, it must be accepted for "people" systems, just as for certain physical systems, that they cannot be encompassed by any simple model, even in principle.

Advocates of synthetic experiential learning point out that synthetic experiential exercises include elements of chance, ambiguity, and uncertainty. Perhaps the strongest point favoring the synthetic approaches is that while participation may initially have negative impact on those who do not do well handling these variables under strange conditions, they have the opportunity to improve. They very well might not have this opportunity in their work venue.

Arguments in favor of synthetic experiential learning include the following:

- Experience in the work venue involves so many variables in the system, its environment, and the personal environments of the individual managers that relevant variables for learning are rarely identifiable and their relationships to outcomes determined.
- The work venue does not present a sufficient amount of learning and density of reinforcement opportunities to have a strong enough impact on managers' behavior to make a significant or lasting difference.

Critics of synthetic experiential learning have used these very arguments to support the superiority of natural experiential learning. They note that synthetic experiential techniques, whether simple cases or elaborate simulations, present only simplified versions of complex organizational situations. Experience in solving the problems presented tends to mislead participants into believing that the actions taken by them, or proposed by the instructor in the critique, will work just as well in real life. It can lead to limiting analysis of work venue situations by discounting many of the operative variables, oversimplifying functions that relate variables, and discounting uncertainty in dealing with people.

A danger in extensive use of analytic synthetic experiential materials is that the exercises introduce and reinforce the belief that the diagnosis is or points directly to the remedy. There is the related misconception that the master role of management is to solve problems. The experience downplays the importance of sensitivity to problem situations and opportunities and the art of defining the appropriate problems. There is not the same risk or test of the will to accept risk as there is in the work venue. Also, feedback from other participants in a synthetic experiential situation is never the same as feedback from other stakeholders in a natural experiential situation. They also note that so much time is taken up in simulations that there is usually insufficient time for effective analysis and tieback to previous learning to make the experience cost-effective.

Well-designed and -implemented synthetic experiential approaches have both significant advantages and limitations. Their advantages include the following:

- planned, directed opportunities to apply learning and identify the need for specific learning
- risk-free opportunities to take actions to test strengths and weaknesses in design and implementation
- high learner involvement
- ability to compress or expand time and space, add new data, introduce complications or eliminate them as experience indicates the need, stop the action to change course or to point out interesting behaviors, and to tie action into previously identified needs
- feedback can be both immediate and focused
- collaborative analysis with a friendly, helpful group.

While experiential exercises should be more than "fun and games," "fun and games" can be useful to break the ice, reduce tension and boredom, and unfreeze set positions.

There are also limitations of synthetic approaches:

- the limited number of variables with narrow ranges
- participants' tendency to act to bring credit to themselves in the exercise rather than to act as they would on the job
- generalizations based on a single experience.

As simulations are made more real by adding variables and extending the ranges of values, exercises become less efficient, less clear, less focused, and, in some cases, counterproductive. They become time-consuming. Memory and the ability to understand and act on complex instruction can become the ends. The compression of time and space, focused attention, and virtually immediate feedback are in some circumstances advantages. They also can be dangers that distort the real management situation to a degree that the learning is made counterproductive. Interpersonal relations in exercise are just as synthetic; people tend to become actors rather than managers.

Many trainers see the limited number of variables in a synthetic exercise as an advantage rather than as a disadvantage. It permits directing learning to specific behaviors and competencies without the distraction of variables unimportant in the specific context. They say that even if they could, they would not duplicate the work venue with its variables, uncertainties, long-delayed feedback, and lack of advantages of permitting practice in the use of a technique and repetition using alternative management models and implementation modes.

The pluses for well-designed and -implemented synthetic experiential learning far outweigh the minuses. It is of great value in unfreezing, of value in changing behaviors, and occasionally of value in refreezing for transfer to the job. Major problems can develop when the limitations are ignored and the assumption is made that use in the learning venue will lead to use in to the work venue.

CONCLUSION

Passive learning is motivated by the pleasure from gaining knowledge rapidly. Experiential learning is motivated by the pleasure of using learning and testing and demonstrating competence. In Kolb's (1984) analysis, managers have "a strong orientation toward task accomplishment and decision making." Their learning style favors abstract learning. Thus it may be that they transfer more from passive learning to the work venue than do people in other occupations.

Experiential learning tends to provide the following opportunities:

- to be active participants in meaningful situations
- to use learning in experiences related to the work venue
- to discover new relationships and gain new insights
- to strengthen independent analysis and learning
- to learn from group analysis and feedback.

Passive learning is more effective for transmitting knowledge and may be the only approach for such learning as complex analysis. Synthetic experiential learning is of greater value for helping managers acquire the competencies the time span requires. To develop a tight feedback loop from theory to performance, output, and analysis, and back to theory is too great for natural experiential learning.

The usefulness of experience for experiential learning, in general, depends on the compatibility among what is to be learned, the experience, and the characteristics of the participants and the work venue. The key variables, the venue and experience, can be changed as necessary in synthetic approaches but not in natural approaches.

Synthetic experiential learning has its greatest value in helping participants to acquire technical competencies—such as statistical, engineering, and accounting techniques—rather than in such areas as negotiating and supervising.

The major danger in synthetic experiential learning is that the preferred theory is rarely challenged; the exercises are structured to demonstrate and provide practice in the use of the model. However, to paraphrase Kierkegaard, any model, no matter how close to the truth, is free and useful only up to a certain point. When one overshoots the mark, it becomes a nontruth and counterproductive.

10

NATURAL EXPERIENTIAL LEARNING AND MANAGEMENT DEVELOPMENT

INTRODUCTION

Both synthetic and natural experiential learning involve analyzing a situation, making a decision, taking action, and dealing with the consequences. It is the last two elements—taking an action and dealing with the consequences—that constitute the key activity implementation, which distinguishes experiential learning from passive learning. The critical difference between synthetic and natural experiential learning is the venues in which the action and the learning take place. Natural experiential learning theory assumes that whether the learning and work venues coincide is important for learning and the transfer of learning.

Natural experiential learning has additional values that will be discussed and illustrated in this chapter. An important one is that problems, opportunities, and issues are not givens. They have to be identified and defined in the course of learning.

Synthetic experiential exercises are favored by most managers. But it is not clear to what extent learning from these exercises is transferred to the work venue. Different managers face different issues, opportunities, and problems. Only rarely are those faced by any manager presented as exercises. Where an exercise is constructed from a real experience, the reality is drained out in the attempt to increase general applicability, reduce the number of variables, and control the time frame.

The transfer of learning to the work venue may depend on variables that are not subject to change by training activities. Among these are the system's environment and organizational characteristics (e.g., objectives, power structure, and maturity). Other variables, such as selection of participants, are only occasionally subject to control by the trainer. The only training efforts that may be worthwhile are those in which these variables can be realistically discounted.

Management competencies, including solving management problems, are not identical in practice with similarly named competencies in other work-related activities. "Relates well with people," a characteristic of good salespersons, does not necessarily mean the same when applied to good sales managers. People who do well in management training games may not make the best managers. Competencies that are discussed, illustrated, and even practiced in a simulated experience (e.g., risky decision making) do not necessarily carry over into practice on the job. A major reason is that the possible consequences of taking an action are not clear. Whether the action will be accepted by senior management is unknown.

The learning theory we advocate calls for application in the course of the learning or soon after the initial learning takes place. This is not the case in management development, which does not include substantial natural experiential learning. All programs use passive learning to add potentially useful information to participants' life-banks. The key word is "potentially." Only in natural experiential learning is there the direct effort to ensure transfer of learning to the work venue.

The value of natural experiential learning for management development is generally accepted. However, beyond traditional approaches such as mentoring and rotation, use of structured natural experiential approaches tying learning and experience have been strongly advocated only since the end of World War II. Sampson (1953) points out the need to put academic learning to immediate use in order to increase understanding and skill and to refreeze the new behavior. Bennett (1956) goes further, stating that programs must focus on specific organizational needs. This, he postulates, requires careful selection of participants, developing content as "intellectual conditioning" to meet the organization's needs, and, as soon as possible, application aided by skilled mentoring. Livingston (1971, 1983) claims that experience must come before learning theory as well as after. He believes that theory is meaningless unless participants have experience that integrates the learning as an active life-bank element.

Advocates of use of the case study recognize the need for natural experiential learning. Unable to bring the work venue into the classroom or to move the classroom, they settle for bringing "real" cases into the classroom. The continuing popularity of this passive approach is that it mimics experience and gives students the feeling of being involved with the "real thing." A major difference between passive and experiential education is that in the former, the performance of one participant does not impact on that of another. The impact of relationships among people is a distinguishing feature of experiential approaches. It is a rare individual who can move from passive learning to active use in the work venue. While there are relationships among participants in synthetic experiential learning, they are not those in the work venue, where there is a history and a future.

A review of training (Carnevale 1988) concluded with the opinion that there is a need to increase natural experiential training at all levels from entry to executive. Carnevale believes that by using this approach employers would integrate development into the organization's institutional culture and structure, and encourage and facilitate innovation. From the viewpoint of the individual managers, this would be integrating into their life-banks a more effective metaprocess for learning from experience.

We assume that variables in the work venue determine the nature of effective management and must be taken into account in management development. However we do not have adequate knowledge about the relationships between the venue and management competencies and styles to make definitive recommendations for design and implementation. From these considerations, it would follow that the work venue is the best learning venue for management development. The problem is what form of natural experiential learning would be most effective. We would be well advised to apply Occam's razor, a general principle in the theory of theories. It states that one should use the theory with the fewest assumptions.

NATURAL EXPERIENTIAL LEARNING

Natural experiential learning begins by identifying and correlating work venue characteristics with those assumed and predicated by theory. It uses the relationship between theory and reality to identify opportunities and problem situations, develop and implement plans for dealing with these appropriately, and observe the consequences. Learning takes place as managers analyze and compare the sequences of anticipated and actual events. This leads to confirmation or modification of the theory. The specific learning and relationships are generalized to reinforce the existing model or develop a new one. The learning is incorporated into the participants' life-banks. The metaprocess by which managers perform this sequence and recall useful models from the life-bank is not divorced from the managers' individual learning styles.

The primary objective of natural experiential learning is to increase the efficiency and effectiveness of this metaprocess as it relates to learning in the workplace venue. We will review, in the next section, a number of natural experiential learning approaches, indicating their strengths and shortcomings in achieving this and other learning objectives.

Additional arguments for natural experiential learning approaches in management development are that they do the following:

- give more meaning to and provide greater motivation for learning theory and new approaches
- identify needed competencies and tend to increase them for use in the work venue more effectively than other approaches
- facilitate understanding of the problems and points of view of persons on different levels and in different disciplines
- provide opportunities to explore and test new approaches under natural conditions subject to some controls and safeguards
- facilitate personal growth and assurance by reducing reentry uncertainties
- continue support during test and change stages.

Among basic assumptions are that natural experiential learning addresses the specific needs of both individual managers and the organization and has stronger active determiners simplifying and motivating application than does learning in any other venue. The effectiveness of natural experiential learning varies with the coincidence between the system's needs and the learning content, the participant population, the specific learning approach, and how the work venue is used. Support for these assumptions includes the following:

- These approaches involve all the parameters of the workplace but are less effective when the relative importance of different parameters is ignored.
- Members of the participants' role sets are intimately involved in the learning and change experiences. There must be the will to involve them as participants in the learning process.

Organizational culture that limits the patterns of responses to many inputs and conditions the behavior of managers is considered to be automatically taken into account and analyzed in a planned manner. People in functioning organizations tend to have a stable relationships that are threatened by any significant change which is not recognized as a positive gain. Significant changes in behavior can present a threat to the manager's role set and induce resistance. Recommendations to reduce resistance include the following:

- involving key members of the role set in developing and implementing the change
- providing full information about the nature, rationale, and expected impact of the change and obtaining feedback
- encouraging open discussion of the advantages and disadvantages, problems and opportunities, alternative approaches for achieving the same objectives, trade-offs, and dialectical analysis.

These activities are integral to natural experiential approaches. It is not necessary to transfer new learning to the work venue; learning takes place in the work venue. Participants are subject to the norms of the workplace and expectations of members of the role set who become directly involved in the learning experience. Whatever the form of natural experiential education, learning in the work venue makes the learning more compatible with the learning in the individual's life-bank.

Resnick (1987) cites research comparing formal school learning and work experience. In terms of management development, these findings indicate the importance of reducing the differences between the learning and work venues. Findings applicable to management development are the following:

- In the work venue, managers pool activities to achieve a common objective; they rarely do so in the classroom. While there is pooling in synthetic experiential exercises, it is not of the same nature; pooling is forced by the rules of the exercise.
- Lectures, discussions, and case studies are cognitive activities that may increase knowledge. To a lesser degree, this is also true of synthetic experiential learning. Neither approach requires the application of knowledge as a tool in a real venue.
- When the learning and work venues are not coincident, there is symbol manipulation and symbolic experience. Management calls for contextualized reasoning and application.
- Models and generalized learning are the stock in trade in the academic venue. Specific competencies applicable in the workplace are needed in management.

Further, if "every organization has its own particular pattern of assumptions about the world" (Schein 1986), each management development program should be unique. While they do not solve the general problem, natural experiential approaches are self-customizing.

Examples of Natural Experiential Learning Approaches

The most common form of natural experiential learning is the managerial counterpart of on-the-job training for skilled workers. New managers are expected to come to the job with some knowledge from having observed and talked to other managers, and to continue learning by observing and listening to experienced managers, drawing on supervisory and other nonmanagerial models, and seeking and getting feedback and advice from superiors. This is the least structured form of management development. It presumes that managers, on their own, can determine how to change and effect the required changes in their behavior.

On-the-job training would seem to be the natural experiential learning approach par excellence. The rub is that reliance on on-the-job experience is inadequate. Only rarely can managers generalize from their experiences to a usable model. Without a model to which to refer, data and experience are pretty meaningless for future decision making. Models are needed to make sense out of experience. A necessary condition for learning from experience is conscious exploring and testing of hypotheses about cause/effect, models, and management practices in a frame of reference that organizes observation and analysis, and assists understanding and learning. This calls for having the appropriate lifebank metaelements do several things:

- go beyond the culture, models, and processes of the focal system to consider and accept new learning
- make and test generalizations from specific experience
- accept and operate on the hypothesis that no model is a perfect cause/effect machine, and modify and adapt general models to the specific situation
- select the appropriate models to order experience and data and to help understanding.

As Dewey (1938) pointed out, not all experiences are learning experiences. Many managerial experiences are simply routine repetitions of other experiences.

While on-the-job training and mentoring are seen as major means for developing and improving managerial competencies, they are rarely systematic approaches even in companies that say they are their major development approaches.

Mentoring is probably the oldest planned management development approach. It is a one-to-one, on-the-job relationship between a competent manager and a learning protégée. It is probably the most commonly employed natural experiential development approach in the private sector, where it is seen as essential that managerial behavior be consistent with organizational and hierarchical culture. It includes trumpeting the protégée's competence and performance as a manager, sponsoring the protégée for more challenging tasks, serving as role model, providing support and consultation, and advising about relationships, organizational culture, processes, and technologies. Mentoring activities range from informal discussion and advice to "direct, constant, focused contact" (Lawrie 1987). At one extreme, the mentor does not supervise but helps by asking questions, listening, and advising. At the other extreme, the mentor can use rewards and punishments to shape learning.

The protégée is expected to gain acceptance through the support of the mentor as well as to learn from the models that the mentor points out and from friendly, nonsupervisory feedback and analysis of performance and relationships. The mentor gains from review of application, analysis of performance, and the teaching experience.

In some cases the mentor may become a coach with whom the protégée can discuss issues and problems. The mentor or coach may also provide, in addition to direct assistance in specific situations, theoretical underpinning for the analysis and decision making that will help and challenge the protégée to generalize and adapt the learning to other situations.

Mentoring, as an informal, personal relationship, has always been a common practice at relatively high management levels. At this level usually it is directed primarily to helping the protégée develop relationships and cement security in the position, and to clarifying and making explicit the expectations, the "rules of the game," and the important issues and relationships. Senior managers usually serve as mentors. Appointed higher managers in the public service are less likely to serve as mentors than are managers at similar levels in the private sector. To a significant extent, civil service managers serve as mentors to their politically appointed superiors.

The relative value of the different mentoring activities is a matter of dispute. There is little objective research on the impact. In his review of the literature, Roback (1989) found subjective claims that "everyone who makes it has a mentor," but little hard evidence. Mentoring patterns and effects are not fully understood.

Moravian College in Pennsylvania developed a program for training mentors (Nadler 1983). Supervisors were trained to advise others on how to use instructional resources and education. The preceptor in the LIFE approach (see Chapter 11) plays the role of a mentor. This is a rare example of a mentor from outside the system. The role and rationale for it are discussed in some detail in Chapter 11.

Bandura (1986) links mentoring with a process he calls "abstract modeling." In this process, the manager learns judgment skills and "the rules of the game" by observing the performance of the mentor. Frequently the mentor both models consciously and, by discussing the reasons for taking a specific action, provides the general theory.

Role modeling is a passive form of mentoring. It calls for the learner to observe, analyze, and, through self-directed learning, acquire the characteristics of outstandingly competent managers. A form of role modeling is described by Long (1988). The characteristics believed to be possessed by outstanding managers in the organization are identified and carefully described. Evidence validating the characteristics is presented. After discussion of the model, managers are helped to analyze and describe their own characteristics and performance, and to develop a plan to acquire the desired characteristics.

Coaching and mentoring are related approaches. Both are one-to-one and related to on-the-job training, with assistance focused on specific competencies. Coaching is a more formal, less personal approach. The coach is usually the new manager's superior. The mentor is not. Coaching is more directed to technical and formal interpersonal tasks; mentoring, to the less technical, informal interpersonal relationships. Both seek to help new managers develop and maintain good communications and collaboration with their role sets. Mentoring is particularly useful for managers who are "outsiders," not members of the "old boy" network, who are at a disadvantage without a sponsoring mentor (Zey 1984). Both coaching and mentoring provide enriched, valid experience with limited risk; permit dynamic feedback and instruction; and have direct payoffs to the individual, the mentor, and the organization.

A limitation of modeling, coaching, and mentoring is the restricted range of learning. Limits are set by existing models and practices, the competence of the coach or mentor, and organizational standards. There is more emphasis on output and less on development. The objective tends to be doing the "right" thing and getting the "right" answer rather than developing effective thinking and work processes. If the model, coach, or mentor is not esteemed, neither is the learner. If the senior is a poor instructor or model, the learner may ignore the instruction. If standards are set low, the learner can become very satisfied with mediocre performance.

To be effective, mentoring and coaching have to be carefully planned. Preparation includes establishing credibility and a trust relationship between the partners, acceptance of each other's roles, and an explicit or implicit contract for the process that either party can reopen at any time. This should include agreement on objectives to be achieved, the process for achieving them, the nature of the dialogue, the guidance to be provided, the circumstances under which it will be provided, the degree of the mentor's involvement, and the feedback mechanism. Obviously, success depends on the motivation and competence of the mentor or coach. Approaches based on a one-to-one relationship, such as mentoring, coaching, and role modeling, have a number of phases: initiation, cultivation, acceptance and trust, change, separation, and redefinition. It is assumed that the relationship will be positive in each of these phases. Failures indicate that this is not always the case. The relationship is not easy. If acceptance comes easily, separation may be very difficult and the protégée may never develop a natural individual style. If the relationship is very close, it may lead to a mutual dependency relationship and strengthened authoritarian personality patterns. There are special problems when the players are of different sexes (Kram 1988).

Along with the descriptions of the roles played by the models and the ways in which they perform their roles, managers and a counselor discuss the differences between their roles and performance and why the model performance is felt to be superior. It is then left up to the managers to decide what changes are desirable and how to effect them. The approach described by Long (1988) is a form of behavioral modeling.

Studies of managers and others who have been given special assignments as career development *activities* indicate a generally favorable reaction to their experiences. A study by Taylor, Giannantonio, and Brown (1989) found this to be the case but also pointed up difficulties that reduce the value of the experience. These include difficulties in transition back to the regular job, less-than-satisfactory personal relations with the members of the assignment role set, a high dependency on the state of general life satisfaction, and less benefit felt by older participants.

Other natural experiential designs characterized as "planned learning opportunities" have different objectives (Lombardo and McCall 1983; Long 1988). These approaches include enriched and new assignments, "start up" assignments, "fix it" assignments, and serving on a task force. The assumption is that the increased challenge from new or more difficult tasks and opportunities for self-fulfillment will motivate independent and continued learning.

The task force and project have traditionally been used to deal with specific situations and problems that either are not or cannot be handled by an existing unit. The assignment gives the manager focused experience in developing and carrying through to conclusion a complex activity directed toward a specific, attainable objective. When used for development, it is important to identify the values of the venue's variables and to plan the learning opportunities in the planning, operating, and assessment stages. The managers assigned may be involved in only one or two stages (e.g., the implementation or the analysis of outcome). What is new is that the assignments are designed both to accomplish specific organizational objectives and to provide learning of theoretical models and experience in their application under controlled, but still natural, conditions.

Job rotation is commonly used to prepare managers for new or higher assignments. The manager is given specifically designed, relatively short-term assignments in different units. The objectives include providing opportunities to gain competencies needed in the tasks the manager is expected to perform at the end of the rotation; to gain a better appreciation of the operations of the entire system; and, by widening the friendship circle, to become better able to function in boundary-spanning roles. For rotation to be an effective learning experience, the trainee should be fully involved in managerial work in each assignment, with complete responsibility for specific functions. This is difficult, considering the temporary nature of the assignment. It is a major reason why rotation is more often announced than used in planned development. Sometimes mentoring and rotation are combined by providing a mentor in each new assignment.

The McDonnell Douglas program (Settle 1988) to develop future managers is a good example of a combination of rotation and mentoring. Four supervisors with high potential are selected for two-year rotating assignments proposed by each participant. Each participant is given a senior-management mentor who volunteers for an assignment and is selected by the participant. The role of the mentor is spelled out. It includes meeting with the participant and discussing the tasks and other career and development matters, reviewing and discussing performance appraisals, ensuring appropriate assignments, and meeting with the development committee. The carefully selected mentors are competent and motivated to serve.

Two natural experiential offshoots of role-playing are transactional analysis and role analysis technique. Transactional analysis also makes use of psychotherapeutic techniques. It uses the manager's natural behavior and the actual role set as the starting points for synthetic exercises. It focuses on the participant's personality and perceived behavior, and the reactions of others, primarily members of the role set, to effect changes in both behavior and personality. Role-playing derived from work venue experiences is used for both analysis and practice. Frequently members of the role set attend role-playing sessions and discuss actual versus role-playing performance.

Role analysis technique is not a form of role-playing but a natural experiential approach in which the type of analyses common in discussions of role-playing are adapted to a natural experience. It is a group activity directed toward clarifying role set expectations through the discussion of experiences on the job. The objective is to reduce ambiguities that lead to disagreement, failure to cooperate, and conflict among co-workers. The technique is most often employed in organizational development but can stand on its own (French et al. 1984).

Both transactional analysis and role analysis technique focus on changing inappropriate or counterproductive behavior in personal relations. There is no strong evidence that they produce either greater understanding or a significant, lasting change in behavior.

There has always been training of work teams. This has been extended to management teams. Individual management development focuses on personal objectives, which may lead to suboptimization. Management team training focuses on organizational objectives, vision, and innovation. It includes organizational theory, strategic planning, and development of alternative practices and procedures, in order to broaden managerial views and concerns. Teams work on improving communication, standards, assessment, contingency plans, coordination, cooperation, and trust. The managers in a training group interact in their day-to-day operations. Sometimes, in a series of programs, teams are set up with overlapping members (i.e., the senior member of a lower-level team is the junior member of the next-higher-level team). Some programs are one-shot; some, continuing. Some involve a few sessions each year on a scheduled basis; some have planned agendas. Some focus on problems and issues presented by top management and participants; some are directed to massive change (e.g., the culture of the entire system and developing strategic plans); others focus on more immediate issues relating to a specific area, such as personnel. The participant is the system; development is the means for achieving system objectives.

Programs designed to change the behavior, relationships, and competencies of a natural family group are related to team training. A family group consists of managers who are employed in the same organization or managers in different organizations in the same discipline or providing the same service or product. In a family group, the managers face similar environments and issues. The actual degree of kinship can vary considerably. The programs tend to be a combination of passive and synthetic experiential learning in the unfreezing and change stages; in the refreezing stage they use natural experiential learning by application, observation, and feedback analysis. Some programs include organizational development (Verlander 1988). The LIFE program described in Chapter 11 was developed for a family group. Kurt Lewin's action research approach, the major theoretical process for many of these team approaches, includes a continuing sequence of data collection, feedback, team analysis, action planning, action, leading to a higher-level data collection, and so on. Where the participants are from the same system, major objectives are to reduce suboptimization, gain acceptance for the primacy of the system's objectives, and increase cooperation.

Contract learning is an approach focused on developing and strengthening independent learning. A program contract, defining both learning objectives and means for achieving them, is agreed upon by the participating manager and the trainer. Development and implementation of the contract and assessment of achievement are the natural experiential activities. Designing the program is a collaborative effort. Passive and experiential learning approaches are employed. Immediate application of learning, followed by participant's and role set's feedback and analysis of the feedback, are used to refreeze change and reinforce independent learning. The training staff provides support and consultation to reduce fears of change and risk taking. This is a very useful approach. However, the press of routine and the willingness of trainers to accept less than contract commitments tend to limit its effectiveness.

Management by objectives as a development technique is a contract learning approach. It has elements of work planning, supervision, and development. It is most useful if employed for development. When used for supervision, it tends to lose its effectiveness for development. It is the experiential approach most directly related to the real-life situation. It employs operational objectives, techniques, feedback, and criteria. The approach has four key elements: relatively short-term operational objectives; focus on organizational goals; agreement on the individual manager's role, objectives, plan, and criteria for acceptable performance; and joint assessment of performance by the manager and superior, leading to the next agreement. However, as noted, its use for control and supervision sharply reduces its value for development. Risk taking, unless it is part of the agreement, tends to be inhibited.

Organizational development has evolved into a discipline for development and change with its own theory and techniques. From the point of view of management development, it is a natural experiential approach that seeks to promote individual and systemic development by making changes in individual life-banks and interpersonal behavior. Its goals go beyond individual management development to improved systemic coordination and cooperation, and increased understanding among managers. Organizational development practitioners usually do not consider themselves to be engaged in management development. Most make little effort to integrate the two fields. A view advanced by some is that dealing with the problems and competencies of the individual, apart from the welfare of the organization as a whole, leads to harmful suboptimization in which the welfare of the manager and the manager's unit are put ahead of that of the organization. Organizational development's focus is the functioning of the organization. Competencies stressed are those required by the organization for coordinating and integrating operations (Hornstein and Mackenzie 1984).

There are attempts to integrate organizational development and individual development. One such effort is described by Frizell and Gellermann (1988). Organizational development efforts are focused on achieving long-range planned changes in the culture, relations, and processes that affect the system.

Since the mid-1970s, human resource specialists have assumed the responsibility for helping to bring about change in the culture of organizations. The discussion in Chapter 8 indicated the difficulty in obtaining such a change. Nevertheless, there are many programs designed to accomplish cultural changes. This is not a simple objective that management development can be expected to achieve on its own. Efforts to achieve this level of change must involve all human resource activities, including work assignment, recruitment, supervision, and incentives. For management development to be useful, extensive use must be made of natural experiential learning.

Dechant (1988) describes the management development role in a program to help the Equitable Company move into a new domain that required more competitive and more aggressive management. Roles for managers were redefined. Development prepared managers to communicate the new system objectives, processes, and stance to the people below them; train subordinates to carry out the new objectives; respond to the needs of subordinates as problems arose; and build a consensus for the new culture. The program included passive learning to provide information about the new philosophy and objectives, and the roles and tasks to achieve the objectives. There were case studies and synthetic experiential learning to provide analysis and develop skills in communicating and solving the types of problems that could be expected. This was followed by extensive natural experiential learning, including meetings to describe experience and analyze the feedback.

Organizational transformation is a natural approach that seeks to combine aspects of management development and organizational development. Its purported strength is helping organizations to make the transition to a new culture as the need is dictated by the enacted environment (Frame and Nielsen 1988). Elements of the approach include a modified standard management training program consisting of modules such as "the environment," "organizational structure," "a team-building organizational development intervention," and "manager as change agent." A specially designed assessment center is employed to select individuals whose skills and values are consistent with the new culture. Top management participates in the organizational interventions by providing long-range vision, the new mission, and a definition of the new values and norms to be expressed in the operating philosophy. These are discussed and "sold" to each successive level of management. Objectives are established for each unit and provision is made for continuous feedback to managers. Achievement and rewards are linked.

The Blake-Mouton "managerial grid" (1978) is one of the few attempts to move management development toward increasing operational effectiveness by integrating concern for expressive and instrumental managerial roles. Training and development activities would be strongly natural experiential learning.

The American Management Association's Competency Program (Daloisio and Firestone 1983) makes extensive use of Knowles's theory. Additional rules of adult learning that are postulated include the following:

- Adults prefer not to discuss general theories or be given an overview of the content.
- Learning must directly help participants solve current problems they face.

Generic management competencies were determined by a form of task analysis of the jobs of some 2,000 managers. Based on these data, the competencies of model managers were identified and a program to help participants learn the competencies was developed. Participants' competencies were assessed by a variety of tests. Managers were provided with feedback and motivated to attend didactic sessions to learn about the competencies. They met individually with advisers and engaged in group discussions to gain competencies and to form individual competency development plans. These were regarded as learning contracts. They then worked with an adviser on a one-to-one basis to carry out the plan. The primary objective was gaining management skills through experiential learning (i.e., application of learning on the job).

Competency development plans emphasize experiential learning for skill development. Participants work on implementing their plans for six months. During this time they communicate with an adviser at regular intervals to receive guidance and support. In a "feedback week," working in five-person study groups, they discuss their learning during the six-month period. At the workshop they receive feedback from group members and faculty to enhance readiness to learn in the next cycle.

In the study of managerial activities, eighteen competencies were identified and arranged in four clusters that form the basis for both analysis of participants' competencies to determine need and the content of the program. The clusters are "goal and action management," "directing subordinates," "human resource management," and "leadership."

The U.S. government's program for senior managers (Newell et al. 1988) is a yearlong activity that integrates training with on-the-job application of learned skills. The objective is to provide a more effective learning environment and immediate results to demonstrate the value of the training. The report on the program indicated that the gains hypothesized were achieved. However, there were some difficulties. Participants found it difficult to meet the time demands of their full-time jobs and those of the training program. Although there was direct, continuing communication with superiors to make them part of the support system, many superiors resented the time that participation required and either did not support the program or were "mildly hostile."

Revans, possibly the most outstanding European scholar and practitioner of management development, does not believe that management can be taught but must be learned by experience, performing and taking the responsibility as a manager. Competence as a manager is demonstrated by action, not talk. Revans's sophisticated natural experiential approach has several different forms. Four learning characteristics are identified and programs are tailored. These are derived from the values of two variables, tasks and venue. The basic program components are identifying a project that would be useful to a host organization (participants conduct projects in organizations other than their own), developing and learning the theory and techniques to carry out the project, planning to carry out the project, implementing the plan, and receiving feedback from managers in the host organization. Revans's students are placed into real situations to develop needed solutions to urgent problems (Revans 1974 and McNulty 1979).

Revans has used the approach both to train managers to deal with existing problems in their organizations and in the Inter-University Programme, an advanced development program for managers. In the latter program, participants with some managerial experience work with a tutor on an individual basis for six months before the formal start of the program to ensure that they have and will have the necessary academic backgrounds. The formal program includes a three-month diagnostic phase (for the project) and a four-month action phase. There is review and feedback on the work during and at the end of each phase. In a form of Revans's approach called action learning, some of the analysis of a participant's plan and work is by fellow participants.

Revans's assumptions (McNulty 1979), in addition to those noted, are the following:

- Managers learn more effectively by discussing real problems (that they and others face) with other managers.
- A manager's disclosure of anxieties, "if shared, will lead . . . to managerial understanding."
- "Managers are all different and each can act only within the limits of his or her character, ability and past experience."
- The advisers of the participants and the small sets of participants have to be carefully selected from experienced managers and trained in their new roles.
- "New knowledge is but the reorganization of what has already been written on the cortical slate. It is not fresh facts that we absorb but the ability to make better use of those we already know." (pp. 12–16)

Revans was one of the first academics to make a successful transfer to consultation that included management development using natural experiential learning. His design remains one of the most sophisticated. Although widely used in other countries, it is not used to any significant extent in the United States.

In the course of their analysis of the roles and competencies of managers in organizations open in different degrees to their environments,

Lawrence and Lorsch (1969) suggest that it may be more effective to select managers with the appropriate "emotional orientation" than to attempt to make and maintain any highly significant changes through development. Without agreeing with this view, it is obvious that the "emotional orientation" variable cannot be ignored. However, to the extent that development can help, natural experiential approaches which select participants (Settle 1988) and those which tailor content and/or learning approach to both the individual and the environment would seem to be more effective approaches (Frame and Nielsen 1988; Daloisio and Firestone 1983; Hoberman and Mailick 1988).

Evaluation of Natural Experiential Learning

Natural experiential approaches assume that there is a fairly stable, historical organizational culture and body of behaviors developed over time that people in an organization exhibit and expect. Since these serve as the basis for measuring performance, successful managers tend to have similar guiding principles of observation, attention, and inference. They tend more readily to see and accept certain things and relationships while opposing, concealing, or filtering out others (Dery 1986). It is these limitations that make reliance on on-the-job experience inadequate. For the introduction of new concepts and approaches, it is necessary for managers to add to their life-banks through learning outside of experiences in their own work venues.

Probably the most uncertain and difficult task in management development is for the trainer to take into account and adjust for the participants' life-banks and work venues, and the relationships between these and the trainer's own life-bank. A major advantage of natural experiential approaches is the ability to adjust the learning approach and specific content as more is learned about these factors and their interrelationships with each other and with program objectives. If internal and external environmental factors are constant and all relationships are known, on-the-job learning might be an effective approach. But our knowledge is always incomplete and becoming outdated. Further, learning is influenced by the relationship between the culture of the participants' focal systems and the culture of the change agent. Where a change agent is from a culture different from that of the individuals whose behavior is to be changed, serious miscalculations are almost inevitable.

Synthetic experiential learning has advantages that cannot be duplicated in natural experiential approaches. Two of these are

- the ability to focus concentration on a single learning objective
- the ability to compress time and adjust the space of the experience to the fit the learning venue's time and space resources.

In most organizations in the Western world there is a conflict between the policies for risk governing the behavior of top management (in government, elected and senior appointed officials) and people in the rest of the organization. The policy at the top tends to be "Maximize profits to the risk taker and the organization with acceptable risk to the organization." Below the top, it tends to be "Minimize risk for the risk taker, with some expectation of profits to the unit." Trainers usually do not know enough about participants and their work venues to advise them how to act in situations in which risky actions are irreversible. The best that trainers can do is to serve as consultants and counselors during such activities. This role is possible only in natural experiential approaches.

Despite the emphasis of New Age approaches on encouraging risk taking, participants can probably be conditioned more effectively by natural experiential learning approaches to accept the risk in transfer of learning to the work venue. These approaches involve members of the managers' role sets in the learning process and condition them to accept the changed behavior and the risk involved, and to provide useful feedback and reinforcement.

We believe that assumptions made by some natural experiential learning approaches may be open to question. Among these are the following:

1. Learning is more effective when participants face problems in an unfamiliar work venue, one to which they will not return after the training.
2. Discussions of general theory should be avoided, because adults want answers and direct application.
3. There is a single set of managerial competencies that all managers can use effectively in their work venues.

Even if the first assumption were the case, the problem of use on reentry is far greater than the questionable benefits of more readily unfreezing and changing in a strange organization. Further, effective managers must be able to place their organizations in a historical context, understand why the temporal sequence of events leading up to the present took place, and learn to identify and use these parameters. Without such knowledge and understanding, the manager is fixated in the present, unable to learn from experience and unable to influence the development of the system and its adaptation to change.

The second is a strange assumption, almost implying that every manager must reinvent management. One does not learn which management competencies are important and how to use these competencies without some understanding of and ability to use theory, whether developed by the manager or introduced by another. A most important element in management development is to learn to induce and adjust learning from specific experience to new situations by means of models. Lifelong learning requires the continuous adaptation of general means to specific ends.

As for the third assumption, natural experiential learning assumes a contingency model. It assumes that managers have in their life-banks not one set of known "perfect" managerial competencies but the knowledge and skills needed to develop and select from alternatives, employing concepts and estimates of probabilities and possibilities from their own venues. The necessary alternative life-bank elements can be acquired only by managers who can learn and generalize from their experiences, and apply their general concepts in specific situations. This is a circular or helical sequence of cause and effect. Natural experiential learning uses the contingency model to explain progressive learning. In a circular fashion, acquisition of life-bank elements that lead to the effective use of a contingency model is based on natural experiential learning. According to Dewey (1935), the essence of natural experiential learning would be making the connection between an action and its consequences. He calls this a backward-forward connection. We note the need for a base that may be changed with experience but is needed to guide and test the "backward-forward connection."

Some criticisms of synthetic experiential learning apply equally to some natural experiential learning approaches, such as project management and organizational development:

- They do not subject the learner to both stable, continuing expectations and relationships and the complex, ambiguous, unplanned situations that are faced in the actual job.
- They do not duplicate the pressure, risk, dynamics, and competition of actual continuing management.
- They do not require continuous sensitivity to potential problems, issues, and opportunities.

CONCLUSIONS

To recapitulate, arguments in favor of natural experiential learning include the following:

- Learning is directed toward satisfying identified individual and organizational needs.
- There are fewer assumptions about the variables in the participants' work venues.
- Reentry and use of learning are simplified and incremental.
- Learning is effectively incorporated into participants' life-banks, reinforced, and transferred to the work venue.

- Processes and habits for independent learning from experience are developed and reinforced.

Managing complex organizations calls for more than charisma and knowledge of organizational theory and practices, more than individual competence. It requires continuity of culture, objectives, and processes and relationships. Incremental change tends to be safer than sudden, great change. A necessary condition for effective functioning over an extended period is the presence of a community of people who know and trust each other, understand and accept their interdependencies and support the system's basic values. Members must have compatible beliefs, practices, and processes. At the same time, managers have to be sufficiently flexible and adaptable to meet changing and sometimes unexpected situations. Management development can help prepare managers, but it is not the total answer.

Natural experiential approaches that emphasize, but are not restricted to, a specific, limited objective can prepare managers to accept and deal with the stress, ambiguity, and risk which accompany unanticipated, major change. Programs that do not have strict time limits or many participants or other inhibiting factors can more readily adjust to individual participants' needs. Trainers (or coaches or mentors) need to have time and opportunities to adjust content and teaching styles to evolving situations and learning styles of participants.

In natural experiential learning, participants learn to identify and use opportunities that provide occasions for obtaining and testing new learning. This is the most difficult and most profitable element in this approach. It is the condition for incorporating competencies for lifelong learning into life-banks.

11

LEARNING INDUCTED FROM EXPERIENCE (LIFE)

INTRODUCTION

This chapter is devoted to a discussion of a natural experiential learning approach for management development, Learning Inducted from Experience (LIFE). This is an approach that we developed based on our experiences in a program for senior managers in the New York City civil service. It started using passive and synthetic experiential learning approaches. After a while we incorporated some natural experiential learning. Based on our experiences, LIFE was designed, using primarily natural experiential learning, for the New York University program in mental health policy and administration. It was later used as the primary management development approach in the Administrative Staff College of Israel.

The New York University program was a special degree program in the Graduate School of Public Administration. All participants were serving as managers at some level in a public mental health system and had at least a master's degree in a related field. Since they all took the same modules, participants remained together until the last few modules, which related to the research and writing of the doctoral dissertation. Superiors agreed that participants would be permitted to attend scheduled sessions and to introduce and use new learning in their jobs.

They also agreed to provide us with feedback from use of learning in the work venue.

Some of the issues that arose in our experiences in the design and conduct of management development programs and that LIFE was designed to address included the following:

- strengthening transfer of learning to the work venue
- dealing with different values of key parameters for different participants (e.g., work venue characteristics and learning styles)
- reducing counterproductive effects of fragmented, inactive, and inappropriate learning
- decreasing time away from the job
- maximizing the values of passive and synthetic experiential learning through coordination with natural experiential learning
- helping managers learn to cope better with risk and contingency
- learning about use of learning in the work venue to permit modifying content, design, and learning approaches as we went along.

We were neither the only nor the first to be concerned with the need for management development to deal with these issues. More management development programs are being designed to meet the individual organization's objectives and fit with its culture and environment as well as its work force (ASTD 1989). To the extent that the effectiveness of this training is assessed, it is on the transfer of learning to daily activities. Implementation is the most specific management function. It is the key managerial function in the entire input-throughput-output sequence. To perform this function, managers must know and be able to use models that will provide them with assumptions for cause/effect relationships in their work venues.

However, the job calls for more than understanding relationships, the meaning of managerial concepts, and how to analyze simulated managerial problems. Learning about the psychology of work may not lead to improved relationships between managers and their subordinates. Managers need more than theoretical knowledge of budgeting, planning, organizing, and other managerial functions. Management is action, hands-on competence to use the required knowledge, skills, and judgment.

In the absence of conscious theoretical underpinning, natural experiential approaches such as rotation and project assignments are less effective. Analysis of experience to identify what can be learned and to add to the active part of the manager's life-bank depends on having a theoretical frame of reference and a process that can be used to organize, simplify, and make available learning from disorganized, complex experience.

Management development cannot provide all the learning that managers need to grow on the job. Experience in managing is necessary but not sufficient for growth. LIFE assumes that two major development objectives are to help managers to generalize effectively from their experiences and to develop and maintain motivation for lifelong learning. LIFE uses the same approach for both objectives. It is directed to applying, testing, and gaining experience in specific theory and models on the job.

Some development approaches focus on "doing the right thing." In LIFE, participants study the literature and, with the guidance of preceptors, develop an arsenal of alternative approaches. They test and adapt these based on experience in use in the work venue. Continuous self-directed learning is necessary if there is no one best management style or model.

LIFE programs include the following:

- content modules, usually three months in duration, that concentrate (except for the first module, which is an overview of the entire program) on a single content area (e.g., leadership and strategic management)
- biweekly preceptorial sessions in which two to four participants meet with a preceptor to discuss, assess, reinforce, and plan to use new learning; assess impact of use; and develop new learning
- one-to-three-day plenary meetings at the beginning and end of each module, in which half of the time is used to introduce and integrate new content and half to reinforce learning from the module being completed.

LIFE continues after the plenary session to focus on learning in the work venue. Like Organizational Development, its objective is to help participants gain the competencies to make the desired changes in the work venue. Organizational Development frequently focuses on change of organizational characteristics without helping managers gain the competencies needed to function effectively in the changed organization.

There are many good experiential learning approaches in addition to LIFE. Some are described in Chapter 10.

THE THEORETICAL BASE FOR LIFE

Much of the theory discussed in this chapter was not identified in advance and used consciously to develop the LIFE model. Theory was added, modified, and discarded as we gained experience. One example, the concept of the "life-bank," followed design and implementation of LIFE as an operational program rather than preceding it. We now start with the integrating concept of the life-bank as basic for both learning and use. We feel that this concept is implicit in the work of the educational theorists on which we based our first designs.

Development is seen as adaptive, evolutionary, and complex. It is a pragmatic, heuristic process in which learning can lead to unfreezing, change, and refreezing by adding to, subtracting from, reorganizing, and reinforcing the contents of the individual's life-bank. LIFE does not assume that there is a single management development package with a rational, comprehensive model for appropriate managerial behavior that is best for every manager.

LIFE is based on assumptions in four areas: the learning venue, processes, and styles; the life-bank; objectives of management development; and LIFE in relation to other experiential learning approaches. We will discuss each of these.

Learning Venue, Processes, and Styles

One does not use theory that is an inactive life-bank element (i.e., without a base in experience) or learn from experience without an organizing principle (i.e., guidance from theory). Learning is added to the life-bank as an active element by a dialectical interaction between theory and experience. Theory helps the manager learn what can be generalized from one unique experience and applied in another unique situation. Theory provides the categorizations for storing learning in the life-bank. Defined categories permit competent, goal-directed managers to select and adapt from past learning to meet current needs and conditions. Categorization not only eases recall and adaptation of past learning, it tends to keep learning active and not, to use Dewey's term "inert."

Using a different categorization, we assume that there are two categories of elements in the life-bank useful for management. The first is a not very well organized, untidy bank of logical and managerial models and individual experiential, empirical conclusions and assumptions. The second includes all the metaelements (e.g., the processes for learning and adding to the life-bank that are used to evaluate and select the appropriate sets of elements from the bank and to organize them for use in particular situations).

The learning assumption (similar to an assumption by Piaget) is that learning takes place in the interplay between these two sets, in the cycle of testing models by experience and using feedback from experience to adapt and develop generalized models whose usefulness is again tested by experience. The LIFE approach seeks to convert the learning cycle into a learning helix directed toward incorporating skills that facilitate the transfer of learning as an active metaelement in the manager's life-bank by using feedback from experience not only as reinforcement of transfer skills but also as input to the next learning ascent.

The physical and psychological characteristics of the educational venue in which learning takes place, including the characteristics of faculty and other participants, have significant impact on the manner in which learning is integrated and potentially activated in the life-bank.

If learning is inducted from and tested against experience, there is less chance of misguided application of new learning. A danger in learning general models and new practices by either passive or synthetic experiential education is that the more convincing the model or the new practice is, and the better it is learned, the greater the possibility of the learning's becoming an isolated element in the participant's life-bank. This is almost certain if participants do not gain the competence to modify and adapt the models to local circumstances. Upon reentry the attempt to apply the learning tends to emphasize the process and to downplay the real objectives.

Whether managers are helped to unfreeze and become prepared for change through external incentives or new learning is irrelevant. Both forces are operative. Learning for use occurs in the conflict among managers' needs for achievement, affiliation, and power (Campbell 1957) and their expectations of a reward for success and fear of the consequences for failure. This conflict, as a force for management learning, cannot be experienced in any venue but the work venue.

While application is holistic, acquiring knowledge and more difficult technical skills is easier and more effective when focused on a specific management area (i.e., use of a modular structure). The modular structure, modified to focus on use of a set of related competencies, is also frequently more effective in experiential learning. Use of holistic structure in passive and synthetic experiential learning tends to limit the level of content of knowledge and skills and, to a lesser degree, the other competencies. Modules can be as advanced as the life-banks of the participants will allow.

"Learning time" is an important variable. Time is required to change and refreeze, to coordinate and integrate learning through use of theory and reinforcement through feedback. The less time there is between learning and use of learning, the greater the motivation to learn and use, and the greater the chance that there will be continued use.

Lifelong learning must be self-directed. This is accomplished most effectively by strengthening life-bank metaelements relating to processes for determining learning needs and strategies to meet these needs, and assessing, adapting, integrating, and retaining useful new learning. These processes can be made automatic by repeated application in the ultimate use venue. Learning should be planned to reduce participants' dependency on faculty and to increase independent learning capabilities.

One might ask, "Why spend time on models when we advocate using the actual job for development?" Experience comes to us in a kaleidoscopic flux of impressions and discrete patterns and relationships. These are not completely random but are organized in categories and typologies dictated by the metaelements in our life-banks. The metaelements themselves are functions of our language, unexpressed theoretical concepts, assumed cause/effect relationships, and deep behavioral and cognitive habits. We can do little to change some of these. We cannot change the structure of English to make it more like Japanese. We do have the ability to consider new issues, new ways to act, new models and concepts and, to a limited degree, to categorize and reorganize knowledge and experiences in new ways.

The Life-Bank

Adults have complex, rich life-banks. These include simple elements like those which relate to knowledge and skill competencies; more complex elements such as behavioral abilities; and complex process metaelements of categories like decision making and learning. Much of the contents of adult life-banks has been reinforced to an extent that makes them very resistant to change. Simple elements such as knowledge and skills are the least difficult to change. Complex metaelements such as those which relate to values and judgment are the most difficult.

Only some life-bank elements seem to be applied in every venue. There are many elements that are venue-specific (i.e., values and competencies that are not transferable between venues).

Where all persons involved in a program have equally rich life-banks, although not necessarily in the same categories, effective learning situations have to be open and symmetrical with respect to participation. Both learners and faculty have to be equally able to initiate discussion, provide analysis, and question assertions, approaches, and interpretations. Participants must be able to criticize themselves, and others, without opening themselves to adverse actions.

Discussion with peers of plans and feedback from implementation are important for learning content. There is a very strong tendency to make sense of what we experience, observe, or read in terms of our own beliefs, language, interests, and experiences (our life-banks). Without outside challenges, there is a tendency to reinforce the point of view or conclusions with which we are comfortable. Discussions with others tend to bring into play other positions and conclusions. This also provides experience for open discussions with peers in the work venue. Acquiring this competency is an important objective for lifelong learning.

Different sets of elements in the life-bank are activated by different venues and patterns of stimuli. The venue in which the learning takes place tends to define the venue in which the learning is useful. It takes extraordinary motivational and adaptability metaelements in a person's life-bank to be able to transfer competencies easily from the playing field to the work venue or everyday life.

The life-bank metaelement "learning style" affects both learning and transfer of learning to the work venue. Consideration must be given to differences in participants' life-banks and learning styles. Obviously learning styles are functions of life-banks. However, there is little research on this relationship. The relationship between learning style and life-bank should affect the learning approaches used. As noted, Kolb (1984) presents evidence that persons from different technical disciplines are more comfortable with different learning styles. Even though all of the participants are managers, they may have specialized in different disciplines. Significant differences in participants' work venues may necessitate employing a variety of learning approaches. For example, the degree to which a system must be open to its environment to prosper may determine the values and competencies that its managers must have and how they will approach learning (Lawrence and Lorsch 1969).

Learning, introduction of new elements into a person's life-bank, does not necessarily come from planned experiences. One of the strong points of natural experiential learning is that it is open to learning from chance occurrences. Repetition of the known and expected reinforces existing competencies, it does not lead to new knowledge or competence. It is the new problem, the new relationship, the chance occurrence, the novel and unexpected in experiential learning that force new life-bank combinations that result in new learning. Experience by itself is rarely sufficient; the learning from a chance occurrence does not come to the unprepared mind.

The definitions and constructs of reality in participants' life-banks limit their imagination (the play of elements in their life-bank) and, consequently, determine the nature of the solutions that they tend to develop. The role of the preceptor includes inducing participants to construct new definitions and constructs of their experience and using the models and theory being studied to lead to alternative solutions.

Management Learning Objectives

The primary objective of LIFE is to motivate and help managers to engage in lifelong learning and to learn how to learn from their work experience. Improving current performance and potential for advancement are important for participants and sponsors. In LIFE, these are also seen as means for motivating learning to learn.

Management development must focus on the work venue. Development, which stops at decision making in the educational venue, is of little consequence if there is no transfer of learning. The work venue, in LIFE, is both the key action venue and the learning venue. A managerial decision is meaningful only if it is followed by action. Managerial action takes place in the work venue through delegated and decentralized activities performed by a chain of subordinates who may or may not know, care or not care, be able or unable to carry out the decision in the manner intended by the manager. Decisions are frequently subject to the approval of superiors who may or may not have the same objectives. Development, to be effective, must carry the manager through taking and reporting on the action to achieving the desired objectives.

Management theory and management practice are not necessarily consecutive. It is not a matter of which is in advance of the other, whatever "advance" means. It is that they are different although overlapping fields. The meaning of the same terms can be quite different in the two fields. There are no universally applicable theories or models for managerial behavior in all situations. Managers need competencies to use different models for management activities, to play different roles, and to determine the appropriate role and model for each situation. Management theories and models tend to be extremely reductionist simplifications that are stated in terms of loosely defined variables. Interpretation of their meaning depends to a great extent on the conditions under which they are applied. These conditions not only can change from system to system and from manager to manager but also can change significantly for the same manager, in the same system, over time. Different theories and models are more effective for different managers. Managers must have at their command an arsenal of models. They need to acquire an active arsenal in their life-banks and sensitivity to changing conditions in their work venues to be able to change and adapt models and modes as dictated by circumstances. One precaution: management theories are at best useful paths for understanding. It is disastrous when, through emphasis in management development, they become rutted roads.

Managers add to their life-banks and integrate and organize new learning for application in different ways, depending on the characteristics of their life-banks and those of their work venues. To learn to induce from experience, managers must have opportunities to use models as frames of reference for planning and analyzing experience.

Learning from experience and feedback are maximized when these are freely discussed with competent, nonthreatening colleagues. This is particularly the case for learning to live with ambiguity and to take and control risk. Managers can learn these only in the work venue.

The anticipated reaction of managers' role sets strongly influences the nature of change to which managers are open. The role set's actual reaction strongly influences transfer and refreezing. Managers are more likely to try to change behaviors incrementally, in order to minimize adverse reactions from their role sets, than to take actions certain to be opposed by the members of their role sets.

A manager's prolonged absence from the work venue makes application for which the manager's role set is not prepared more difficult. Except for a small population of strong-willed, convinced individuals, changes in behavior resulting from management development will not persist in the face of continued resistance on the part of the manager's role set.

While higher management may play the dominant role in determining the objectives and content, the participants are the major players in determining the most appropriate learning styles.

LIFE and Other Experiential Approaches

Experiential approaches emphasize the importance of realism (relationship to the work venue), challenge, risk, feedback, and historical and future relationships.

A basic LIFE assumption is that both learning and organization of life-bank elements for use are strongly situational. A major difference between synthetic and natural experiential learning approaches is that the former assume the differences between the learning venue and the use venue do not significantly affect transfer of learning adversely. The latter do not make this assumption. LIFE and other experiential learning approaches differ from "learning from experience" and "application of common sense" in two crucial factors. Most experiential approaches provide theory and operational models to use as frames of reference for learning and cause/effect rationales for action. These link experience and learning. LIFE goes one step farther. It introduces learning for developing models and theory from experience. Experiential learning structures experience to add efficiently to participants' life-banks an arsenal of techniques and competencies for future analysis and action. We are forced to rely on our subjective experience. But if learning is to take place, it is essential that it be tempered by objective analysis.

The work venue is the most effective learning venue in which to strengthen the will and competence for lifelong learning of managerial competencies. LIFE provides theory, models, and illustrations from current practice in group workshops using the full range of passive and synthetic experiential learning approaches. Participants develop occasions for utilizing the learning in their current job assignments. Preceptorial activities before and after use in the work venue are directed toward increasing model-building and utilization skills and motivating continuing learning.

The number and complexity of the relationships among variables that determine the effect of managers' changed behavior make attempts to develop simple predictive models foolhardy. Among the variables involved are the following:

- the degree of the change
- the managers' competency and will to change
- the managers' status and the respect accorded the individual manager
- expectations of the consequences of change or failure to change
- the relationships among managers and between them and top management
- managers', organizations', and role sets' flexibility, adaptability and openness to change, and ability to cope with ambiguity
- the state of the environment
- the cost of unfreezing, changing, and refreezing, and the risks for both the managers and their role sets
- the reliability and validity of the change model
- the learning styles of individual managers.

LIFE tends to decrease problems stemming from lack of knowledge about the work venue and unpredictable developments unrelated to management development. During the program, it has the capacity to change content, learning approaches, and application in the work venue. Content of modules can be changed to mesh with opportunities for use in the work venue. It has been possible in a number of cases to develop opportunities to use learning in the work venue.

Integrating each module into a holistic frame of reference and extending learning over a long period of time have increased the flexibility of the approach.

LIFE IN PRACTICE

Group programs are concerned with two different sets of objectives. One is the objectives for the program as a whole (i.e., for all participants and their organizations). The second is achieving each individual's learning and use objectives. Integrating work and learning venues in LIFE tends to merge these two objectives.

The LIFE process includes program planning to determine objectives and content, and activities to achieve these; formal plenary meetings to introduce content and synthetic experiential exercises to unfreeze and initiate the change stage; independent learning from the literature and related assignments; work venue activities to test, practice, and reinforce learning; and preceptorial meetings to join passive and synthetic experiential and natural experiential learning, and to strengthen motivation and competence for independent learning. Feedback from participants and preceptors is analyzed for planning future modules.

The ideal LIFE preparation would include the following:

- a needs analysis, including the current and expected states of the system, its environment, and the participants
- a statement of objectives agreed to by the participants, senior management, and the trainer
- agreement by senior management that participants will be encouraged to utilize learning in the work venue
- identification of the current and anticipated jobs and competencies of the participants, defined in terms of objectives and tasks
- agreement by participants, senior management, and faculty to objectives and design, including resources, activities, responsibilities, and standards. (Development and program objectives may not be identical.)

We have never been able to accomplish this ideal. However, the way the program is designed makes it unnecessary to design the ideal to have a successful program. Changes and adjustments are possible during implementation.

In the initial planning session, the information and findings are discussed with potential participants and their superiors to get agreement and commitment by both participants and senior management with respect to goals, training time, learning venues, resources, content, process, and other program elements. These are not absolutes; trade-offs are possible. Participants and sponsors understand that the program may change as more information becomes available during implementation.

In the second planning session, the proposed design is presented. Agreement is reached on the responsibilities and commitment of each party.

The customized assignments, individual implementation, and preceptorial sessions make it possible to adjust design during implementation for such variables as level of competence and learning styles of the participants. During implementation, preceptors and participants provide feedback on program design, implementation, and learning and use in the work venue. The feedback is analyzed to determine what changes are desirable. The feedback, analysis, and conclusions are discussed with participants individually and in the plenary session. Agreed-upon changes are made.

If the work venue is to be the primary learning venue for LIFE, participants must be both faculty and learners. Not only must the managers be ready to play both roles, but the managers' role sets must be prepared to accept the managers' playing the two roles. Playing these two roles is an important component of learning to learn. Senior management has to be prepared not only to accept the managers' new roles but also to provide constructive feedback both to the manager and to the training staff. Getting top management to carry out this role is difficult. This may be the weakest element in the LIFE process. Many senior managers lose interest once a program is under way. Indifference on the part of senior managers may make it virtually impossible for participants to transfer learning to the work venue in the course of regular managerial activities. This can induce conflict between the preceptor and the senior manager, invalidate feedback from the senior manager, affect motivation, weaken the trust relationship between participant and preceptor, and seriously compromise the program.

Only the content of the first module is completely determined in advance. During this module the program design, contents of future modules, openness to change, and related matters are described and discussed.

At the plenary sessions, which are usually held every three months, a training team and the participants engage in an interactive program. Both passive and synthetic experiential approaches are employed. These include case study analysis and discussions, short lectures, discussion, small team exercises, management games, and descriptions of participants' use of learning. In a one-day plenary session, half of the day is devoted to the module being completed, to review, clarify, and reinforce the learning; to integrate the learning into learning from earlier modules; and to prepare to integrate the learning into future learning. The other half of the day is spent introducing the content of the next module. The use of the content in management is discussed. The content is linked to past and future modules and to the jobs of the participants. The objectives of the preceptorial sessions and reading lists are discussed.

During both plenary and preceptorial sessions, participants and faculty are expected to observe and analyze the impact of their own behavior and that of others. This is a continuing exercise to increase participants' powers of observation, their sensitivity, and their ability to report on behaviors and interpersonal interactions. Learning to increase knowledge and skills to grasp and use abstract concepts, theory, and models is provided by passive learning such as assigned reading, short lectures, and discussions in which participants demonstrate their learning and the relationship of the learning to their work assignments. Actual work activities in which participants are engaged are used as case studies and exercises. Participants are required to suggest how the learning can be used in various work venues, including their own.

Organizing the content into modules has both advantages and disadvantages. Among the advantages are the following:

- The content can be more readily adjusted to meet needs in the work venue.
- The content of a module is clearly defined, and passive approaches are more effective.
- The effectiveness of use of learning is more readily recognized; it is not buried in the effects of numerous other management activities.
- It is simpler to relate all competencies to performance of specific tasks.
- Participants are better motivated to change if they can relate the new learning to improved performance.
- Spending three months on one aspect of management provides time to identify opportunities for practice, application, and refreezing of specialized learning.

The disadvantages are fewer:

- It is rarely possible to use the learning from any one module relating to expressive tasks without involving learning from other modules.
- Modular learning tends to become inactive learning.
- There is a tendency to focus on instrumental roles.
- Techniques rather than general skills are emphasized.
- Natural experiential learning may not be possible.

Three techniques are used to increase the effectiveness of the modular approach. Overall they seek to integrate the learning into the entire corpus of management theory and practice. The first is to provide, in the first module, an overview of the entire program and how it relates to the needs analysis and management. The second is, in plenary and preceptorial sessions, to integrate each module into both earlier and later modules. Third, and most important, is the emphasis on use in the work venue. This, by its nature, involves integrating the new learning into the entire management activity. The continuing integrating activities clarify the supporting role of the content of each module, make relationships between tasks and competencies clearer, and weld them into a stronger, more flexible vehicle for management.

The number, content, and sequencing of modules are determined by the objectives and resources set for the program in the design agreement. The modules are both instrumental (i.e., directed to increasing a specific skill, such as financial management or strategic planning) and expressive (i.e., directed to improving a specific ability such as oral communication). Competencies and techniques in such areas as problem solving tend to be treated in every module in dealing with issues and problems as they arise.

Content modules in a program for the Israel Administrative Staff College included managerial behavior, management practice, decision making and management science, change in complex organizations, the environment, and policy analysis. The program included training in the role of the preceptor. There was also a module on the history, rules, practices, and style of Israel's public service and the structure of the government.

Preceptorial Sessions

The preceptorial sessions are crucial. In these sessions, participants are motivated and helped to learn from their experiences, to induce and generalize learning from experience, to link group and their own learning experiences, to integrate cognitive and experiential learning, to deduce specific applications of models, and to integrate the contents of the different modules. In these sessions, participants learn to receive and provide consultation effectively. The success of the preceptorial sessions depends on participants and preceptors fulfilling an implicit contract on objectives and responsibilities to achieve them.

Preceptorial sessions provide a learning venue for improving learning metaelements. Discussions of plans to implement learning in the work venue with the preceptor and peers are designed to provide positive reinforcement and to introduce new learning approaches. Analysis of implementation gives participants experience in generalizing from specific experience (learning induced from experience). This process puts into motion helical learning. The discussions before action increase the learning potential in implementation as well as expectations and chances of success. The discussions after implementation focus on learning and the learning process. They also increase the chances for success in the next planning-implementation cycle.

At a secondary level the increased success in implementation tends to encourage greater investment in participating and learning during preceptorial sessions. However, probably the most important learning gain is the encouragement of lifelong learning by the demonstration of the value of the time invested in reading, analysis, and testing of new models.

Preceptorial meetings use feedback from participants' experiences, analysis of reading, and other learning activities as the subjects of discussion to stimulate reflection on experience as the raw material for both learning and use of learning. The group analysis is directed toward inducing change by generalizing learning from experience and developing plans for future application of learning.

The concepts that there is no one best way to manage, and that behavior (e.g., leadership style) should change as circumstances change, are disturbing to many managers. The need to identify the operational variables in a specific situation and determine the appropriate model and theory and managerial role and behavior can make some managers feel like jugglers working in a strobe light show, confused by the ambiguity and complexity of the moving objects and the changing colors. Participants are prodded and assisted by both questions and suggestions from the other participants and the preceptor to analyze the situation, identify possible models to explain what could take place or is taking place, and identify and evaluate possible alternative actions. A major purpose of the consulting process is to help reduce anxiety and to encourage acceptance of reasonable risk in action. Reinforcement is used to encourage refreezing. Discussion is directed to increasing skill in identifying learning opportunities in advance of action. This is a skill needed for lifelong learning.

To a far greater extent than the plenary sessions, the preceptorial meetings foster reciprocal relationships among the participants. The participants help, criticize, and teach each other. They gain experience in receiving and giving advice, in explaining their own analyses, and in analyzing and discussing those of others. Where in passive and synthetic experiential learning the level of content tends to be at the competence level of the lowest one-third, in preceptorial sessions the tendency is to challenge each participant to come to the highest level. Critical analysis of planned implementation is a better learning experience when it is done with the assistance of two or three friendly peers in the nonthreatening venue of the preceptorial session.

Plans for application include activities to obtain support and feedback from members of participants' role sets. This tends to make members of the role sets participants in the learning experience. The role set, as well as the manager, is engaged in testing and evaluating models. Participants become faculty members for this crucial aspect of their own development. A major effort in preceptorial sessions is directed to preparing them to carry out this role.

During the preceptorial sessions, managers practice distancing themselves from their performance on the job so that they objectively observe, record, and report on their own behavior and the results of their actions. The objective is to help them become motivated and able to criticize their own performances without responding defensively to questions and criticism. They become their own mentors.

The preceptor facilitates, confronts, and challenges the participants to be sensitive to the force field in which they function. Participants become sensitized to intersystem relationships, and conflicting and overlapping interests and points of view, and become more attuned to others and more understanding of, without necessarily accepting, other viewpoints.

If participants have different learning styles, the preceptorial sessions can provide a good learning venue for adjusting teaching styles. Preceptors are able to change assignments for the members of a preceptorial group. The only restriction is that it must be possible to design the plenary sessions so that all participants are on an even footing. Some groups may want to review earlier material, some may want more advanced material, and some may want to spend some time on integrating materials from different modules. Sometimes, when a need is identified, a preceptorial session will be spent on a general technique such as problem solving.

An interesting concept discussed by Kolb (1984) and attributed to L. S. Vygotsky is the "zone of proximal development" as the zone in which learning takes place. The zone is defined as "the distance between the actual developmental level as determined by independent problem solving and the level of potential development as determined through problem solving under adult guidance or in collaboration with more capable peers" (Kolb, 1984, p. 133). In terms of the LIFE process, the zone is the difference between the solutions and learning from feedback that the participants develop independently and with peers in preceptorial sessions. In LIFE most learning, both for direct program content and for lifelong learning habits is focused in this zone. The learning gained from peer analysis and discussion is related to Vygotsky's concept.

Faculty

The key faculty member is the preceptor. The role of preceptors is both complex and difficult. Their major objectives are to help participants learn how to learn (i.e., prepare for lifelong learning) and integrate new learning as active life-bank elements (i.e., refreeze new learning). To achieve these objectives, preceptors have to be effective catalytic agents, sounding boards, mentors, coaches, resource consultants, gadflies, personal counselors, and management consultants. They have to have the competence to help participants learn from experience, independent reading, and analysis of both to increase their competence for lifelong learning.

Faculty members serving as preceptors assume a role radically different from those of the teacher in the classroom and the facilitator in most experiential learning. The participants' statements of their work venues and their situations, and the degree to which a specific set of theories or models is relevant, are authoritative. While these and the accuracy and interpretation of feedback may be open to question, they are not changeable on the basis of the preceptor's dictum.

Preceptors have the responsibility to help participants prepare and implement their individual learning plans (self-enforcing contracts). Their roles go beyond helping participants. While preceptors are not usually involved in the needs analysis and the original planning of a LIFE program, they are key actors in revising and determining the nature of the continuing program. They are expected to assess and report on the program design; the appropriateness of content; the degree to which participants unfreeze and learn new approaches, techniques, and behaviors; and the use that they make of their learning. They participate in program design and recommend how to strengthen the program to increase its value to participants. They make suggestions for reading, assignments, the content and learning approaches to be used in the plenary sessions, the content of future modules, and linking modules to provide an integrated, comprehensive learning experience.

Preceptors and other staff members at the plenary sessions work as a team, not as specialists who lecture, discuss, or involve participants in an exercise for one or two hours and then leave. All activities and approaches are integrated and coordinated. Faculty members who are content specialists integrate their specialties into the role of the manager. They are role models, facilitators to involve participants, discussion leaders, discussants, critics, and observers. They assess learning and give feedback to program planners. Since preceptors come from the ranks of academics and practicing managers, their past experience tends to make them intervenors, doers or talkers—not passive listeners. Helping preceptors acquire listening skills is part of preceptorial training. The preceptors need not be training professionals. The most successful have been practicing managers who became academics and experienced managers who practiced independent learning and consequently have good knowledge of current theory and practice.

As in the Israel program, it is desirable to orient and provide guidance for preceptors to play their roles. It may be necessary to conduct an orientation program for other faculty as well. Few academics or practicing managers have served as members of a learning team or have the background needed to integrate and coordinate the content from all the modules. Few have had any previous experience with the combination of learning approaches used in LIFE.

The orientation has had to be kept short for practical reasons. It has included aspects of the following:

- LIFE theory and practice
- objectives and content for both the entire program and the specific modules
- information about the characteristics of participants, their work venues, and the needs assessment.

Participants

Participants play several overlapping roles. Among these are learner, manager, discussant, planner, reporter, assessor, resource, and consultant. It is desirable that participants have some commonalities in addition to being managers, so that they can play these many roles effectively. In the New York University program all participants were managers in mental health systems. In the earlier classes all came from a New York State system. In later classes participants came from different states and from local as well as state systems. In the various Israel programs participants came from three distinct populations: central government officials, elected representatives in the Knesset, and mayors of cities. Sometimes there was an entire class from one of these groups.

As distinct from many other programs, particularly most university programs, LIFE requires that participants be managers. This is obviously necessary if participants are to apply the managerial content in their work venues. We do not assume that persons who have never managed can learn to become effective managers in a passive or synthetic experiential training program.

When participants come from the same organization or the same type of organization or perform related work, work venue commonalities make it possible to design programs with more specific content and application. If participants come from different work venues with different disciplines, passive and synthetic experiential learning have to be varied to facilitate incorporation into participants' life-banks and maximize transfer of learning. This may make it necessary to increase the generality of content in the plenary meetings. Adjusting for individual learning styles in the plenary sessions is difficult, but it is possible in the preceptorial sessions. Adjusting may be made easier by assigning participants with common characteristics to the same preceptorial group.

If participants in a preceptorial group are from significantly different work venues, it may be necessary to structure assignments and analyses of work experience differently than if all come from similar work venues. In the latter case, learning can be in terms of directly applicable content. In the former, a variety of synthetic experiences can help learning to make valid deductions and generalizations.

Some researchers of learning style believe that teachers should adjust their teaching styles to participants' learning styles. Others advocate that participants should be challenged to adjust. Still others come down in between. Some favor sometimes adjusting teaching styles to meet individual learners' needs and sometimes consciously ignoring individual learning styles to force learners to accommodate varied teaching styles (Guild and Garger 1985). Whichever assumption one makes, all agree that there are different learning styles. Trainers should be aware of these and take them into account in training activities. As indicated earlier, we not only accept the concept of learning styles, we extend it to transfer to the work venue. LIFE assigns the preceptors the task of helping to adjust learning approaches to patterns required by participants' learning styles.

Lifelong Learning

Only strong, formal mentoring programs focus as directly as LIFE on individualized learning in the work venue. LIFE goes further to focus on lifelong learning. This is the most difficult objective of LIFE—to increase the will and competence of participants for independent, lifelong learning. LIFE plans activities to strengthen metaelements in participants' life-banks for lifelong learning.

The structure of preceptorial sessions is a primary means. Three principal means are employed to build and maintain the structure. The first is by equalizing the status of participants and faculty, particularly in the reciprocal relationships in preceptorial sessions. The second is by the continuous questioning in preceptorial sessions focused on learning and strengthening the "learning" metaelement. Participants are asked: "How did you use learning?" "Why?" "What did you learn from use?" "How did you learn?" "How can you use this learning?" "How could more have been learned from the experience?" "What could others learn from your experience [i.e., how should the content learning you started with be modified]?" The third, and most important, is by making the individual manager responsible for his or her learning.

Other planned activities to achieve lifelong learning objectives are discussion and use of learning techniques to integrate specific learning into a broader frame of reference, experience in group analysis and planning, individual reading, feedback and analysis of experience, and continuing effort to reduce the dependence on the preceptor during the course of the program.

Other techniques and activities used to increase lifelong learning skills include the following:

- inculcating participants with the will and competence to learn from reading, not only "how to" and "they did it, you can" popularizations but also professional texts and periodicals. (This is crucial, since reading is the one way managers can, independently and for a lifetime, draw on the thinking and experiences of others to enrich their life-banks.)
- developing the habit of moving from passive learning to self-directed natural experiential learning by seeking and implementing ways to utilize and test the value of the passive book learning
- requiring participants to identify and define specific management problems and opportunities, and to use learning to develop and implement plans to take action
- providing opportunities for participants to practice critical analysis in preceptorial sessions of the literature, individual plans for application, and feedback from implementation
- gaining competence in developing rational arguments in defense of their po-

sitions in preceptorial sessions without being defensive and, where the evidence indicates, learning from the arguments of others and changing their positions
- serving as consultants to other participants.

ASSESSMENT AND COMPARISON WITH OTHER APPROACHES

Most traditional management development presents information about the expressive role and some exercises relating to instrumental management tasks. The theory tends to be based on a single human model (e.g., "economic man") and simple, general psychological rules. These are easy to comprehend. But people do not normally react on the basis of a rational calculation of the return to them from their actions. Further, their reactions to the same stimulus can be quite different in different circumstances. LIFE does not assume that the behaviors which are taught and reinforced outside of the work venue are easily transferred to the work venue or that competencies, values, or points of view from one venue transfer automatically to another. LIFE focuses on change and refreezing in the specific work venue and provides training in transfer. Although useful, passive and synthetic experiential learning do not provide significant opportunities to change, test, and refreeze changes in emotional relationships and responses such as friendship, anger, fear, dependence, and moral outrage, which develop over time in the work venue. LIFE takes these as givens and builds on existing emotions and relationships. Learning is tested in the crucible of real life in the work venue.

LIFE incorporates as integral to the learning process creative thinking techniques for both individuals and groups to introduce new ideas and concepts not learned from experience or the literature. Creative outputs may stem from a combination of directed, focused search and the happenstance of life-bank elements joining together (Hadamard 1954).

Nevertheless, while using these approaches the assumption is not made that a single insight or "shock treatment," which may produce a seemingly significant change in the short term, is effective for any sustained productive and significant change in managerial behavior.

There is not a one-to-one relationship between intervention in a development activity and a lasting change in behavior. There are many unknown external intervenors and other variables mediated through integration in the life-bank. The inability to control or even to know these intervening variables drastically limits the design of management development. LIFE can respond as more is learned.

In full-time programs away from the work venue, application is not attempted until the participants have completed the program. This, in theory, ensures that the participants return to their jobs fully prepared to use their new learning and makes them responsible for this. It ignores the fact that the most difficult stage of management development is use of learning upon reentry. In LIFE there is no "reentry problem"; learning and its use in the work venue are integrated.

The time allocation for LIFE, the plenary session and the two-hour preceptorial sessions, is unique. LIFE reduces the problems for executives who "can't spare the time away from the job" for themselves or their subordinates. In one eighteen-month program, participants were away from their jobs seven days, no more than one day in any three-month period. They met in preceptorial sessions biweekly for two hours in a location convenient to their workplaces.

LIFE is different from other natural experiential approaches, such as rotation, that do not introduce significant new concepts, models, and techniques. The introduction of these is necessary for new learning. In denying that new learning can be derived solely from experience, we are asserting, in a metaphoric sense, the Second Law of Thermodynamics for management development (i.e., that managerial entropy in an isolated system must increase).

The content of LIFE is based on the concept of contingency management. The role of chance in determining the state of the focal system and the consequent changes in the demands on management is recognized. The contingency management content seeks to give managers the tools and technologies to cope with significant chance occurrences.

Sometimes senior management's objective is to change the culture of the organization. Participants are expected to learn and accept new organizational values, goals, and approaches. Managers are expected to accept significant systemic change and to serve as change agents for their subordinates and peers. LIFE is an effective development program for achieving this objective. The cultural objectives of the program can serve as the subject of the holistic initial module. Changing behavior of others becomes the matrix in which technical skills and behavioral abilities are embedded in later modules.

We have discussed the problems of reliability and validity in assessing management development activities. The relative lack of success in assessing management development has been documented. These findings apply, of course, to demonstrating the value of LIFE. However, many of the research shortcomings identified (Campbell et al. 1970; Baldwin and Ford 1988) are less relevant for LIFE. This is a consequence of the design. Feedback from independent learning and individualized learning, and the use of learning in the work venue, provide the basis for assessment and the need for change in design and implementation.

Reinforcement for refreezing is provided in the preceptorial sessions by the preceptor and other participants. Among issues that are less relevant for LIFE than for other approaches are the following:

- differences between the training and work venues
- identification of training cues that transfer to the work venue
- integrating new learning into participants' life-banks
- using learned behaviors upon reentry
- learning to generalize from specific experiences
- learning to apply general models to specific circumstances
- making a fit between teaching and individual learning styles.

We can report two studies of the impact of LIFE. These use, for the most part, subjective reports from participants and preceptors. The latter reports not only give information on the learning and use of learning by participants, they also provide information on the development of the preceptors.

An assessment of the program for the Israel Staff College (Tapuach 1980) reported the following, on the basis of interviews, questionnaire responses, and anecdotal feedback from participants:

- behavior changes in decision making and participation as team members and leaders in the work venue
- increased competence as managers and policymakers
- greater sensitivity in interpersonal relations
- an interest in maintaining contact with the Administrative Staff College and attending future programs. (This led to the formation of an alumni association to sponsor additional programs.)
- strong support for the modular approach and the preceptorial sessions.

Spiro (1979) evaluated the LIFE approach used in the New York University doctoral program in mental health policy and administration. Information was obtained from participants' and preceptors' logs kept during the program, questionnaires, and interviews with participants some time after completion. The analysis of the comments in more than 500 logs kept by both participants and preceptors supported the information gathered through other means. The logs of both groups were analyzed separately to identify and classify comments with respect to knowledge acquisition, application, and behavior change. Participants' logs were also analyzed for attitudes toward the preceptor, the LIFE approach, and the doctoral program as a whole. More than 400 unsolicited statements concerning these six factors were obtained.

- 95 percent of participants' statements about knowledge acquisition and use were positive.
- 72 percent of the preceptors' comments, using somewhat higher standards, were positive.
- 93 percent (91 of 97) of statements relating to application of learning were positive.
- Behavioral change to the extent that it was commented upon was positive.

Some of Spiro's conclusions are presented below:

> Sixty-three percent of entering participants remained with [this] challenging program . . . [which] enabled them to bring [new] techniques back . . . to their jobs . . . enhancing job performance. [It] increased . . . work/study habits . . . giving them new resources.
>
> The program enables participants to use their workplace as a laboratory for learning.
>
> The attributes which were most frequently cited as most positive were: individualized learning, application of theory to practice, and use of the workplace as a laboratory for learning. Learning . . . is incremental; with continuous reenforcement. . . . [It] encourages self-development after completion of the program. (Spiro 1979, p. 80)

LIFE depends less on end-of-program assessment; results are continuously assessed by both participants and preceptors. Feedback from use and discussion of results provide the basis for strengthening or changing managerial approaches and enriching participants' life-banks. They also provide evidence for assessing the value of new learning and the development of approach and techniques. Although the feedback provides useful operational information for design and implementation, it does not yield the statistically significant evaluative evidence that most researchers want.

CONCLUSION

To summarize, the LIFE design uses a seven-stage learning process. The stages are not necessarily sequential, and no stage is ever assumed to be completed. A helical learning process is assumed in which, with additional learning, each stage recurs at a higher level. The stages are the following:

- identifying and assessing competency needs
- developing specific learning objectives and a learning agreement
- implementing the learning agreement
- applying the learning in the work venue

- observing use of learning and cause/effect relationships
- analyzing feedback and developing new learning that leads to the next level in the helix and a new cycle of learning, use, and new learning
- reinforcement, modification, and improvement of competencies and their use on the job.

Techniques and processes employed in the seven-stage learning process include those listed below:

- use of participants' work venue roles, assignments, issues, problems, and so on as sources for passive and synthetic experiential learning content and exercises
- use of their work venues for application of learning and natural experiential learning
- identification of opportunities for direct, immediate application of new learning in the work venue
- use of feedback for improving observational and analytical skills
- use of analysis of feedback for initiating a new learning cycle
- periodic input of new content (i.e., management models, concepts, and approaches) and integrating this content into participants' life-banks
- reinforcing learning and refreezing new behaviors by feedback, repetition, and integrating learning.

In LIFE, the process for obtaining any significant change in behavior from unfreezing to refreezing is slower than in most programs. Significant change in managerial behavior can be brought about by practice in the use of the changed behavior with accurate, helpful feedback leading to competence in performance and by demonstration to the manager that the consequences of the change in behavior are beneficial. Refreezing may be an incremental process. Management development that does not put primary emphasis on refreezing may be valueless. Significant, lasting development is not a deterministic, short-term, one-shot process. Development not only should refreeze behavior but also should provide, through development of lifelong learning processes, the means for unfreezing and changing that very behavior. Even this may be possible only for changes that do not run counter to the manager's value system. LIFE recognizes the difficulty, and in some cases the virtual impossibility, of obtaining significant, lasting change.

The following are some shortcomings of the LIFE approach and indications of how we attempted to solve the problems presented:

- In some cases participants do not have opportunities to use new learning on their jobs. In these cases, it may be necessary to rely on passive and synthetic experiential learning approaches to integrate learning into their life-banks. If there are others in the work venue who do have opportunities, participants are asked to observe these managers and to describe how they could have used the learning and how their performance would have changed.

- In LIFE, as in other natural experiential learning, it is not possible to complete a cycle of strategic management and to get reliable feedback in any training period, even if it is as long as eighteen months. One technique is to have participants define a current situation and trace its development back as far as they can. In some cases, it is possible to go back as far as twenty years. After the development is traced, the participants identify the planning, if any, and the management decision points and decisions that were involved; analyze how these affected the course of events; and develop a plan that would have led to a better current situation.

Despite the strong conviction that the work venue is the most desirable learning venue when the objective is use in the work venue, we do not assert that it is always the best learning venue for all managers, all content, and all times. For example, it is not best when the objective is to do well on a written test on management and organizational theory or to conduct esoteric research testing of mathematical models. Learning that is beneficial for the manager may not be beneficial for the employing organization. Unless the consequences of suboptimization are taken into consideration, improved individual performance may be counterproductive for the focal system.

LIFE differs from most other natural experiential learning. Two of the most important ways are the nature of the thought that precedes experience and the reflection that follows. The thought that precedes is the selection and adaptation of a model from the life-bank to guide decision making and action. The reflection following the action is the analysis of the usefulness of the model in various circumstances for learning adaptation principles and techniques and for integrating the learning into the life-bank.

Most natural experiential programs separate cognitive and experiential learning. In LIFE, cognitive learning, application, analysis, and reentry are integrated elements of the learning content. Feedback from use of learning and discussion of the results provide a continuing assessment of content, both theory and implementation of educational and training technologies and plans. The information is fed directly into the planning process to shape the design of future modules. The continued reinforcement and use of learning are effective in reducing "fade-out" of learning, which is common in programs that do not emphasize and review immediate and repeated application.

Other ways in which LIFE differs from other programs include the following:

- The objective of lifelong learning is explicit and primary.
- There are planned activities to strengthen integration of work and learning venues.
- Use is made of immediate application of learning, feedback, and development of new learning as the basis for a learning helix that leads to continuous enrichment of the participant's life-bank.
- The modular approach, which facilitates in-depth learning in a specific area, is integrated into a holistic presentation and application, to facilitate use in the work venue and integrate all the learning.
- Learning is spread out over a much longer period of time. This permits increased opportunities for use, feedback, analysis, adaptation, and helical learning.
- Time away from the work venue is minimized. This decreases disincentives to participate and reentry problems.

Below are some conclusions from our analysis of feedback and our own observations:

- Depending on their predisposition, homogeneous groups tend to be more resistant or more open to change in the unfreezing stage.
- Increased knowledge of theory and good practice does not lead to use.
- Teachers must be accepted as authoritative and benevolent by learners if they are to significantly affect the learning process.
- Learning experiences are more effective when structured to utilize and build on participants' life-banks and the venues where application is expected.
- Reinforcement has to be related to use of learning.
- Approaches and content that are obviously correct in a situation in one venue may be unthinkable in others because of differences in organizational environment, culture, long-term strategy, objectives, incentives, and interpersonal relations.
- Routine responses, without much thought, may be more efficient. This is usually desirable, but one does not learn from routine behavior. If the behavior satisfices, it simply reinforces past learning. Selecting from among alternatives without planning to test and generalize is not a learning process. Acquiring competency in the learning processes a necessary condition for lifelong learning.
- The time structure (i.e., the occasional plenary meeting and the biweekly preceptorial sessions) makes it possible to use LIFE in national and international programs in which participants come together in plenary sessions for one or two days every three or four months. The flexibility with respect to content and approaches to coordinate with the work venue and participants' life-banks permits use of content applicable in different organizational and national cultures. The content in preceptorial sessions can be changed to meet the needs of the specific participants.

- Spreading LIFE learning over a much longer period of time than other development programs and making it a full-time activity, by considering all activities in the work venue as learning opportunities, helps participants absorb and integrate learning into their life-banks.

The LIFE approach could be employed in Organizational Development and group counseling and consultation. It could be used with Revans's (1974) natural experiential project approach. In Organizational Development, the work venue for natural experiential learning would be the organizational development project. In Revans's project approach, the work venue would be the individual's project. LIFE could be employed as a therapeutic process, combining the group session (plenary) and sessions of two or three persons with a therapist (preceptorial sessions). The individual's life would be the venue for natural experiential learning.

12

FINAL OBSERVATIONS

INTRODUCTION

The state of management development and many issues that should be considered by both theoreticians and practitioners have been discussed in the preceding chapters. In this concluding chapter, we review the state of the art and a few of the more important issues. In the course of our discussion we will make recommendations for improving the effectiveness of management development.

There is extensive subjective, and to a much lesser extent objective, evidence that most management development activities are beneficial. The increasing investment and importance assigned to management development by managers and both private-sector and public-sector organizations is one piece of this evidence. We agree, in general, with this assessment. We believe, however, that management development can be, and should be, more effective and have greater impact on the competence of participating managers and the functioning of their organizations.

We have made two principal recommendations, derived from assumptions based on our experience as both managers and management development professionals, that indicate how management development can be made more effective. The first is that management development must be directed toward helping managers become motivated and competent to engage in lifelong, self-directed learning. The second is that the most useful core around which to build learning activities to achieve the first objective and to increase managerial competencies and improve organizational functioning is individual experience through natural experiential learning.

In the course of our analysis, we introduced a number of concepts and relationships and distinguished sharply between types of learning experiences. The key learning concepts introduced include the life-bank, passive learning, and synthetic and natural experiential learning.

The life-bank concept will be further reviewed in the course of this chapter. At this point, it is sufficient to repeat that it is an artificial construct which we believe is useful for identifying, discussing, and utilizing assumptions about learning. We recognize that some of the concepts and definitions, such as "metaelement," are a matter of convenience rather than new entities.

The types of learning approaches between which distinctions are made include the following:

- passive and experiential learning
- synthetic and natural experiential learning
- learning from experience and natural experiential learning.

The review, analysis, and recommendations fall generally into four overlapping categories: management theory and practice, learning theory, management development, and assessment and research. While the recommendations based upon experience and derived from our theory are, we believe, extremely useful, they are still contingent and tentative. We attempt to point out, as we go along, the degree of confidence and the caveats that we have with respect to the recommendations.

MANAGEMENT THEORY AND PRACTICE

Few management theories and recommended good management practices are invariant with respect to the focal system's characteristics, the state of the environment, and the competencies of the specific manager. Expectations of managerial performance, as measured by rewards and promotions for managers, vary in time and space, not only from century to century and country to country, but from decade to decade and from industry to industry, among organizations in the same industry, and according to the background and status of the person making the decision (Unseem 1989). There is usually far greater validity in the criteria and assessment for technical than for managerial competence. Even when selection of managers is on the basis of merit, it is rare that organizations select managers solely on the basis of general managerial competence. They tend to look for financial experts, legal gurus, technical professionals, production people, and other specialists who, they hope, can manage. Many seek persons with a solid liberal arts background.

In the past, the focus in the private sector was on executives who had the financial and legal competencies to take over or rebuff being taken over by another company. Now there tends to be an emphasis on those with generalist (liberal arts) backgrounds or on persons competent in specific production and service-related technologies—the first, in the belief that managers with this background can make greater contributions to long-range planning; the second, in recognition that emerging technologies are playing, and will continue to play, a greater role in determining organizational success.

There has been a shift in emphasis from considering organizations as closed systems to seeing them as open systems. This has led to greater concern with the environment and has resulted in a related shift in the role and tasks of managers. There has been an increase in the perceived importance of scanning and enacting the environment, boundary spanning, and strategic management.

Executives have always been concerned with their customers and their competitors, with the system's task environment. What is new is the interest in the contextual environment. Organizational leaders are concerned with the international as well as the national contextual environment. They are turning with increasing frequency to consultants who assess potential risks and opportunities by analyzing political, social, and economic conditions worldwide and in specific countries and regions. There is a Council for International Risk Management.

Management theory using incremental or equilibrium models of the workplace environments is no longer seen as adequate for most systems. It is recognized that there are events, the consequences of nonlinear changes in the environment, which can cause systems to experience shock. These are unexpected, uncontrolled, major discontinuities in the functional relationships among key variables in the social, economic, and political environments. In these situations chaos theory seems to be more appropriate than equilibrium theory. While there has been some investigation of chaos theory in relation to mathematical and physical systems (Gleick 1987), there has been little with respect to socioeconomic systems. In chaotic environments, a minor random disturbance may amplify the nonlinear relationships to make systems subject to the environment unstable. It is not possible to predict how systems subject to these conditions will restabilize (Kiel 1989).

Although Emery and Trist (1969) describe a possible turbulent (i.e., chaotic) environment, they do not consider in any depth how chaotic conditions develop and how managers should behave to increase their systems' chances for survival.

Ansoff (1979) distinguishes three types of turbulence and suggests response behavior for each. However, these are quite general, and several of them are not appropriate for turbulent, unpredictable environments in the Emery and Trist sense. Several theoretical models dealing with chaotic conditions are discussed briefly by Kiel (1989).

Chaotic conditions may arise when there is radical devolution of power and authority. Such a transfer occurred in the Soviet Union in 1990. The confusion that arose is indicative of the usual inability of managers to stabilize their systems in these circumstances. Where there is no confidence that rational analysis will provide usable projections, nonrational approaches frequently take over.

Managers tend to know much more about the internal venue and closed-system management theory and practice than about open-system theory and the environment. They tend to have good experience in evaluating and using internal information but little experience and competence in converting partial and ambiguous evidence obtained from environmental scanning and reporting into signals for specific actions. Sensitivity, awareness, and analysis of environmental factors provide the basis for lessening the likelihood of unpreparedness for action in response to significant environmental change.

Strategic management has come into prominence as a rational means to anticipate and prepare for both normal and chaotic change. Emphasis on the environment is a major element in strategic management. Gaining competence to be sensitive to, enact, and respond to normal and turbulent environments is most effective in natural experiential learning. Competency gained in normal environments can be expanded by passive and synthetic learning to provide some ability to function when the environment becomes turbulent.

Study commissions' recommendations to improve the functioning of organizations in the 1970s and 1980s have been so repetitive that one can only conclude that few of the recommendations have been effectively implemented. More recommendations relate to structural and cultural characteristics of organizations than to managerial performance. However, even the structural recommendations usually have implications for managerial performance. Recommendations in *Made in America: Regaining the Productive Edge,* the 1989 report of the M.I.T. Commission of Industrial Productivity, are typical:

- greater cooperation between individuals and groups within organizations and between organizations
- eliminating rigid hierarchies and tight boundaries between units

- increasing technology and know-how transfer between major producers, their suppliers, and their customers
- increasing employee participation and unions' role in decision making
- more industrywide programs for training, research, and standardization.

Some participatory management approaches are, upon closer analysis, asymmetrical. That is, some of the persons involved are "more equal" than others. One example is the relationship between senior managers and managers in MBO. Goals and rewards, if any, are set primarily by the senior manager and, not infrequently, so are the means to achieve the goals. Making some suggestions and agreeing with the senior managers' decisions do not add up to very much participation. When managers realize this, teaching "participatory management" becomes a cynical exercise.

Managers in different nations tend to have different managerial styles (Crozier 1964). There is greater dependence on problem-solving and analytic techniques related to those of the sciences in the United States than in other countries (Locke 1989). While Japan and Germany, for example, have used some American production models, their motivational approaches are quite different (Locke 1989). Workers in a given culture expect managers to behave in a given style. American managers are expected to confront differences with both subordinates and superiors. French managers are expected to try to ignore differences with the people who work for them, particularly with members of the "working" class (Crozier 1964).

Multinational companies try to make management independent of national cultures and to develop their own management culture. Unless managers are separated from their native cultures and subjected to an extraordinarily strong and reasonably compatible organizational culture they tend not to adopt the organization's standards to replace their native national standards.

There is a hypothesis that America is losing world markets because American top management has lost the zest for competition. Nothing could be farther from the truth. If anything, there is too much competition. The problem is not competition but the focus on the wrong short-term objectives. The emphasis on short-term incentives and personal success, even in many of our sports which call for team play, has been translated into a management style.

In the past there always has been some concern with personal satisfaction. However, personal satisfaction has never been so great an overriding desire for such an overwhelming percentage of the total American workforce as it is now. Personal satisfaction is not seen as a long-term objective. The objective tends to be satisfaction now or in the immediate future. The strength of this objective is affecting the management of all organizations.

It has had important implications for the loyalty of employees. This, in turn, has profound implication for the functioning of the system.

E. M. Fowler (*New York Times*, October 6, 1990) notes, "Loyalty, once prized by both companies and employees has been shaken in recent years. There is no doubt that the many layoffs and downsizings have made workers much more skeptical about corporate America's interest in their welfare." Although Fowler doesn't specifically discuss loyalties of managers, she does note that layers of middle managers have been eliminated. Can there be any doubt that the loyalty of middle managers will also be affected? The reduced emphasis on loyalty of American managers is a marked difference between American and Japanese management. In Japan corporate loyalty is a prime consideration (Locke, 1989). The weakening of corporate loyalty has led to an increased preoccupation with one's own career and financial gain.

The preoccupation with personal gain has not gone unnoticed. Edward Lawler of the University of Southern California's Center for Effective Organizations commented that managers are not being paid for performance and don't seem overly concerned with conservation of company assets. Management needs to look at its own behavior and determine if management's rewards are in line with skills and what it takes to succeed in a global economy (*Labor Relations Today*, January/February 1990).

Internationalization of organizations and increasing numbers of foreign managers involved in running American companies has introduced new problems. In the period from the end of World War II to about 1980, American companies moved overseas. The problem in that period was for American managers to learn to become effective in foreign work cultures. The issue in the 1990s, and well into the 21st century, may be the reverse. The need may be for the American workforce and in particular supervisors and managers to learn to work effectively with top management from different work cultures. The greatest differences seem to be with top management from Japan. A study by T. Mroczkowski and R. Linowes reported in the *Training and Development Journal* (June, 1990) found that American managers are dissatisfied working with Japanese management and often leave the Japanese owned firms. Reasons given include: too much time spent seeking consensus, foot dragging in making decisions and clannishness. Not used to openly, strongly expressed differences, the Japanese are never quite sure whom they can trust among their American co-workers.

In the past, American companies that set up shop in a foreign country imported American management. Until the mid-seventies there was a general acceptance of the superiority of American type management.

This is no longer the case (Locke, 1989). Further, there is now more buying, merging and setting up of cooperative relationships with going foreign companies. This doesn't call for training foreign managers in American management but for top managements in the companies to learn to work with each other.

The need to adjust to different management styles can also stem from different sex related socialization in the same culture. Helgesen, in her study of women managers and executives (1990), found that "... women in business [tend to] ... disdain the most tradition[al] of business structures–the hierarchical ladder. ... [They] desire to be in the center of things, rather than at the top, which they perceived as a lonely and disconnected position. ... [They] desire to be connected to all those around them as if by invisible strands or threads constructed around the central point. ... [The] hierarchy and the web are in a way mirror opposites."

In a study of changes which could have significant effects on management development, McLagan (1989) identified increased pressure for productivity and a movement to "flatter and more flexible organization designs." The study points to an increase in the pace of change in customer and worker expectations and to globalization of the arena for organizational planning and action. Each of these projections indicates significant changes in the nature and state of organizations' contextual environments that could result in significant changes in their task and functional environments.

There has been more management theory enunciated and more management research conducted since the 1950s than in the preceding 4,000 years. The explicitness of these theories and models makes them easier to apply, compare, and adapt for new conditions. They are so much easier to present in management development that they form the basis of virtually all the content. The models tend to focus on a very limited number of variables, frequently only one or two. This tends to present a very simplified picture of complex systems. Answers and models that are developed from a contingency approach can never be complete or final or even completely satisfying. Doubt and impermanence are characteristic of contingency. The ambiguity and uncertainty are too much for many managers to bear. This may explain the great desire for solutions provided by simple models.

There are differences of opinion about the relative importance of the expressive and instrumental roles of management. An example of the intensity of feelings is the publicized conflict in the Yale School of Organization and Management. The school, which had been one of the leading academic proponents of the human relations approach, decided to shrink its very strong department of organizational behavior by not renewing the contracts of about three-quarters of the faculty. The justification given was that the emphasis on "organizational behavior" was one of the reasons that the school had a "continuing budget deficit." Since the objective of the school, in the words of the new dean, is "preparing people to manage in public service and . . . private business," this is a clear judgment of the relative importance of the two sets of tasks. Students, graduates, and affected faculty protested to no avail (*New York Times*, November 9, 1988). Yale was not being revolutionary; it was adopting the policy of other schools of business administration.

However, many theorists continue to advocate participatory management and other assumptions of the human relations school as appropriate for our society and good for business. An example is the recommendations of the M.I.T. study referred to earlier. The difficulty is to develop a practice that makes this approach a win/win game rather than the win/lose game that many perceive it to be.

The principle "have decisions made by the lowest-level person who has sufficient information" has been converted in some organizations into the concept of empowerment of lower-level managers. This is, in a way, an example of an application of the principle to increase participation at lower levels. However, the devolution of power, coupled with bonuses for productivity and punishment for failure to reach norms, which are set primarily by higher-level management, can produce incentives that closely parallel those in the demand administration common in authoritarian regimes. Supervisors and managers are encouraged to submit inaccurate reports and to ignore potential problems, such as needed maintenance. The practice can exacerbate poor relationships with the work force, leading to a spiral of poorer quality and maintenance, and greater deception.

Many studies, including those by McLagan (1989) and those by the U.S. Department of Labor during the 1980s, predict that there will be changes in the competencies of workers needed and in the characteristics of the persons in the work force. Many of the projections are based on already observable changes. Management theory and practice developed for the anticipated conditions call for significant organizational changes. Among these are the ability to develop and use a more versatile work force, a less well-defined organizational structure, fewer command levels, and more team operations.

Some observers expect that the number of persons who are primarily managers will decrease, while the number performing managerial functions will increase—that the number of persons who combine productive and managerial tasks will increase while the number of persons who perform only managerial tasks will decrease. Some predict more jobs for less-skilled workers. Some predict more jobs for more-skilled workers. The projections are confused. Some studies indicate a continuing increase in the number of executive, administrative, and managerial positions.

Those who expect that there will be less need for general managers at the middle and lower management levels assume that computer-based information systems will permit workers, particularly technical specialists, to communicate directly with senior management. One consequence would be that senior technical workers would serve as lead technicians rather than as managers. Another consequence would be that companies would have a smaller pool of qualified middle managers from which to select top managers. The top managers would require even greater general management competencies than now, since there would be less time spent in face-to-face meetings and routine decision making and more in leading, strategic planning, and communication via computer with the lead technical people.

Theories about "principles" of administration have moved from Gulick and Urwick's (1937) position that there are principles which govern the functioning of organizations as certainly as "engineering principles which govern the building of a bridge." In a 1947 article, Robert Dahl asserted that so many issues in public administration could be resolved only by normative considerations that the construction of an absolute science was doubtful. Herbert Simon (1947) went considerably further, in his comment on Dahl's article, to an overwhelming attack on the concept of "principles." In *Administrative Behavior* (1947) he specifically laid bare the questionable assumptions of the "principles" enunciated by Gulick for either public or private sector administration. Gulick, the least doctrinaire of theorists and possibly the most respected practitioner-theorist of the century, did not demur. However, the fact that "principles" keep cropping up, particularly in connection with the expressive role, indicates that strong differences continue today.

Organizational structures designed to debureaucratize are frequently coupled with a behavior model in which three-piece suits give way to shirtsleeves, rational analysis to "creativity" and intuition, and continuity to hoopla and project-based flexibility. There is acceptance of findings such as those of Peters and Waterman (1986), which indicate the effectiveness of this type of organizational structure and behavior. There is a tendency to downplay the difficulty of changing the culture of stable systems to move from a system with a more restrictive culture to the new model. There is a tendency to downplay the impact that the history and experience of an organization have on its functioning and response to change.

The passage of time enriches a language with multiple meanings and nuances that are felt and understood to a far greater extent by people who were born and have lived their lives in a country than by well-trained, intelligent foreigners. The natives learn and use the language with all its complexities as part of their own growth. They not only communicate in terms of similar concepts and symbols, they think in terms of them. The same happens in an organization with respect to communications, acceptable behavior, response to challenge and risk, and every aspect of organizational life. Each generation brings its own vision and techniques to the organization. While new techniques may be accepted, the vision cannot long be unaffected by the visions of the earlier generations. The continuing impact of organizational culture on management and on management development cannot be ignored.

An issue that has great impact on the design of management development is the determination of the appropriate role and tasks of chief executive officers. The resolution of this issue tends to determine the roles and tasks of managers at all lower levels. The issue derives in part from differences in normative definitions of the role and tasks and in part from differences between normative definitions and the actual roles and tasks as reported by trained observers. There are also differences in the reports of observers on the tasks performed and the importance of each of these tasks. There is even wider divergence between the predictions of how the role and tasks will change in time.

The Board of Governors of the American Society of Training Directors (Galagan 1990) believes that the role of the chief executive officer is to create the vision for the organization and set its values, goals, and policies. In the course of carrying out this role, the executive has to extrapolate effectively from the past to the future, serve as the organizational knowledge and power center, demonstrate caring for individuals, and inspire trust in the board and shareholders. The report also noted the loneliness of the solitary decision maker and executives' continuing primary concern with domestic operations and organizational stability.

Other normative definitions of chief executive officers emphasize other roles and tasks. Some focus on the executive as the boundary spanner, some on the charismatic leader, some on the creative genius, and some on the super salesman. Each definition is probably useful in come circumstances, but no definition is useful in all situations. However, if we think in terms of an executive team rather than of an individual, many of these roles and tasks are performed in all organizations. This indicates that there may be a need for training executives to be able to identify the role and tasks that they are capable of performing and want to perform, and to select and train others in their teams to perform the other roles and tasks.

Galagan (1990) also projected the roles and tasks that executives would have to perform in the twenty-first century. Some of these, such as "intuiting the future," do not seem to be in the province of management development as we know it. However, preparing managers to adapt to change is a proper development objective. We believe that this is best accomplished by training managers to continue to learn from their own experiences, supported by learning from current theory and recorded experiences of others.

One reason that normative roles and tasks do not jibe with observed roles and tasks may be that the observers focused on an individual rather than on a team. Another may be that the circumstances were not taken into account. Some of the factors that influence the nature of executive roles and tasks are the age of the organization, the environment, the competition, the level of regulation, the organization's history, its attractiveness to raiders and investors, the relationships between management and board, the product produced, and the technologies and processes employed.

The issue of the role of the executive is a corollary of what is for some perhaps the most basic issue: the universality of management theories and practices. For others, as we indicated, this is a nonissue. And there are theorists and practitioners holding a complete range of views between these extremes. Our position is that there are some models and practices which are common to many different types of systems. Which models and practices are useful are functions of the use to which they are to be put, the individual managers, the variables characterizing the systems, and the environments in which they are to be used. Characteristics, models, and practices that are universal are so general as to be virtually useless for design of programs. For example, a universal characteristic of all functioning complex systems is that there is a decision-making process and authority. The process may involve everyone voting, or face-to-face interactions among some of the stakeholders, or a single decision maker convincing followers, or any one of a large number of other alternatives. In university departments the process tends to be collegial, arrived at by discussion and consensus. In an army in combat, decisions tend to be made by individual commanders with hierarchical primacy. It would be meaningless to assert a single "best process" for all of these. For management development to be effective, its content and processes must follow the organizational principles of the systems in which the participants are employed.

One last word on management style. There has always been a management school that emphasizes the leader. This has been, from the earliest times, the province of the publicist rather than the academic. When rational leadership is ineffective, particularly in a time of turbulence, there is a tendency to assert that effective leaders must be inspired, visionary, and prophetic. The true path is revealed to the few creative leaders. Leadership must be based on inspired (never explained) superhuman vision and insight. The leader demands and deserves unquestioning followers. Not only is there no explanation of how the leader arrives at the intuitive decisions, there cannot be; to explain would be to open the decisions to rational analysis and possibly destroy the leader. There is an analogous rush to the irrational in the sales of books about prophecy and religion. The sales of these books become extraordinarily great in times of political upheaval.

Some theorists and practitioners question the significance, reliability, and validity of much of the research on the beneficial results of inspired leadership and what is, in many respects, its opposite, a totally open participatory culture. We feel that not every organization would benefit from changing its leadership and structure and culture to either of these models. However, many, infatuated with the success stories, have sought to adopt one of these—sometimes with success. There is a feeling that if an approach has been followed by an improved company bottom line, it cannot be wrong.

One characteristic of the new "success" criterion is that short-term financial gain has become the primary objective of the private-sector elite. The focus of many executives has turned from production and sales to financial manipulation. The observation of Akio Morita, chairman of the Sony Corporation (*New York Times*, June 6, 1987) bears repeating:

> The big attraction in American business today is the money game, in which profits are not made by manufacturing or selling goods but by guessing whether the dollar will rise or fall—how can you expect your people will be motivated to work when they are traded like merchandise.

Ironically, American industry may be saved by firms of other nations falling into the same trap, as some Japanese companies have already done. "Like many other industrial companies whose earnings from exports have been hurt by the appreciation of the yen, Tatcho Chemical had come to rely heavily on profits from the financial markets" (Michael Quint, *New York Times*, September 9, 1987).

Learning Theory

Conscious use of learning theory in design and implementation of management development is essential if we are to learn and to improve management development theory and practice. Some learning theory attempts to isolate and then integrate the elements of thinking and learning. These theories hypothesize how the mind operates. Other theory relates to processes such as operant conditioning and seeks to explain how these processes lead to decision making and other outputs. We do not believe that it is necessary to get too deeply involved in controversies relating to how people learn. We created the concept of the life-bank solely to provide us with the frame of reference we needed. It is a frame of reference that assumes the primacy of experiential learning.

The life-bank assumptions are not derived from either cognitive or "Skinnerian"-type assumptions. They do, however, incorporate concepts from various learning theoreticians in combinations that we have found useful in the design, conduct, and assessment of management development. The life-bank is a pragmatic model from which most of Knowles's assumptions can be derived. The principal assumptions of this model are the following:

- Each person develops a unique life-bank that is one key to determining what the person learns (i.e., adds to the life-bank).
- The other key is the learning venue and the relationships between the life-bank and the venue.
- The individual's life-bank and the venue jointly determine what learning will be used in any specific situation.
- Competencies (i.e., sets of life-bank elements) are venue-specific, although some are applicable in many venues.
- Adding new learning to combine into usable competencies tends to be more efficient and effective if the learning takes place in the venue in which the competencies will be used.
- Metaelements (i.e., sets of elements that function as a unit) serve as processes for learning, categorizing, and organizing sets of elements, and establishing new sets of elements for specific functions.

The life-bank model assumes two principal learning sequences. The first is that the need to react to a specific situation triggers a life-bank search for an appropriate model to guide action; use or adaptation of existing models or creation of a new model is considered (use of metaelements); and the sequence is concluded by use of the model and incorporation of new elements into the life-bank. The second sequence originates in feedback from an activity or observation of an activity. The event is compared with existing life-bank models; if no model fits, the data are organized by means of the learning metaelements and integrated into the life-bank by inducing new elements, a generalization that explains the cause/effect and can help the person understand the activity and its consequences.

We have described the life-bank as if it contains only one level of metaelements that define and control the processes for organizing and using elements. However, in terms of logical analysis, it is clear that there are numerous metaelements, some of which have to do with organizing and using other metaelements. In logic the practice is to establish levels or types of metaelements in order to avoid contradictions and paradoxes. We see no need for this level of rigor in our presentation.

Experiential learning is strongly supported by American educational theorists. This support is derived in part from the principal native philosophy, pragmatism. John Dewey, one of the trio of founders of the pragmatist school, was a leader in developing the theory of experiential learning from pragmatism. Two related assumptions are the following:

- Content and learning approaches consonant with the learner's life-bank and characteristics of the work venue are more effective in unfreezing, changing, and refreezing new behavior by integrating the learning into the learner's life-bank.
- Learning is most effective when content is seen by managers as satisfying perceived needs.

Total reliance on natural experiential learning may bring a number of problems in its wake. One is misuse of induction based on limited experience. Two possible, diametrically opposed examples of this misuse are generalizing to significantly different situations without monitoring consequences, and limiting induction to situations with precisely the same parameters. There is also an inability to help participants experience a sequence of activities that in the work venue would take place over a long period of time and from which short-term feedback is either not possible or not reliable or valid. Further it is rarely possible to identify specific problems and issues in participants' work venues to illustrate or provide practice in a specific learning area. It may not be possible to observe and analyze the cause/effect relationship and to get feedback. Contemplation stemming from each of these activities is a crucial learning element in natural experiential learning. This is a problem whether a holistic or a modular course structure is used. If the content is to be broad enough to deal with all aspects of a real situation and deep enough to make a meaningful contribution to any significant behavioral change, considerable time is required for learning content, applying it, and obtaining feedback. There always is a trade-off between breadth and depth of learning in use of natural experiential approaches.

In LIFE we try to solve the problem in two ways. The first is to start each program with an overview of management and the management development process. The second is to bring into each module, particularly in the preceptorial sessions, the salient, related elements in other modules.

A difficult problem that is present in passive and synthetic experiential learning is how to get participants to think through a situation and not automatically give the "right" answer to a case study or exercise. We have been so trained to be good examination takers that we automatically ask ourselves, "What is the expected answer?" and give it. Where written tests are used to evaluate training, the compulsion is even greater than in the "happiness" evaluation.

MANAGEMENT DEVELOPMENT

The principal goal of management development is to increase managers' competencies by achieving two objectives:

1. to inform managers of what is expected of them now and in the near future, and to help them gain and improve the competencies needed to carry out their assigned tasks
2. to help managers to increase and strengthen the competencies that will be required in all managerial assignments, whether at a higher level or in a different department, and no matter how the managerial role changes over time.

Management development is derived from a combination of management theory and practice, and learning theory. There is no standard mix used in design of management development programs. Many management theories are myths (i.e., models without any significant empirical foundation). Nevertheless, it is probably necessary to treat the theories as theorems in management development, so long as they are useful in practice. Even if change is an objective, it may not be desirable to attack a myth head-on in order to avoid early defensive reaction. We have already discussed the validity of learning assumptions.

The differences among programs are in the specific content objectives and the learning approaches used to achieve these objectives. Variations in expectations for managerial performance tend to lead to changes in the content and processes of management development. There are, however, a number of common assumptions underlying design of most management development. Some of these are the following:

- The functioning of the focal system has shortcomings that should, and can, be remedied. Some of these needs can be satisfied by management development.
- The resources are available, including will on the part of all concerned, to implement the program and use the learning.
- Top management will support and provide resources for the program and encourage participants to use the learning in the work venue.
- Uncontrollable changes in the focal system's environment will not affect the state of the focal system significantly.

Program designs run the gamut from the most general content presented by passive learning approaches (e.g., college lectures on the global village), to a great variety of synthetic experiential learning using games and techniques focused on expressive areas (e.g., developing work teams), to natural experiential learning approaches directed at solving specific operating problems in the work venue. Many programs fail to go beyond presenting abstract concepts and constructed issues and cases to realize actual management in terms of the concrete, specific circumstances in which managers manage.

Content can be categorized as instrumental, expressive, or general. The currently popular areas of each of these are the following:

- instrumental—organizational theory, planning, cost/benefit analysis, productivity, and quality control
- expressive—leadership, communications, interpersonal relationships, and motivation
- general—problem solving, decision making, and negotiating.

Until very recently, we assumed that the American models for organizing, managing, and management development were the most effective under all conditions. We stated, and got worldwide acceptance for, the assumption that the rest of the world should learn from us. Our management development model is based on the assumptions that all issues can be converted into well-defined problems and that all problems can be solved if we have enough information and are competent problem solvers. This has led to an emphasis on quantitative analysis with economics as the core discipline. A corollary is that problems should be tackled even if we do not know how to solve them; we can always improve the situation. A second assumption is that differences between people should not be ignored but confronted.

Emphasis in the business schools and schools of public administration is on the quantifiable aspects of management. These management tasks provide better research opportunities and are better adapted to the classroom and passive learning approaches. This emphasis tends to strengthen the problem-solving attitude toward management and to play down the ambiguous, unpredictable behavior of individuals. Another consequence is that analysis of the contextual environment becomes strongly directed to single-discipline (e.g., financial) models.

Related to the problem orientation but much broader in scope are prescriptions for individual behavior that are more appropriate for a democratic, egalitarian contextual environment and for more harmonious, effective organizations. From a philosophical point of view, these seem to be based on Kantian and utilitarian thinking and approaches to self-understanding and relations with others. Some of the prescriptions are the following:

- "egalitarian individualism" (i.e., opportunities for individual contributions must be as equal as possible)
- integration of individual and organizational goals
- increased involvement and participation by individuals, both managers and other workers
- maintenance of a culture of trust, openness, and confronting of issues
- equalization of power
- greater importance to managers of efficient and effective operations and organizational goals than of maintaining status and power and increasing their own opportunities for advancement.

Many of these, such as equality and decentralization, are basic, core American values noted by Tocqueville (1945) near the middle of the nineteenth century.

The content of development programs provided by consultants (including university faculty members) tends to be derived from assumptions focused on managers' expressive role rather than the quantitative and instrumental role. Trainers also show a preference for exploring the benefits of debureaucratized structures and the participatory and equalized relationships that such structures presuppose. This makes for much more exciting workshops. Trainers can develop great exercises. Participants frequently leave with the firm conviction that they have experienced the true path to greatness. This is reinforced by the popular research management texts that support the success of the approach.

Few of the consequences of these assumptions are carried out in most American organizations. They are among the many American assumptions that are not accepted in many other cultures. The primary assumption and the incentive for organizations to invest in management development is that it will increase the quality and reduce the cost of the product or service. The driving incentive is not to increase the quality of life and the work satisfaction of members of the work force, except as these are secondary objectives to support the primary objectives. It is not surprising that the companies which send their managers to these programs do not entirely adopt the human relations and participatory approaches recommended, in the way intended. If this human approach is to survive and grow, organizational cultures and structures must be changed so that these approaches can have achievable win/win objectives which are accepted by all concerned. The Japanese, while not adopting the democratic, egalitarian assumptions, have done this with their quasi-feudal guaranteed employment and loyalty to the company objectives.

Passive learning can be very useful in the unfreezing and change stages. However, competencies that we believe managers must have which cannot be acquired by passive learning include the following:

- to work effectively with others
- to communicate so that the objective of the communication is achieved
- to handle any difficult human relations situation
- to determine the timing and nature of appropriate responses to situations flexibly
- to interpret and use ambiguous and contradictory evidence
- to identify and assess the importance of different variables in a problem
- to select appropriate models to consider and to determine which would best fit the situation
- to adapt and combine known models to improve their applicability in a given situation
- to generalize learning from an experience for future use
- to evaluate expectations and possible costs, and to be willing to take reasonable risk
- to develop new models and approaches when the known are inadequate
- to make timely, appropriate decisions.

Moving from passive to synthetic experiential to natural experiential learning approaches, management development seems to be progressing into the past. Until about the 1890s, the only paths to acquiring management competencies were by managing and learning from experience, or observing or reading about other managers, or being coached by a mentor who served as an adviser and sponsor. Although these paths are still used, the twentieth century has seen the proliferation of other learning approaches. In the first half of the century, the new approaches were primarily didactic and normative. In the second half there has been increasing use of synthetic experiential learning. The movement now is to natural experiential learning. The workplace is again seen as the most effective venue for management development. Although it is the same principal learning venue, the learning theory is quite different from "learning from experience."

There is considerable support for the view that the work venue is the most effective venue for transfer of learning.

> Most of the skills required of the new manager are best learned where the learning applies to the job. Skills such as leadership, communication, interpersonal effectiveness, teamwork, negotiation, learning, counseling, and teaching are difficult to teach in school but easy to teach on the job. (Carnevale 1988, p. 28)

"Remembering" for use (Sacks 1990) is not usually simply recalling fixed, invariant elements from the person's life-bank. It is an imaginative reconstruction built from the relevant remembered elements and organized groups of elements stemming from other experiences and reconstructions. It is our position that recalled elements are more transferable for use in a venue when the learning took place in the venue.

Life-bank elements, to be useful in a specific venue, have to have been recently introduced in connection with use in the venue or actively used in the past in the venue. Inactive elements can with some effort be activated for use in the original use venue. Transfer for use in other venues is more difficult. Training in creative thinking techniques tends to facilitate this sort of transfer. Use of life-bank elements evolves with experience in the use and transfer of elements and the need for the element or metaelement in a specific situation in the work venue.

The role played by the manager and members of the manager's role set, the script that is played out, the enacted environment, other venue variables, and the learning processes and activities planned around these are the crucial elements in experiential learning. In natural experiential learning, we can exercise some influence on the learning processes and activities and the way roles are played by participants in their interpretations of the script. This is about the limit of the trainer's influence. Trainers can have little or no influence on the values of other venue variables. There is much more control when the participants are taken out of their natural work venues and spend a training period in another venue. In synthetic experiential exercises it is possible to write the script defining interpersonal relations and the sequence of happenings, influence through role definition the performances of all the actors, control the analysis of cause/effect to focus on a predetermined learning objective, and determine the importance to be attached to values of variables, incidents, and issues. Besides these advantages there are problems. They include the complex problem of introducing new learning upon reentry, adapting the learning to different and usually more variable and more complex situations, and having the will to risk using the learning. We need more experience and experimentation to learn how to maximize use opportunities in participants' own work venues in natural experiential learning and how to minimize the disadvantages when learning takes place in a "foreign" work venue.

Experiential approaches and techniques that provide experience in use of alternatives are of greatest use for helping managers to acquire the competence to learn from experience in conjunction with contingency management theory. The rationale for this statement is similar to that proposed by Edelman (1987) in his model for the development of the brain and the thinking processes: flexibility is learned only if the learning-specific situation stimulates more than one possible model and thus enriches the life-bank.

Theory and practice emphasize that management is a group activity. While some programs are devoted to developing, leading, and working with teams, there is a more general issue relating to the transfer of learning. The opportunity to use learning from management development is dependent upon the acceptance and support of the manager's role set. This may be impossible if the new behavior is not consistent with the expectations of the role set and the underlying culture of the system. This problem is frequently discussed in management theory and management development. But few management development programs that employ passive or synthetic experiential approaches can deal with the issue effectively.

Along with devolution of power, there is greater emphasis on managers' being motivated to take risk to achieve both organizational and personal objectives. In government there is constant disparagement of bureaucrats who play it safe. However, in practice, in both the public and the private sectors, managers who take chances and lose are not rewarded and may be penalized. This is a crucial issue in the transfer of learning, which always involves risk. Should management development advocate and teach approaches that tend to minimize possible losses or maximize gains, or more complex "mini-max" approaches? Obviously there is no one correct answer. There is a time and a place to minimize and a time and a place to maximize. The "correct answer" of how much and what kind of risk is appropriate is almost completely determined by individual style and the work venue. In passive and synthetic experiential learning, managers can discuss models and alternatives and test their application. The learning is of limited value when the manager returns to the work venue.

Most executive development programs sponsored by academic institutions have traditionally provided little experiential learning. They have used a variety of passive learning techniques ranging from lectures to elaborate case analyses and "in-basket" exercises. There is movement in some institutions to employ more experiential approaches.

Livingston (1983) and other observers have repeatedly criticized the traditional approaches. It has been said many times that the purpose of education is to help learners to use knowledge. This involves helping the manager identify the conditions and the situations in which specific learning could be useful and to evaluate and take the risk that making the change entails. Consequently the tailored case studies and experiential exercises in the best classroom instruction may inhibit rather than motivate use of learning.

Training organizations tend to make greater use of synthetic experiential learning. Their distinguishing techniques are games and elaborate interactive exercises. More recently, there has been some use of a challenging real experience and natural experiential learning. Few learn to perform a difficult, complex task in a single exposure. Repetition and reinforcement, essential to refreeze new behaviors, can take place only in the work venue. This is an additional argument for using the work venue as the primary learning venue and helping managers learn from their on-the-job experiences.

Some programs called management development seem to be directed at relaxation and fun and games rather than at increasing competence. In terms of reducing stress and unfreezing old ideas, they may have greater impact on performance in the work venue than serious academic presentations on the newest analytic techniques or analyses of foreign markets.

Fun and games vary from corporate theater to mountain climbing. Corporate theater has moved, according to Poe (1990), from pure entertainment to "such weighty topics as buyouts and downsizing." Bolt (1990) claims that wilderness programs now give executives "hard-hitting learning they can use." They provide effective experiential learning for handling crises, developing leadership, and working in teams. There is no reliable and valid evidence of what from these experiences translates into changed behavior in the work venue. It is our view that they may be of some value to unfreeze some states, but little else.

It seems clear that managers must learn to tolerate increasing ambiguity and to use less-than-adequate information. They will have to be able to deal, as the need arises, with changing workplace needs and a changing work force. Unless the evidence for a specific change is very strong, natural experiential learning can only help managers to gain competencies needed for making incremental changes in operations and for scanning and enacting their environments more effectively. These competencies will help them to be sensitive to environmental change and to possible need for changes in strategy. Managers could be prepared to change plans and management behavior as information indicating the need becomes available. Passive and synthetic experiential approaches could help them incorporate alternative courses of action and gain competence in adapting and selecting from among these in particular situations. Natural experiential learning would come into play for learning during the course of activating an alternative. Management development that provides these competencies becomes increasingly important in a period in which there is a rapidly changing environment.

The LIFE approach is one technique for achieving the objective of preparing managers to deal with an incrementally changing environment. It does this by providing theoretical models of possible changes and how to deal with them and by giving managers opportunities to practice responding to change and testing the value-specific approaches on the job.

We have noted the importance of risk taking and that learning to be an effective risk taker must take place in the work venue. But this is not helpful, since opportunities for risk taking are not always present. We have not found any program that provides good training in this area. The truth is, we do not know how to advise people to act in a risk-laden environment in which actions can have severe impact and are irreversible. As good as any process is Benjamin Franklin's advice to a young man who did not know whether to marry. Franklin suggested that the young man draw up two lists, one with potential advantages, the other with disadvantages; cross out pairs of equal plus and minus expected values; and look hard at what was left. This issue of risk taking is related to support by higher management for use of the learning from management development in the work venue.

Since change is inevitable, a primary objective of management development must be to motivate and prepare managers to engage in a continuous independent learning process, both to deal with new situations and to improve competencies. The motivation for self-directed, lifelong learning is the result of the interaction between the managers' life-banks and the learning and use venues. The stronger the learning metaelements (i.e., the competence and confidence in self-directed learning) and the greater the incentives from the anticipated use venue, the greater the motivation to learn. But the motivation to use must come from the interplay between life-bank and use venue elements.

In the LIFE approach the preceptor and the other participants motivate and help the individual manager to develop a learning plan, to test it in both the learning and the work venues, and to evaluate its implementation. The manager plays two roles: learner/actor and training adviser to other managers. It is our assumption that the elements of these two competencies coalesce as a result of repeated, reinforced activities over an extended period to produce a strong metaelement for independent learning. Integral to the approach is practice in the development and use of self-assessment instruments.

Learning contracts used in various independent study approaches and MBO are of value if they focus on their continued use for learning to learn rather than as techniques for evaluating performance. Unfortunately MBO objectives are frequently used as standards and criteria for rewards.

Acquisition of some management competencies is most effective using passive and synthetic experiential learning rather than natural experiential approaches. Some obvious examples are learning to deal with anticipated, unique, not repeatable situations and long-term activities such as strategic management. In some situations, it may be too risky or costly to attempt to implement an approach without prior passive analysis to evaluate alternatives and synthetic experiential learning to develop technical competence.

Management education and development curricula follow the tradition of educational curricula by dividing programs into distinct courses and sequences of modules in specialties. This is a Cartesian model which postulates that complex phenomena are more easily analyzed, understood, and dealt with if subdivided into relatively homogeneous components or specialties. The hypothesis has reasonable validity, except that in management (as well as in other social science fields) the components in real life are interrelated so that there is no reality to the individual elements without consideration at the same time of the impact of the entire set of elements. While focusing on a single subject matter area, such as leadership or financial systems, is less confusing and easier to present as a result of the partial isolation, it may be of little value, and perhaps counterproductive insofar as application is concerned. Interrelations among the elements, from the operational point of view, demand simultaneous consideration.

Based on the theory of experiential learning, the holistic structure is more directly related to use in the work venue and to independent learning and use. However, a modular structure is more effective for achieving depth of learning and analysis of the usefulness of alternative approaches in a limited time frame. Both are needed in management development, but they must be integrated. Problem solving and case studies are integrating approaches. Natural experiential learning is probably the most effective integrating approach. It is the primary one in LIFE.

Decision making is seen as the key managerial task. Many programs are directed toward helping managers improve decision making. These usually provide instruction and practice in rational decision making. Others purport to increase creativity and intuitiveness and to improve thinking skills. To what extent are these teachable? If some can be learned in a classroom, to what extent is competence, including will to seek innovative solutions, transferred to the work venue? Some practitioners play down systematic problem solving, which to some extent can be taught, in favor of intuitive problem solving. Their rationale is that managers usually do not engage in a systematic process to obtain answers to the problems they face. Isenberg (1984), reporting the findings of a study, noted, "It is hard to pinpoint if or when senior managers actually make decisions . . . on their own" (p. 82). They seem to depend more on intuition than on pure rational thinking. Five situations in which Isenberg found intuition to predominate are sensing a problem, carrying out behavior responses strongly embedded in life-banks, synthesizing and integrating discrete learning in life-banks, validating rational analysis, and arriving at "reasonable solutions to problems without deep analysis."

Although no one has devised a satisfactory definition of " 'intuition' or of the process of intuition, many theorists and practitioners believe in the efficacy of intuition and that one can learn to become an intuitive decision maker" (Agor 1989).

Even if one accepts the existence of persons with unusual visionary and intuitive powers, it does not follow that these competencies can be learned by means of any current process. The programs that are described are very similar to the brainstorming sessions which were very popular in the 1960s and 1970s. These broke the creative process into two parts. In the first, the critical faculty was blocked to encourage developing a great number of solutions. Free association and structured techniques were employed to develop many solutions. In the second part, the critical faculty was brought into play. There was careful, rational analysis of the alternatives to select those which would best satisfy the given conditions. Having conducted such workshops, sometimes as synthetic experiential learning in the LIFE program, we can say that, on the basis of our experience, they can be both operationally and educationally useful. We do not believe that participants gained in intuition. They acquired techniques to reduce inhibition in suggesting and considering possible solutions they would not otherwise have considered. They also learned the importance of subjecting these unusual alternatives to rigorous analysis and the techniques needed to do so. In all cases, the importance of the "prepared mind" was evident.

The techniques used for improving intuition include guided imagery, self-hypnosis, and journal keeping. Our work in creativity indicates some possibilities relating to the issue. We have assumed that there are metaelements in each individual's life-bank relating to organizing, selecting, and rearranging other elements and evaluating the effectiveness of specific sets to solve a given problem. We assume that if priority in use is given to the evaluative set, the activities of the selecting and rearranging set tend to be restricted. Consequently, practice in the free association and list-making techniques of brainstorming, coupled with avoidance of evaluation until many alternatives are developed, would tend to improve intuitiveness. This view is supported by some subjective research which indicates that creative people tend to have many more ideas and the competence to identify the valuable few.

However, depending on being intuitively right seems to us to be more chancy than reliance on systematic analysis of alternatives. There is no evidence that off-the-top-of-the-head intuitive solutions are totally new answers, a set of elements never before contained in the manager's life-bank, and not a rearrangement of existing elements, variations on old themes. In our analysis, the manager who has the most effective intuition is the one with the "prepared mind," the possessor of a rich life-bank and strong selecting and arranging metaelements.

We believe that significant new solutions which are not the product of systematic attack, including use of creative thinking techniques, are modifications of solutions to related problems or stem from solving a simplified form of the problem. Useful answers to problems in technical fields—and management is a technical field—come from "prepared minds." A. N. Whitehead took the position that it is desirable to dispense with the need for thought in as many situations as possible. He compared occasions requiring thinking to occasions in a battle calling for a cavalry charge. These he said are few in number and should be made only at decisive moments. Many confuse Whitehead's position, which assumes development and repeated use of basic solutions, with intuition, which is quite another matter.

A point of view opposite to Whitehead's seems to be expressed by Kaplan (1964):

> The price of training is always a certain "trained incapacity". The more we know how to do something, the harder it is to learn to do it differently. . . . I believe it is important that training in behavioral science encourage appreciation of the greatest possible range of techniques. (p. 29)

The rationale for this conclusion is illustrated by Kaplan's "law of the instrument." This is, in simple terms: "Give a small boy a hammer and he will find that everything he encounters needs pounding." This caution does not invalidate the Whitehead position. Both managers and management development practitioners are better practitioners for knowing what has worked in the past. However, they must continue to be sensitive to possibilities and unexpected opportunities for using a variety of approaches, including those which have been discarded.

Career development, with its parallel objectives of advancing the purposes of the individual manager and of the employing organization, is an enlightened approach and perhaps the only feasible one. However, it is obvious that these are very different objectives which under many circumstances may be antithetical. In the public sector the possibility of a conflict between the objectives of politically appointed executives and career managers is regarded as almost certain.

The specifics for motivation and processes for individualized, lifelong learning, which is regarded as a major aim of management development, are not focused directly at achieving short-term organizational objectives. They include having the manager set the learning rate toward objectives relevant to the manager's (not the organization's, except as these coincide) immediate and long-term objectives. The only continuing force to motivate achieving individual and organizational objectives is the desire to deal effectively with the problems and opportunities that occur during the workday.

The differences between individual career objectives and organizational objectives cannot be ignored. The goals, objectives, policies, culture, and processes of the employing organization and the career objectives of the individual manager must be taken into account. Resolution of the differences is an important task for the training specialist. In packaged programs, the issue is avoided because neither set of objectives plays an important role in determining content and process. In programs tailored for an organization, the usual needs analysis is an estimate of the organization's needs and only secondarily of the needs of the individual managers.

Only when top management sets a developmental objective and leaves it up to the individual manager to determine how to achieve it is the individual free to reconcile organizational and personal objectives (Long 1988).

Most management development focuses on the role of the manager in the organization. The system's environment is considered only in organizational theory or when it impinges on decision making, as in strategic management. While there are some passive and occasional synthetic learning activities to improve scanning skill, the most rewarding approach is natural experiential learning. It is the only approach in which scanning from the viewpoint of the task environment is possible. This is crucial for learning how to influence these elements. To some extent this is done in marketing training. However, there the effort is largely directed to viewpoints of consumers, not to those of competitors and other key elements in the task environment.

How successful can ethics programs be in getting managers to put ethical considerations above the interests of their companies and themselves? How should managers act when there are significant differences between the values of their employing system and those of the contextual environment? In some cultures and to many in our culture, these are absurd questions. The answers are obvious. Nevertheless, these are questions at the heart of an ethics program. Only recently, and only in selected situations, has the rule of personal responsibility in carrying out the order of a legal superior been imposed. In most cases persons who refuse orders for moral reasons tend at best to be not rewarded, and in most cases they have been punished with little redress. The experiences of most whistle-blowers in the United States are indicative of what happens in the most favorable contextual environment when managers put society's interests first. When managers put moral considerations and society's interests first, it is not because they were convinced to act that way in management development.

One of the few populations that changed its religious beliefs in order to survive, about which we have significant information, are the Marranos, the Spanish Jews who converted to Catholicism under the threat of the Inquisition. The Marranos spent much of their intellectual energies in subsequent years on the philosophical question "Can one change one's moral and religious beliefs at will, as prudence or public policy requires?" (Hampshire 1990). The Marranos never arrived at a complete answer. But by their practices, it would seem that, after one or more generations, some people can, and some cannot. The Marranos were not faced by a boss who wanted a change or a workshop on ethics or even a law that could mean a fine or imprisonment. They were faced by the choice of conversion or the auto-da-fé.

If the culture of the contextual environment cannot get successful managers to conform to ethical standards or values significantly different from those imposed by their life-banks and the culture of the focal system, no training course can. While management development is concerned with all facets of managerial behavior, there are behaviors and value systems that, we do not believe, can be changed in any significant manner by management development.

Management development cannot always lead to improved management. In a review of management development in the United Nations Secretariat and the United Nations Development Program, Hoberman (1990) concluded that management development is of little organizational value where there is emphasis on short-term results, rapid turnover of the most senior administrators, and political pressures exerted on decision makers, and selection, assignment, and promotion are dependent on political and personal loyalty.

Some have attributed the failure of management development in the Secretariat to its international character. However, Hoberman (1990) and Reymond and Mailick (1985) noted that other United Nations organs, which do not have the same structural characteristics, have conducted management development which compares favorably with management development in other public and private organizations. Hoberman further pointed out that there tends to be poor management development in organizations with conditions similar to those in the Secretariat. These conditions are not unusual in organizations in the American public sector and are not unknown in the private sector.

An assignment of one of the authors was to design a management development program for an international organization. During the needs study, it became apparent that the explanation for seemingly inappropriate managerial behavior was managers' rational response to the challenges presented by the members of the board of the agency. While the directors were high-status persons in their native countries, they had little real decision-making power in the agency. They resented their subordinated roles and played out their resentment in a game directed at challenging the managers' technical competence. The managers in turn spent a great deal of time and effort anticipating and responding to the directors' challenges. This involved increasing technical rather than managerial competence. Management development to change managers' behavior to obtain more effective and efficient operations would have been pointless without changing this relationship. Improvement in the functioning of this agency would have to focus on the power structure before attempting development approaches.

From being the world's teacher in management in the post-World War II period, many advise American business leaders to become students of management in other countries. The countries suggested most often are Japan and Germany (Locke 1989). Even some developing countries are mentioned. The assumption of the "economic man," with the resulting overemphasis on quantitative analysis, and the relative neglect of experiential learning approaches are given as causes. Locke (1989) gives as a primary reason that the Germans have instituted the most effective management education. It makes far greater use of experiential education.

Research

Our review of the literature identified a number of theories relating to experiential learning and independent learning. However, we found no research that had any high level of reliability or validity. We found no reliable and valid evaluation instruments for measuring performance. The postprogram "happiness" questionnaire is the most common instrument. It is clearly not acceptable for any serious research. The written and oral tests of knowledge gained may be reliable, but they provide very little evidence of use of learning in the work venue. The single "treatment-test" design, which has limited reliability and validity, is repeated over and over, as if it were the feasible and acceptable research design.

Even if we accept the positive findings, "twenty-five years of research have identified the need to make executive programs more explicitly developmental, but fall short on identifying how to design and conduct them" (Verlander 1988, p. 32).

As indicated earlier, we have doubts about the ability to implement classically designed, useful, reliable, and valid studies relating to management development that include a pretest, a posttest, and randomly selected pre-test and posttest populations. Few hypotheses related to management development are defined so clearly that they could be subjected to rigorous research. There are no generally accepted definitions or standards of performance for key managerial tasks. There are no universally accepted criteria and standards to measure changes in a system's efficiency and effectiveness that do not involve numerous intervening variables.

Most practitioners and researchers recognize these difficulties. However, feeling the need to justify their activities, they use less valid designs. Some accept subjective "happiness" reports by participants as reliable estimates of program value. Others measure participants' competence to answer questions about the knowledge content of their programs. Measuring knowledge gained is attractive because it is objective and easy to determine. Measuring use of the knowledge in the work venue and the impact of learning is not. The objectives of most management development include increasing participants' competence and having a positive impact on the functioning of the focal system. Achievement of these is not easy to measure objectively.

Virtually all research in human relations is conducted by academics and students in fulfillment of degree requirements. The Toppins (1989) survey found that almost two-thirds of this research was devoted to training-related activities. It far outweighed such other activities as work force planning, compensation, benefits, information systems, organization and job design, union and labor relations, selection and staffing, and incentives. Although the research was carried out by academics and students with training in research design and statistics, only 6 percent of the project designs were of an experimental nature. The greatest percentage of the designs, 35.7 percent, was descriptive.

Imel's (1982) review of the research literature to determine the extent to which adult learning theory is used in practice found that "Although teachers perceive adults as being different, these perceptions do not automatically translate into differences in approaches to teaching."

There is research evidence that participation in experiential learning programs has a positive impact on the social, psychological, and intellectual development of high school students. Managers are not high school students, and the conditions for experiential learning in a workplace for students are not those of natural experiential learning for managers. However, the conditions of the high school experience are similar to those involved in rotation and special assignment for development. What is necessary is to add the careful observation, reflection, and induction activities that are usually slighted in rotation and special assignment, where the emphasis tends to be on accomplishment.

There are few articles dealing with failed programs. In the many reviews of the research literature in Campbell et al. (1970) and in our review from 1970 to date, we found no significant negative findings.

Meta-analysis, a technique for combining the findings from a number of studies, may provide a means for obtaining more reliable findings. Until now, however, attempts to use the technique have been flawed by failure to take into account the incompatibility of the different studies. There should be an attempt to develop uniform designs, terminology, and reporting. This seems to be a necessary condition for this technique to be useful.

There are many areas in which exploratory and formative research would be useful. Some of these relate to the following:

- the impact of the manager's role set
- the use and value of learning theory in design and implementation of management development
- techniques and content as functions of population and environmental variables
- use of research findings in design and implementation of programs.

There is need for preliminary studies to identify and define learning variables and to posit relationships on which to base hypotheses that can be subjected to test. Even if we are not totally successful in this effort, the activities involved and the alternatives considered would give us greater insight into the nature of the learning process and conditions under which use of learning in the work venue is increased.

There is inadequate research into the reliability and validity of needs analyses. How do needs vary, depending on one's point of view? Some views that should be considered are those of top management, potential participants, and their role sets. How do development needs relate to other factors that affect a system's functioning? Some factors that affect a system are structure, incentive systems, and the task and contextual environments.

There is little evidence that prior to implementing research, practitioners determine whether the design will yield the evidence needed to answer their questions. It is essential to make this assessment if research is to be useful. It involves, among other things, identifying the pertinent variables and clearly stating the theoretical relationships among the variables that are the hypotheses. Relevant and irrelevant variables, and test and intervening variables, have to be distinguished.

There is need for developing theory and designs for experimental and longitudinal studies of processes and techniques for improving management performance. There are none now because there is little theory and no techniques for dealing with the great difficulty of subjecting functioning organizations and living persons to the constraints and ambiguities that this would require.

FINAL REMARKS

There are many needs that neither a manager nor a training needs analyst can detect because of the blinders and bounds that experiences place upon their life-banks, and consequently on their thought. Their life-banks contain deep-rooted assumptions and "givens" about roles, capabilities, processes, cause/effect relationships, and even the nature of organizations. The blinders and the aversion to risky change are particularly inhibiting for learning and the transfer of learning in successful organizations and for successful managers. The manager's life-bank and work venue determine the questions posed; the information sought, accepted, and used; the environment enacted; the learning that takes place; and the use to which learning is put. Refreezing broader vision and the will to go beyond the boundaries of their self-enacted domains and take the risks that accompany the use of new learning can take place only in the work venue, in the course of natural experiential education.

The uncertainty of environmental and organizational changes has had a profound effect on the loyalty of both managers and nonmanagers. To be fully effective, there must be a means for demonstrating to the managers that the organization is concerned not only with improving their value to the organization but also with their career development as individuals. Management development can be the means if top management demonstrates continued support, defines acceptable risk, and encourages managers to use learning.

The changing environment has resulted in an increase in managers' boundary-spanning tasks in terms of both internal networking and relationships with the task environment, and of the importance of continuous independent learning.

Views that are rarely considered in management development include that not all problems are solvable, not all issues can be resolved in a manner satisfactory to everyone, and Kaufman's (1985) comment that outstanding managers have just been lucky. Each of these points up the importance of being able to respond effectively to the unexpected. This competence is not gained through passive learning but through experiential learning. To the extent that it is venue-specific, it can be acquired most effectively in the venue.

Beyond the individual manager's learning and competence is the matter of organizational learning, the ability of the organization to change its mode of functioning through unfreezing, changing, and refreezing the ways in which it does business.

> The old way was to learn from the outside in. . . . Knowledge originated at universities and government think tanks. . . . In the new economy, knowledge also comes from inside organizations through incremental learning gained as products and services are made and delivered to customers. . . . It is continuous incremental improvements that gain the lion's share of commercial success. (Carnevale 1990, p. 41)

Natural experiential learning is the necessary ingredient for programs to help managers learn to identify opportunities for improvement and to determine and make the desirable changes. It is an essential component of development for transferring learning to the work venue. But, beyond these, it is the only approach that can, to the extent that management development can help, improve the ability of an organization to deal with the full range of management issues and situations we have described.

GLOSSARY

Active Learning—learning that can be usefully applied directly or in the immediate future, or for which the learner can clearly see how and where it can be applied.

Behavior—activities (primarily observable) of a manager that interact with or have impact on others in the focal system and its environment or on the functioning of the system.

Boundary—defined in several different but related ways, including "criteria for distinguishing between elements inside and outside of the focal system, and the limit of the domain in which the system's controls prevail."

Bounded rationality—the necessity of making decisions within the cognitive limits of rationality (e.g., knowledge of alternatives, their consequences, and their utility) (March and Simon 1958).

Career development—a planned program implemented for an individual manager by using a range of approaches, of which management development may be only one, to satisfy current and future management needs of the organization and personal aspirations of the individual. It may extend to a lifelong process involving sequences of experiences that include avocational as well as managerial learning and development.

Change (also referred to as "moving")—a stage in the Lewin model in which the new learning is defined and accepted.

Closure—skill in completing and making sense of incomplete and ambiguous information. We assume that closure is related to the skill to retrieve life-bank elements on the basis of limited and fragmentary identification of desired elements.

Coaching—helping another, usually a subordinate, improve job performance by a one-to-one relationship. The focus is on the whole person, feedback, consultation, and task analysis.

Coalign—to bring all the variables that determine the functioning of a system into agreement. Coalignment is seen by Thompson (1967) as "the basic administrative function" bringing into agreement not only the human actors but also the "streams of institutionalized action."

Competencies—both the behavior and the thought process needed to perform a task or job and the behaviors and thought processes of which an individual is capable. There are many ways to categorize competencies. We distinguish five categories:

- knowledge—information
- skill—competence to use information without involving others (e.g., operate a machine, design a statistical study, develop a legal brief)
- ability—competence in relating to other people (as a supervisor, a subordinate, a social worker, a mentor)
- judgment—competence in identifying issues, problems, and opportunities; developing and determining reasonable alternative solutions and decisions; anticipating consequences; and selecting the most appropriate alternative
- will—motivation, determination, and persistence to undertake and complete a task, achieve an objective.

Content—the knowledge and other competencies that participants are expected to gain from a management development program, or the substance of a program dealing with management and managerial-related behaviors.

Critical incident—an incident that provides significant insight into the nature of the managerial role or the competencies required to perform a specific task, or behaviors that differentiate between performing a task effectively and ineffectively.

Culture—in an operational sense, those factors which characterize and influence the members of an organization, or a subset of the members of an organization (e.g., managers), to exhibit thought and behavior patterns different from those of members of other organizations or other subsets in the same organization. (see Chapter 8.)

Design—the completed plan for a management development program, including objectives, activities, assessment and feedback plans, and alternative approaches as a function of assessment.

Domain—the activities of a system that are recognized by its enacted environment as appropriate. It also is the area recognized by systems in the task environment as that in which the focal system has distinctive competence.

Element—the individual unit of the contents of a person's life-bank. Among the elements are learned information and competencies, and combinations, sequences, and patterns of these. There are active elements that can readily be employed, less active elements that require effort to retrieve and employ but are of potential use, and inactive or inert elements that were once learned but are no longer available for use, cluttering and reducing the effectivensss of the life-bank.

Enacted environment—the elements of the environment that a manager takes into consideration in decision making. "Enacted environment" is the relevant environment for a specific manager. It is not the same for all managers in the same organization. Managers create and define (i.e., enact) the environment to which they respond. People enact their environments differently in different venues. However, in every case the enacted environment is the result of scanning and a search process.

Environment—in an organization or system, everything that is not within the focal entity (i.e., is outside its boundaries). We distinguish three categories of environment:

- task environment, the systems in the environment with which the people and machines in the focal system have a direct, one-to-one relationship
- functional environment, the systems in the environment with which the people, subsystems, and machines in the focal system have an indirect, more remote than a one-to-one relationship that nevertheless is well defined and traceable through intervening entities
- contextual environment, the entity's environment other than task or functional. It includes the totality of forces affecting the functioning of the focal system (e.g., the political, social, and economic conditions of the society of which the focal system is a part).

Environmental scanning—planned, cognitive search of the environment to identify and evaluate elements that have, or have the potential to have, significant impact on the focal system. It is an effort to make the enacted environment more relevant.

Experiential learning—learning based on feedback and analysis of experience. It is a planned activity that involves observing, interacting with others, acting, experiencing the consequences of actions, noting the impact on others and their reactions, reflecting, learning from the reflection on the cause/effect relationship, incorporating the learning in the person's life-bank, and providing raw material and opportunities for generalization. We distinguish between experiential learning that takes place in the work venue and in other venues. We categorize experiential learning as either synthetic or natural. (See the definitions of synthetic experiential learning and natural experiential learning.)

Expressive role—the set of social-emotive tasks in which relationships with others are of primary importance. Examples of these tasks are leading, motivating, resolving conflict, and coaching.

Family group—a group of participants who have significant work venue-related commonalities that permit using work-related, specialized cases, exercises, and other learning materials and approaches. Most of the time, the term refers to people from the same organization. However, it is also used for managers from the same industry or service, or those from the same functional area (e.g., sales).

Feedback—relating to management, information about the input, functioning, and output, and the relationships among these and the impact on the work venue. The information may be for an individual manager, a subsystem, or a total productive system. Feedback usually describes elements of performance (i.e., throughput) and achievement of defined objectives (i.e., output). The objectives of feedback include providing the information for learning, modifying goals, models, and activities, and assessing and improving performance for goal achievement. In communications, feedback is information that completes the communications loop by indicating what the designated receiver understood and is doing about the message from the sender.

Focal system—the system or organization that is the subject of discussion and analysis.

Holistic—refers to the approach in which the content of the program is presented as a totality rather than in terms of specialties in separate sessions or modules.

Imagination (used interchangeably with "intuition")—the faculty that includes imitation, intuition, and creation. It is as important in management as memory and reason. Imagination is not independent of the "prepared mind." Mandelbrot, one of the most innovative of present-day scientists, said, "Intuition is not something that is given. I've trained my intuition to accept as obvious shapes which were initially rejected" (Gleick 1987, p. 182).

Inert learning—learning the manager does not use and that serves only to clutter an individual's life bank.

Instrumental role—the set of managerial tasks that do not involve extensive relationships with other people and are primarily directed toward task achievement. Examples of instrumental tasks are planning, statistical analysis, problem definition, resource allocation, and evaluation.

Leading system—the element in the focal system's task environment that has the greatest influence on its functioning.

Learning style—the set of processes by which individuals incorporate new elements into their life-banks. These are assumed to be different for different individuals (Guild and Garger 1985; Kolb 1984).

Life-bank—the totality of values, assumptions, competencies, habits, expectations, motivators, concerns, thought patterns, learning style, attitudes, worldview, and other behavioral determiners with which a person is born, develops through growth, or acquires in some manner over a lifetime. It includes the unique set of parameters that determine how an individual can and will interpret and react in a specific situation, as well as processes and criteria for responding to and accepting, acquiring, and integrating new experiences and learning into itself. Dewey refers to a similar construct in the realm of purely personal events that are always at the individual's command and that are his exclusively. Weick, extending an assumption of Mead, suggests: "Response repertoires control noticing. The person carries this repertoire and its implications for noticing wherever he goes" (1969, p. 26).

Lifelong learning—the continuation during a person's lifetime of a self-motivated process for adding active learning to one's life-bank.

Management development—an organized effort to motivate and help managers change their behavior in a defined manner through education, training, and experience.

Management development program—includes the needs analysis, program objectives, design, implementation, and assessment. Design elements include content, learning approaches and venue, the participants, relationships between these, and the process and criteria for making the decisions relating to these.

Metaelement—one of a set of special life-bank elements that functions in connection with utilizing other elements in the life-bank. The functions include joining elements in new sequences and patterns, discarding or changing elements, retrieving learning for use, converting and organizing experience and elements into new learning (creativity), and integrating learning into the life-bank. We make no assumptions about how metaelements accomplish these tasks. We simply assume that they do so in some way. A number of outstanding scientists have described how a sudden flash of insight led to the solutions for which they are famous. These experiences provide a clue about the functioning of the metaelements. Poincaré, possibly the most famous French mathematician at the beginning of the twentieth century, stated that after working on a problem for some weeks with no result, the solution came to him when he was unable to sleep one night: "Ideas arose in crowds. I felt them collide until pairs interlocked, so to speak, making a stable combination." (Hadamard 1954, p. 14)

Model—a set of assumptions about the relationships among a class of defined activities and their consequences that is useful for identifying and defining relevant variables, providing guides and a frame of reference for understanding and interpreting relationships, and analyzing cause/effect and other functional relationships.

Module—a unit of a development program. The modular design is the opposite of the holistic design.

Natural experiential learning—learning that takes place in the venue in which the learning is expected to be used (in management development, the work venue), by performing work which is expected to continue after the completion of the specific training. The experience can be preceded or followed by consideration of theory or models related to the activity and its effect. The experience is followed by observation and analysis of the outcome. Based on this analysis, new theory may be developed (usually when the experience precedes), or theory may be modified, discarded, or reinforced. The activity takes place in real time and with real work relationships. The activities are of some consequence to the individual and the focal system. To the extent that learning in school is expected to be used in school (i.e., the focus on testing), school learning could be considered natural experiential learning.

Needs analysis—includes both the process and the findings of the process used to determine desirable objectives, contents, and learning approaches of the management development program for an organization or an individual.

Organizational development (OD)—an experiential educational and training strategy to help an organization and the people in it adapt to specific, significant changes in goals, technology, staffing, and the enacted environment through planned organizational change. The change agents are, in general, persons from the organization who, in the course of OD, are trained for their roles. Assumptions include that change is more effective when it is a collaborative effort of the persons involved, directed toward establishing a more humane and participatory system. Objectives of OD activities include improving competence in interpersonal relations, team building, learning to resolve conflict productively, and identifying and remedying structural weaknesses and inadequate processes. Techniques include data gathering, group analysis, and collaborative problem solving.

Passive learning—any learning methodology that does not require the participants to engage in an activity to implement a decision and actually deal with the consequences. Passive learning is opposed to experiential learning. Examples are reading, lecture, discussion, case analysis, problem solving, and the "in basket."

Plenary session—in the LIFE approach, a session attended by all participants. Plenary sessions in LIFE are employed to introduce or to complete a learning module.

Preceptor—a faculty member who acts as consultant, mentor, information source, role model, and gadfly in the formal small group (preceptorial) session. (There is a detailed discussion of the role of the preceptor in Chapter 11.)

Preceptorial sessions—formal sessions in LIFE that are the integrating venues for natural experiential learning. The focus is on inducing learning from experience. They are devoted to increasing learning and planning, reporting on and analyzing the impact of implementing learning, and identifying learning that results.

Progressive learning sequence—a sequence in which each learning experience in a set of learning experiences both adds to the learner's life-bank and prepares the way for the next learning experience.

Rational man (or "economic man")—a model of human behavior. The individual is assumed to make optimal decisions in some utility frame of reference, on the basis of sufficient knowledge.

Reentry issue—the problem of gaining acceptance and support from the manager's role set for the manager's changed behavior resulting from application of learning from management development activities.

Reference group—a set of people to whom the focal person relates in a venue different from the work venue (e.g., home, training program, golf club). Members of a reference group expect specific behaviors from the person both in the specific venue and in other venues.

Refreeze—the stage in the Lewin model in which new learning becomes a stable, active element in the learner's life-bank.

Risk and *uncertainty*—used interchangeably, although technically they are different. We use them to mean both that the consequences of alternative actions cannot be predicted and that there probably will be different consequences to a decision maker from choosing an alternative.

Role conflict—a situation, leading to confusion and dissonance, that arises when there are two or more role expectations such that carrying out one would make it difficult, if not impossible, to carry out one or more of the others.

Role set—the set of persons in the work venue with whom the individual manager interacts and who have specific expectations of how the manager should act. Their acceptance of the manager's behavior can influence the manager's performance.

Satisfice—a term introduced by March and Simon (1958) in their description of decision making. It indicates decision making in which the decision maker selects the first adequate solution rather than continuing to search for the best solution.

Scanning—includes searching, collecting, processing, and evaluating information about the environment. A major activity in enacting one's environment.

Self-directed or independent learning—a process in which managers assume responsibility and actively seek, with or without the help of others, to determine their learning needs, define their learning objectives, develop and implement a plan for achieving these, and assess their progress toward the objectives.

Senior management—the term we use to designate the superiors of the program participants.

Structure—as a verb, the activity that includes determining the tasks to be carried on by people and machines to achieve assigned objectives, packaging tasks into jobs or units, defining relationships among jobs, and establishing motivators and standards. As a noun it is the result of the activity.

Synthetic experiential learning—learning derived from engaging in physical activities that have real, observable consequences. They usually take place in a learning venue that is not the work venue. The activities are specifically designed to provide an occasion for learning. They usually do not involve real time and work venue relationships, and are not directed toward achieving real organizational objectives. Some examples are role-playing and games.

Uncertainty absorption—the systematic reduction in risk to the total system by reserving decision making on more risky matters to higher levels. Also the reduction in both accuracy and completeness of evidence as information is communicated from level to level or agent to agent in an organization, through summarizing, changing emphasis, and other editing.

Unfreezing, moving or *changing,* and *refreezing*—the three stages of a change model (Lewin 1951). They refer to motivating to change or replace a set of life-bank elements, introducing and gaining acceptance for a new set of elements, and fixing the new set as a stable, active life-bank set of elements.

Utility—the value assigned by an individual to one of a set of alternative consequences.

Venue—in the broadest sense, the physical and psychological factors, and all the other variables associated with the focal system, that have any impact on the participants or their activities. Two venues are intrinsic to the learning process. The educational venue is where teaching and learning take place. The work venue is where learning is expected to be used. In natural experiential learning, the educational and work venues are identical.

BIBLIOGRAPHY

Agor, W. H., ed. 1989. *Intuition in Organizations: Leading and Managing Productively*. Newbury Park, CA: Sage.

American Society for Training and Development. 1989. *The Learning Enterprise*. Alexandria, VA: The Society.

Andrews, E. S., and Noel, J. L. 1986. "Adding Life to the Case-Study Method." *Training and Development Journal* February. 39(3).

Andrews, K. R. 1961. "Reaction to University Development Program." *Harvard Business Review* 3(39).

Ansoff, I. H. 1979. *Strategic Management*. New York: Wiley.

Arendt, H. 1974. *The Human Condition*. Chicago: University of Chicago Press.

Argyris, C. 1962. *Interpersonal Competence and Organizational Effectiveness*. Homewood, IL: Richard D. Irwin/Dorsey Press.

———. 1964. "T-Groups for Organizational Effectiveness." *Harvard Business Review* March–April.

———. 1973. "The CEO's Behavior: Key to Organizational Development." *Harvard Business Review* (51:55–64, March–April).

Argyris, C., and Schon, D. A. 1978. *Organizational Learning*. Reading, MA: Addison-Wesley.

Awal, D., Katzell, R. A., and Katzell, M. E. 1988. "Significant Development Experiences in Careers of Indian Executives: Implications for Management Development." In *The Practice of Management Development*. Edited by S. Mailick, S. Hoberman, and S. Wall. New York: Praeger.

Bagehot, W. 1873. *Physics and Politics*. New York: D. Appleton.

Baldwin, T. and Ford, K. 1988. "Transfer of Training: A Review and Direction for Future Research." *Personnel Psychology* 41.

Bandura, A. 1969. *Principles of Behavior Modification*. New York: Holt, Rinehart and Winston.

———. 1977. *Social Learning Theory*. Englewood Cliffs, NJ: Prentice-Hall.

———. 1986. *The Social Foundations of Thought and Action*. Englewood Cliffs, NJ: Prentice-Hall.

Barthes, R. 1977. *Roland Barthes*. New York: Hill and Wang.

Beer, S. 1975. *Planning for Change*. New York: Wiley.

Bennett, William E. 1956. "Master Plan for Management Development." *Harvard Business Review* May–June.

Bennis, W. G. 1966. *Changing Organizations*. New York: McGraw-Hill.

———. 1969. *Organization Development: Its Nature, Origins, and Prospects*. Reading, MA: Addison-Wesley.

———. 1981. "A Dialogue with Warren Bennis—Organizational Development at the Crossroads." *Training and Development Journal*. April.

———. 1984. "The 4 Competencies of Leadership." *Training and Development Journal*. August.

———. 1989a. *On Becoming a Leader*. Reading, MA: Addison-Wesley.

———. 1989b. "Why Leaders Can't Lead." *Training and Development Journal*. April.

Berry, J. K. 1990. "Linking Management Development to Business Strategies." *Training and Development Journal* August.

Berryman, S. E. 1987. "Breaking out of the Circle: Rethinking Our Assumptions About Education and the Economy." Presentation at 43rd National Conference of the American Society for Training and Development, June.

Birnbrauer, H. 1981. "Reinforcing Your Training Programs." *Training and Development Journal* January.

Blake, R. R., and Carroll, D. A. 1989. "Ethical Reasoning in Business." *Training and Development Journal* June.

Blake, R. R., and Mouton, J. S. 1978. *The New Managerial Grid*. Houston: Gulf Publishing.

Bledsoe, R. 1988. "An Approach to Executive Development." In *The Practice of Management Development*. Edited by S. Mailick, S. Hoberman, and S. Wall. New York: Praeger.

Block, P. 1987. *The Empowered Manager: Positive Political Skills at Work*. San Francisco: Jossey-Bass.

Bolt, J. F. 1985. "Are We Meeting the Management Training Challenge?" *Training and Development Journal* January.

———. 1990. "How Executives Learn: The Move from Glitz to Guts." *Training and Development Journal* May.

Brinkerhoff, R. O. 1983. "The Success Case—A Low Cost, High Yield Evaluation." *Training and Development Journal* August.

———. 1988. "An Integrated Evaluation Model for HRD."

Brookfield, S. 1985. *Self-Directed Learning: From Theory to Practice*. San Francisco: Jossey-Bass.

———. 1986. *Understanding and Facilitating Adult Learning*. San Francisco: Jossey-Bass.

Brown, B. 1989. "The Search for Public Administration: Roads Not Followed." *Public Administration Review* March/April.

Brown, F. G., and Wedel, K. R. 1974. *Assessing Training Needs*. Washington, D.C.: National Training and Development Service Press.

Bruner, J. S., Goodnow, J. J., and Austin, G. A. 1956. *A Study of Thinking*. New York: Wiley.

Bryant, A. L., Jensen, J. O., Thompson, M. Z., and Miletich, R. G. 1978. *Management and Executive Development in Industry, Universities, and the Federal Government*. Rock Island, IL: U.S. Army Management Engineering Training Activity.

Bureau of Labor Statistics. 1976. *Handbook of Methods for Surveys and Studies*. U.S. Department of Labor, Bulletin 1910.

Burke, M. J., and Day, R. R. 1986. "A Cumulative Study of the Effectiveness of Managerial Training." *Journal of Applied Psychology* 71(2).

Burke, W. W. 1976. "Organizational Development in Transition." *Journal of Applied Behavioral Science* 76(3).

Bushnell, D. S. 1990. "Input, Process, Output: A Model for Evaluating Training." *Training and Development Journal* March.

Campbell, D. T., and Stanley, J. C. 1963. *Experimental and Quasi-Experimental Designs for Research*. Boston: Houghton Mifflin.

Campbell, J. P., Dunnette, M. D., Lawler, E. E., III, and Weick, K. E. 1970. *Managerial Behavior, Performance, and Effectiveness*. New York: McGraw-Hill.

Cantrall, A. M. 1952. "Law Schools and the Layman: Is the Law Education Doing Its Job?" *American Bar Association Journal* November.

Carlisle, K. E. 1985. "Learning How to Learn." *Training and Development Journal* March.

Carnevale, A. P. 1986. "The Learning Enterprise." *Training and Development Journal* January.

———. 1988. "Management Training Today and Tomorrow." *Training and Development Journal* December.

———. 1990. "Training America's Workforce." *Training and Development Journal* November.

Carnevale, A. P., and Schulz, E. R. 1989. "Return on Investment: Accounting for Training." *Training and Development Journal* July.

Catalanello, R., and Redding, J. 1989. "Three Strategic Training Roles." *Training and Development Journal* December.

Chapman, R. L., and Cleaveland, F. N. 1973. *Meeting the Needs of Tomorrow's Public Services*. Washington, DC: National Academy of Public Administration.

Chapple, E. D., and Sayles, L. R. 1961. *The Measurement of Management*. New York: Macmillan.

Chenault, J. 1987. "The Missing Option in Executive Training." *Training and Development Journal* June.

Cheren, M. E., ed. 1987. *Learning Management: Emerging Directions for Learning to Learn in the Workplace*. Information Series no. 320. Columbus: National Center for Research in Vocational Education, Ohio State University.

Christensen, D. R., and Kinlaw, D. C. 1984. "Management Training: Managers Can Do It All—Or Almost All." *Training and Development Journal* May.

Clegg, W. H. 1987. "Management Training Evaluation." *Training and Development Journal* February.

Cocheu, T. 1989. "Training for Quality Improvement." *Training and Development Journal* January.

Cohen, M. J., and Ondrasik, A. L. 1988. "Project Management: A Model Case." In *The Practice of Management Development*. Edited by S. Mailick, S. Hoberman, and S. Wall. New York: Praeger.

Collins, E.G.C., and Scott, P. 1976. "Everyone Who Makes It Has a Mentor." *Harvard Business Review* 1976. 56(4):89–101.

Colosi, Marco. 1984. "Who's Pulling the Strings on Employment at Will?" *Personnel Journal* May.

Conner, D. R. 1988. "The Relationship Between Change and Corporate Culture." In *The Practice of Management Development*. Edited by S. Mailick, S. Hoberman, and S. Wall. New York: Praeger.

Connolly, S. 1983. "Participant Evaluation: Finding out How Well Training Worked." *Training and Development Journal* October.

Conrad, D., and Hedin, D. 1978. "Are Experiential Learning Programs Effective?" *National Association of Secondary School Principals Bulletin* 62.

Cook, J. T., and Bonnett, K. R. n.d. "Mentorship: An Annotated Bibliography." San Francisco: Far West Laboratory.

Cook, T. D., and Campbell, D. T. 1979. *Quasi-Experimentation: Design and Analysis Issues for Field Settings*. Chicago: Rand McNally.

Cox, C., and Beck, J. 1984. *Management Development: Advances in Practice and Theory*. New York: Wiley.

Craig, R. L., ed. 1976. *Training and Development Handbook*. 3rd ed. New York: McGraw-Hill.

Crowe, M., and Adams, K. 1977. *The Current Status of Assessing Experiential Education Programs*. Columbus: National Center for Research in Vocational Education, Ohio State University.

Crozier, M. 1964. *The Bureaucratic Phenomenon*. Chicago: University of Chicago Press.

Cyert, R. M., and March, S. G. 1963. *A Behavioral Theory of the Firm*. Englewood Cliffs, NJ: Prentice Hall.

Dahl, R. A. 1947. "The Science of Public Administration: Three Problems." *Public Administration Review* Winter.

Daloisio, T., and Firestone, M. 1983. "A Case Study in Applying Adult Learning Theory in Developing Managers." *Training and Development Journal* February.

Davis, L. E., and Cherns, A. B., eds. 1975. *The Quality of Working Life*. New York: Free Press.

Deal, T. E. 1986. "Deeper Culture: Mucking, Muddling, and Metaphors." *Training and Development Journal* January.

Dechant, K. 1988. "Accelerating Organizational Culture Change Through Management Training." In *The Practice of Management Development*. Edited by S. Mailick, S. Hoberman, and S. Wall. New York: Praeger.

Deming, W. E. 1988. "The Deming Theory of Management." *Academy of Management Review* January.

Dery, D. 1986. "Knowledge and Organizations." *Policy Studies Review* August.

Deutsch, C. H. 1990. "Managing: Bringing the Outside Inside." *New York Times*, May 13.

Dewey, J. 1910. *How We Think*. New York: D. C. Heath. (Reprint)

———. 1938. *Experience and Education*. New York: Collier Books.

Doig, J. W., and Hargrove, E. C., eds. 1987. *Leadership and Innovation*. Baltimore: Johns Hopkins University Press.

Dopyera, J., and Pitone, L. 1983. "Decision Points in Planning Evaluation of Training." *Training and Development Journal* May.

Downs, S. 1987. "Developing Learning Skills." In *Learning Management*. Edited by M. E. Cheren. Columbus: National Center for Research in Vocational Education, Ohio State University.

Dror, Y. 1988. "Advanced Workshops in Policy Analysis for Senior Decision Makers: Lessons from Experience." In *The Practice of Management Development*. Edited by S. Mailick, S. Hoberman, and S. Wall. New York: Praeger.

Drucker, P. F. 1967. *The Effective Executive*. New York: Harper & Row.

———. 1974. *Management Tasks, Responsibilities, Practices*. New York: Harper & Row.

Druian, G., Owens, T., and Owen, S. 1980. "Experiential Education: A Search for Common Roots." *Journal of Experiential Education* Fall.

Dreyer, J. W., Jr. 1988. "Integrating Management Development, Organization Development, and Management Systems for Operating Results." In *The Practice of Management Development*. Edited by S. Mailick, S. Hoberman, and S. Wall. New York: Praeger.

Dyer, W. G. 1983. *Management and Organizational Development*. Reading, MA: Addison-Wesley.

Edelman, G. M. 1987. *Neural Darwinism: The Theory of Neuronal Group Selection*. New York: Basic Books.

———. 1990. *The Remembered Present*. New York: Basic Books.

Edelman, G. M., and Mountcastle, V. B. 1978. *The Mindful Brain*. Cambridge, MA: M.I.T. Press.

ETS Developments. 1989. "Experimenting with the new Technologies: The Highs and Lows of Developing an Interactive Videodisc to Teach Classroom Management Skills." Princeton, NJ: Educational Testing Service.

Edwards, W., and Tversky, A., eds. 1967. *Decision Making*. Baltimore: Penguin Books.

Emery, F. E., ed. 1969. *Systems Thinking*. Baltimore: Penguin Books.

Emery, F. E., and Trist, E. L. 1969. "The Causal Texture of Organizational Environments." In *Systems Thinking*. Edited by F. E. Emery. Baltimore: Penguin Books.

Etzioni, A. 1986. "Mixed Scanning Revisited." *Public Administration Review* January/February.

Faerman, S. R., Quinn, R. E., and Thompson, M. P. 1987. "Bridging Management Practice and Theory: New York State's Public Service Training Program." *Public Administration Review* July/August.

Fanning, D. 1990a. "The Executive Life." *New York Times*, financial section, January 21.

———. 1990b. "Recharging the Batteries of Midlife." *New York Times*, financial section, June 3.

———. 1990c. "A Spiritual Healer for the Workplace." *New York Times*, financial section, June 10.

Faris, J. J. 1983. "Employee Training: The State of the Practice." *Training and Development Journal* 37:85–93, November.

Fellenz, R. A., and Conti, G. J. 1989. *Learning and Reality: Reflections of Trends in Adult Learning*. Columbus: Center on Education and Training for Employment, Ohio State University.

Fiedler, F. E. 1967. *A Theory of Leadership Effectiveness*. New York: McGraw-Hill.

Finkle, C. 1984. "Where Learning Happens." *Training and Development Journal* April.

Fish, S. 1989. *Change, Rhetoric, and the Practice of Theory in Literary and Legal Studies*. Durham, NC: Duke University Press.

Fisher, L. M. 1989. "Sickness in the Cockpit Simulator." *New York Times*, February 20.

Fitzgerald, L. F. 1985. *Education and Work: The Essential Tension*. Information Series no. 304. Columbus: ERIC Clearing House, Ohio State University.

Fowler, E. M. 1989. "University Heeds Advice on Management." *New York Times*, March 7.

Fox, N. 1977. "Action Learning Comes to Industry." *Harvard Business Review* September–October.

Frame, R. M., and Nielsen, W. R. 1988. "Excellence According to Plan." *Training and Development Journal* October.

French, W. L., and Bell, C. H. 1984. *Organization Development: Behavioral Science Interventions for Organization Improvement*. Englewood Cliffs, NJ: Prentice-Hall.

Friedman, T. 1989. *From Beirut to Jerusalem*. New York: Farrar Straus Giroux.

Frizell, R. N., and Gellermann, W. 1988. "Integrating the Human and Business Dimensions of Management and Organization Development." In *The Practice of Management Development*. Edited by S. Mailick, S. Hoberman, and S. Wall. New York: Praeger.

Gagne, R. M. 1970. *The Conditions of Learning*. New York: Holt, Rinehart and Winston.

Gagne, R. M., and Briggs, L. J. 1979. *Principles of Instructional Design*. 2nd ed. New York: Holt, Rinehart and Winston.

Galagan, P. A. 1989. "Mapping Its Patterns and Periods." *Training and Development Journal* November.

———. 1990. "Execs Go Global, Literally." *Training and Development Journal* June.

Gall, A. L. 1987. "You Can Take the Manager out of the Woods, but. . . ." *Training and Development Journal* March.

Gannon, M. J. 1975. "Attitudes of Government Executives Toward Management Training." *Public Personnel Management* January/February.

Gardner, J. E. 1987. *Choosing Effective Development Programs*. New York: Quorum Books.

George, Claude S. 1972. *The History of Management Thought*. 2nd ed. Englewood Cliffs, NJ: Prentice-Hall.

Georgenson, D. L. 1982. "The Problem of Transfer Calls for Partnership." *Training and Development Journal* October.

Giles, D. E. 1990. "Dewey's Theory of Experience: Implications for Service-Learning." In J. C. Kendall and Associates, *Combining Service and Learning*. Raleigh, NC: National Society for Internships and Experiential Learning.

Gilmore, T. N. 1988. *Making a Leadership Change*. San Francisco: Jossey-Bass.

Gleick, J. 1987. *Chaos*. New York: Penguin Books.

Goffman, E. 1961. *Asylums*. Garden City, NY: Doubleday Anchor.

Gold, K. A. 1982. "Managing for Success: A Comparison of the Private and Public Sectors." *Public Administration Review* November/December.

Goleman, D. 1988. *New York Times*. February 7.

Gordon, R. A., and Howell, J. E. 1959. *Higher Education for Business*. New York: Columbia University Press.

Goscinski, J. "New Techniques of Training for Managers in the Polish Management Development Center and Other Training Centers in Socialist Countries." In *The Making of the Manager*. Edited by S. Mailick. Garden City, NY: Anchor Doubleday.

Grayson, C., and O'Dell, C. 1988. *American Business: A Two Minute Warning*. New York: The Free Press.

Grider, D., Capps, C., and Tooms, L. 1988. "Evaluation Evaluation." *Training and Development Journal* November.

Guglielmino, P. J. 1987. "Developing the Top-Level Executive for the 1980's and Beyond." *Training and Development Journal* April.

Guild, P. B., and Garger, S. 1985. *Marching to Different Drummers*. Alexandria, VA: Association for Supervision and Curriculum Development.

Gulick, L. H., and Urwick, L., eds. 1937. *Papers on the Science of Administration*. New York: Institute of Public Administration.

Gurin, A., and Williams, D. 1973. "Social Work Education." In J. C. Hughes et al., *Education for the Professions of Medicine, Law, Theology and Social Work*. New York: McGraw-Hill.

Gutteridge, T. G. 1986. "Organizational Career Development Systems: The State of the Practice." In *Career Development in Organizations*. Edited by D. T. Hall. San Francisco: Jossey-Bass.

Hadamard, J. 1954. *The Psychology of Invention in the Mathematical Field*. New York: Dover.

Hall, D. T., ed. 1986. *Career Development in Organizations*. San Francisco: Jossey-Bass.

Hamblin, A. C. 1974. *Evaluation and Control of Training*. New York: McGraw-Hill.

Hamilton, S. F., and Hamilton, M. A. 1989. "Teaching and Learning on the Job: A Framework for Assessing Workplaces as Learning Environments." Unpublished paper prepared under contract with the U.S. Department of Labor.

Hampshire, S. 1990. "Spinoza and the Happy Few." *The New York Review of Books* May 17.

Harno, A. J. 1953. *Legal Education in the United States*. San Francisco: Bancroft Whitney.

Harrison, C. 1989. *Career Development in the Workplace*. ERIC Digest 86. Columbus: Center on Education and Training for Employment, Ohio State University.

Hauser, W. L. 1988. "Pfizer's 'Environment of Opportunity.' " In *The Practice of Management Development*. Edited by S. Mailick, S. Hoberman, and S. Wall. New York: Praeger.

Hays, C. L. 1988. "Views Collide over Changes at Yale." *New York Times*, November 9.

Helgesen, S. 1990. "The Pyramid and the Web." *New York Times*, May 27.

Henderson, D. E. 1985. "Enlightened Mentoring: A Characteristic of Public Administration Professionalism." *Public Administration Review* November/December.

Herbert, G. R., and Doverspike, D. 1990. "Performance Appraisal in the Training Needs Analysis Process: A Review and Critique." *Public Personnel Management* Fall.

Hersey, P., and Blanchard, K. H. 1969. "Life Cycle Theory of Leadership." *Training and Development Journal* May.

———. 1977. *Management of Organizational Behavior: Utilizing Human Resources*. Englewood Cliffs, NJ: Prentice-Hall.

Herzberg, F. 1966. *Work and the Nature of Man*. Cleveland: World Publishing.

Hilliard, J. 1970. "The Relevance of Medical Education to Medical Practice." *Journal of the American Medical Association* June.

Hobbes, T. 1905. *The Metaphysical System of Hobbes*. Selected by M. W. Calkins. Chicago: Open Court.

Hoberman, S. 1984. "Current Concerns and Trends in Management Development." Paper given at a New York University workshop for training and development specialists.

———. 1990. "Organizational Variables and Management Development." *Public Personnel Management* Summer.

Hoberman, S., and Mailick, S. 1988. "Learning Inducted from Experience (LIFE)." In *The Practice of Management Development*. Edited by S. Mailick, S. Hoberman, and S. Wall. New York: Praeger.

Hogarth, R. M. 1979. *Evaluating Management Education*. New York: Wiley.

Hollenbeck, G. P., and Ingols, C. A. 1990. "What's the Takeaway?" *Training and Development Journal* July.

Holloway, D. 1990. "The Catastrophe and After" [a review of *The Legacy of Chernobyl* by Z. A. Medvedev]. *New York Review of Books*, July 19.

Hornstein, H. A., and Mackenzie, F. T. 1984. "Consultraining: Merging Management Education with Organizational Development." *Training and Development Journal* January.

Horowitz, J., and Kimpel, H. 1988. "Taking Control: Techniques for the Group Interview." *Training and Development Journal* October.

Hughes, E. C., Thorne, B., DeBaggis, A.M., Gurin, A., and Williams, D. 1973. *Education for the Professions of Medicine, Law, Theology and Social Work*. New York: McGraw-Hill.

Huizinga, J. 1955. *Homo Ludens*. Boston: Beacon Press.

Huseman, R. C., and Hatfield, J. D. 1990. "Equity Theory and the Managerial Matrix." *Training and Development Journal* April.

Hutchings, P., and Wutzdorff, A., eds. 1988. *Knowing and Doing: Learning Through Experience*. San Francisco: Jossey-Bass.

Ibn Khaldun. 1967. *The Mugaddimah, an Introduction to History*. Translated from the Arabic by Franz Rosenthal. 2nd ed. Princeton, NJ: Princeton University Press.

Imel, S. 1982. "Guidelines for Working with Adult Learners." ERIC Fact Sheet no. 25. Columbus: National Center for Research in Vocational Education, Ohio State University.

———. 1989. "Teaching Adults: Is It Different?" ERIC Digest no. 82. Columbus: Center on Education and Training for Employment, Ohio State University.

Isenberg, D. J. 1984. "How Senior Managers Think." *Harvard Business Review* November–December.

Jaccaci, A. T. 1989. "The Social Architecture of a Learning Culture." *Training and Development Journal* November.

Jacobs, R. L. 1987. *Human Performance Technology: A Systems Based Field for the Training and Development Profession*. Columbus: National Center for Research on Vocational Education, Ohio State University.

Jacques, E. 1979. "Taking Time Seriously in Evaluating Jobs." *Harvard Business Review* September–October.

Jason, H. 1970. "The Relevance of Medical Education to Medical Practice." *Journal of the American Medical Association* June.

Jennings, E. T. 1989. "Accountability, Program Quality, Outcome Assessment, and Graduate Education for Public Affairs and Administration." *Public Administration Review* September/October.

Johnson, J. S., and Associates. 1986. *Educating Managers*. San Francisco: Jossey-Bass.

Kakabadse, A., and Mukhi, S. 1984. *The Future of Management Education*. New York: Nichols.

Kaplan, A. 1964. *The Conduct of Inquiry*. San Francisco: Chandler.

Katz, D., and Kahn, R. L. 1978. *The Social Psychology of Organizations*. 2nd ed. New York: Wiley.

Kaufman, H. 1985. *Time, Chance, and Organizations: Natural Selection in a Perilous Environment*. Chatham, NJ: Chatham House.

Kearsley, G., and Compton, T. 1981. "Assessing Costs, Benefits and Productivity in Training Systems." *Training and Development Journal* January.

Keeton, M., and Associates. 1976. *Experiential Learning: History, Rationale, Assessment*. San Francisco: Jossey-Bass.

Kendall, J. C., and Associates. 1990. *Combining Service and Learning*. Raleigh, NC: National Society for Internships and Experiential Education.

Kepner, C., and Tregoe, B. 1960. "Developing Decision Makers." *Harvard Business Review* September–October.

———. 1965. *The Rational Manager*. New York: McGraw-Hill.

Kiel, L. D. 1989. "Nonequilibrium Theory and Its Implications for Public Administration." *Public Administration Review* November/December.

Kirkpatrick, D. L. 1979. "Techniques for Evaluating Training Programs." *Training and Development Journal* June.

———. 1986. "Performance Appraisal: Your Questions Answered." *Training and Development Journal*. May.

———. 1987. "Evaluation." In *Training and Development Handbook*. Edited by R. L. Craig. 3rd ed. New York: McGraw-Hill.

———. 1988. "Supervisory and Management Development: Update from an Expert." *Training and Development Journal* August.

Klauss, R. 1981. "Formalized Mentor Relationships for Management and Executive Development Programs in the Federal Government." *Public Administration Review* 41:489–496, July/August.

Knowles, M. S. 1975. *Self-Directed Learning: A Guide for Learners and Teachers*. Chicago: Association Press.

———. 1980a. "The Magic of Contract Learning." *Training and Development Journal. June.*

———. *1980b. The Modern Practice of Adult Education: Andragogy vs. Pedagogy*. Rev. ed. New York: Association Press.

———. 1984a. *Andragogy in Action: Applying Modern Principles of Adult Learning*. San Francisco: Jossey-Bass.

———. 1984b. *The Adult Learner: A Neglected Species*. 3rd ed. Houston: Gulf Publishing.

———. 1987. "Enhancing HRD with Contract Learning." *Training and Development Journal*. March.

———. 1989. *The Making of an Adult Educator*. San Francisco: Jossey-Bass.

Knudson, R. S. 1980. "An Alternative Approach to the Andragogy/Pedagogy Issue." *Lifelong Learning: The Adult Years* April.

Kolb, D. A. 1984. Experiential Learning. *Experience as the Source of Learning and Development*. Englewood Cliffs, NJ: Prentice-Hall.

Komanecky, A. N. 1988. "Developing New Managers at GE." *Training and Development Journal* June.

Kondrasuk, J. 1979. "The Best Method to Train Managers." *Training and Development Journal* August.

Koontz, H. and C. O'Donnell. 1976. *A Book of Readings*. Englewood Cliffs, NJ: Prentice-Hall.

Koprowski, R. L. 1988. "Culture Change at Chase." In *The Practice of Management Development*. Edited by S. Mailick, S. Hoberman, and S. Wall. New York: Praeger.

Korman, A. K. 1966. "Consideration, 'Initiating Structure,' and Organizational Criteria—Review." *Personnel Psychology: A Journal of Applied Research* 19(4).

Koteen, J. 1989. *Strategic Management in Public and Nonprofit Organizations*. New York: Praeger.

Kotter, J. P. 1990. *A Force for Change*. New York: The Free Press.

Kraft, R. J., and Kielsmeier, J., eds. 1985. *Experiential Education and the Schools*. Boulder, CO: Association for Experiential Education.

Kram, K. E. 1988. *Mentoring at Work: Developmental Relationships in Organizational Life*. Lanham, MD: University Press of America.

Kur, C. E. 1981. "OD: Perspectives, Processes and Prospects." *Training and Development Journal* April.

Lawrence, P. R., and Lorsch, J. W. 1969. *Organization and Environment*. Homewood, IL: Richard D. Irwin.

Lawrie, J. 1987. "How to Establish a Mentoring Program." *Training and Development Journal* March.

Leibowitz, Z. B., Farren, C., and Kaye, B. 1981. "The 12-Fold Path to CD Enlightenment." *Training and Development Journal* July.

Lepsinger, R., Mullen, T. P., Stumpf, S. A., and Wall, S. J. 1988. "Large Scale Management Simulations: A Training Technology for Assessing and Developing Strategic Management Skills." In *The Practice of Management Development*. Edited by S. Mailick, S. Hoberman, and S. Wall. New York: Praeger.

Lewin, K. 1951. *Field Theory in Social Sciences*. New York: Harper & Row.

Likert, R. 1961. *New Patterns of Management*. New York: McGraw-Hill.

———. 1967. *The Human Organization*. New York: McGraw-Hill.

Lippitt, G. 1982. "A Dialogue with Gordon Lippitt." *Training and Development Journal* January.

Livingston, J. S. 1971. "The Myth of the Well-Educated Manager." *Harvard Business Review* January–February.

———. 1983. "New Trends in Applied Management Development." *Training and Development Journal* January.

Locke, R. R. 1989. *Management and Higher Education Since 1940: The Influence of America and Japan on West Germany, Great Britain, and France*. New York: Cambridge University Press.

Lombardo, M. M., and McCall, M. W. 1983. "Great Truths That May Not Be." *Issues and Observations* February.

Long, Carl D. 1988. "Establishing New Directions with Senior Management." In *The Practice of Management Development*. Edited by S. Mailick, S. Hoberman, and S. Wall. New York: Praeger.

Lowy, A., Kelleher, D., and Finestone, P. 1986. "Management Learning: Beyond Program Design." *Training and Development Journal* 40:34–37, June.

Lukaszewski, J. E. 1988. "Behind the Throne: How to Coach and Counsel Executives." *Training and Development Journal* October.

Lusterman, S. 1977. *Education in Industry, a Research Report*. New York: The Conference Board.

———. 1985. *Trends in Corporate Education and Training*. New York: The Conference Board.

McCall, M. W., Lombardo, M. M., and Morrison, A. M. 1988. *The Lessons of Experience: How Successful Executives Develop on the Job*. Lexington, MA: Lexington Books.

McEvoy, G. M., and Buller, P. F. 1990. "Five Uneasy Pieces in the Training Evaluation Puzzle." *Training and Development Journal* August.

McGregor, D. 1960. *The Human Side of Enterprise*. New York: McGraw-Hill.

McLagan, P. A. 1989. "Models for HRD Practice." *Training and Development Journal* September.

McNulty, N. G. 1979. "Management Development by Action Learning." *Training and Development Journal* March.

Machiavelli, N. 1964. *The Prince*. New York: Appleton-Century-Crofts.

Mager, R. F. 1968. *Developing Attitude Toward Learning*. Belmont, CA: Fearon Pitman.
———. 1972. *Goal Analysis*. Belmont, CA: Fearon Pitman.
———. 1973. *Measuring Instructional Intent*. Belmont, CA: Fearon Pitman.
———. 1975. *Preparing Instructional Objectives*. Belmont, CA: Fearon Pitman.
Mager, R. F., and Beach, K. M. 1967. *Developing Vocational Instruction*. Belmont, CA: Fearon Pitman.
Mager, R. F., and Pipe, P. 1970. *Analyzing Performance Problems*. Belmont, CA: Fearon Pitman.
Mackenzie, W.J.M. 1967. *Politics and Social Science*. Baltimore: Penguin.
Mailick, S., ed. 1974. *The Making of the Manager*. Garden City, NY: Anchor/Doubleday.
Mailick, S., and Hoberman, S. 1974a. "General Considerations Regarding Managerial and Organizational Development." In *The Making of the Manager*. Edited by S. Mailick. Garden City, NY: Anchor/Doubleday.
———. 1974b. "New Techniques in Management Training: A Future Perspective." In *The Making of the Manager*. Edited by S. Mailick. Garden City, NY: Anchor/Doubleday.
Mailick, S., Hoberman, S., and Wall, S., eds. 1988. *The Practice of Management Development*. New York: Praeger.
Mansfield, H. C. 1989. *Taming the Prince: The Ambivalence of Modern Executive Power*. New York: The Free Press.
March, J., and Simon, H. *Organizations*. New York: Wiley.
Marshak, R. J. 1983. "Cognitive and Experiential Approaches to Conceptual Learning." *Training and Development Journal* 37:72–77, May.
Martin, D. W. 1987. "Déjà vu: French Antecedents of American Public Administration." *Public Administration Review* 47(4): July/August.
Maslow, A. H. 1954. *Motivation and Personality*. New York: Harper and Row.
Mayrides, E. 1984. "Emerging Trends in the Field of Management Development." Unpublished paper. New York University.
Merriam, S. B. 1984. *Adult Development: Implications for Adult Education*. Columbus: National Center for Research in Vocational Education, Ohio State University.
Messick, S., ed. 1976. *Individuality in Learning*. San Francisco: Jossey-Bass.
Michels, R. 1949. *Political Parties*. New York: Free Press.
Miguel, R. J. 1979. *Work-Centered and Person-Centered Dimensions of Experiential Education: Implications for a Typology of Programs*. Columbus: National Center for Research in Vocational Education, Ohio State University.
Miles, M. B. 1989. *Learning to Work in Groups*. New York: Teachers College, Columbia University.
Miles, R. E. 1975. *Theories of Management: Implications for Organizational Behavior and Development*. New York: McGraw-Hill.
Miller, D. B. 1981. "Training Managers to Stimulate Employee Training." *Training and Development Journal* February.
Mintzberg, H. 1973. *The Nature of Managerial Work*. New York: Harper & Row.
———. 1989. *Mintzberg on Management*. New York: The Free Press.
MIT Commission on Industrial Productivity. 1989. *Made in America: Regaining the Productive Edge*. Cambridge, MA: MIT Press.

Mohr, L. B. 1988. *Impact Analysis for Program Evaluation*. Pacific Grove, CA: Brooks/Cole.

Moore, D. T. 1990. "Experiential Education as Critical Discourse." In J. C. Kendall and Associates, *Combining Service and Learning*. Raleigh, NC: National Society for Internships and Experiential Learning.

Moore, M., and Gergen, P. 1985. "Risk Taking and Organizational Change." *Training and Development Journal* June.

Mouton, J., and Blake, R. R. 1984. "Principles and Designs for Enhancing Learning." *Training and Development Journal* 38:60–63, December.

Mumford, A. 1980. *Making Experience Pay: Management Success Through Effective Learning*. London: McGraw-Hill.

Nadler, L. 1983. *Human Resource Development: The Perspective of Business and Industry*. Columbus: National Center for Research in Vocational Education, Ohio State University.

Napier, N. K., and Deller, J. 1985. "Train Right or Don't Train at All." *Training and Development Journal* February.

Naylor, M. 1985. *Adult Development Implications for Adult Education*. ERIC Digest no. 14. Columbus: Center for Education and Training for Employment, Ohio State University.

Newell, T., Wolf, J., and Dexler, A. 1988. "Rescuing Training: Joining Learning and Application in a Federal Agency Training Program." *Public Personnel Management* 17(3).

Newstrom, J. W. 1987. "Confronting Anomalies in Evaluation." *Training and Development Journal* July.

New York Times Book Review. 1990. October 29.

Noe, R. A., and Schmitt, N. 1986. "The Influence of Trainee Attitudes on Training Effectiveness: Test of a Model." *Personnel Psychology* 39.

Odiorne, G. S. 1969. *Management by Objectives*. Englewood Cliffs, NJ: Prentice-Hall.

———. 1985. "The Hard Technologies of Training." *Training and Development Journal* October.

———. 1987. *The Human Side of Management: Management by Integration and Self-Control*. Lexington, MA: Lexington Books.

O'Neill, P. E. 1990. "Transforming Managers for Organizational Change." *Training and Development Journal* July.

O'Rourke, P. J. 1990. Book review. *New York Times*, October 29.

Palumbo, D. J. 1987. Introduction to "Symposium: Implementation: What We Have Learned and Still Need to Know." *Policy Studies Review* 7(1).

Parker, B. L. 1986. *Summative Evaluation in Training and Development*. Bloomington, MN: Process Management Institute; Minneapolis: Training and Development Research Center, University of Minnesota.

Parry, S. B., and Robinson, E. J. 1979. "Management Development: Training or Education." *Training and Development Journal* July.

Peirce, C. S. 1957. *Essays in the Philosophy of Science*. Edited by A. Rosin. New York: Liberal Arts Press.

Perrow, C. 1979. *Complex Organizations*. Glenview, IL: Scott, Foresman.

Peters, T. 1987. *Thriving on Chaos. Handbook for a Management Revolution*. New York: Alfred A. Knopf.

Peters, T., and Waterman, R. H., Jr. 1982. *In Search of Excellence. Lessons from America's Best-Run Companies*. New York: Harper & Row.

Pfeffer, J., and Salancik, G. R. 1978. *The External Control of Organizations*. New York: Harper & Row.

Piaget, J. 1971. *Psychology and Epistemology*. Harmondsworth, England: Penguin.

Pierson, F. C. 1959. *The Education of American Businessmen*. New York: McGraw-Hill.

Pigors, P., and Pigors, F. 1961. *The Case Method in Human Relations*. New York: McGraw-Hill.

Pincus, W. 1971. "The Clinical Component in University Professional Education." *Ohio State Law Journal*, Spring, 32.

———. 1980. *Clinical Education for Law Students*. Meilen Press.

Plant, R., and Ryan, M. 1988. "Managing Your Corporate Culture." *Training and Development Journal* September.

Plato. 1930. *The Works of Plato*. Edited by Irwin Erdman. New York: Modern Library.

Poe, R. 1990. "Company Shows Face the Music." *New York Times Magazine*, June 10.

Poincaré, H. 1952. *Science and Method*. Translated by F. Maitland. New York: Dover.

Porter, L. M., and McKibbin, L. E. 1988. *Management Education and Development: Drift or Thrust into the 21st Century*? New York: McGraw-Hill.

Porter, M. E. 1990. "Japan Isn't Playing by Different Rules." *New York Times*, financial section, July 22.

Pressman, J., and Wildavsky, A. 1984. *Implementation*. Berkeley: University of California Press.

Pugh, D. S., Hickson, D. J., and Hinnings, C. R., eds. 1985. *Writers on Organizations*. Beverly Hills, CA: Sage.

Rachal, J. 1983. "The Adragogy-Pedagogy Debate: Another Voice in the Fray." *Lifelong Learning: The Adult Years* May.

Rader, M., and Wunsch, L. P. 1980. "A Survey of Communication Practices and Business School Graduates by Job Category and Undergraduate Majors." *Journal of Business Communication* Summer.

Ralphs, L. T., and Stephan, E. 1986. "HRD in the Fortune 500." *Training and Development Journal* 69–76, October.

Resnick, L. B. 1987. "Learning in School and out." *Educational Researcher* 9.

Revans, R. 1974. "The Project Method: Learning by Doing." In *The Making of the Manager*. Edited by S. Mailick. Garden City, NY: Anchor Doubleday.

Reymond, H., and Mailick, S. 1985. *International Personnel Policies and Practices*. New York: Praeger.

Rhinesmith, S. H., Williamson, J. N., Ehlen, D. M., and Maxwell, D. S. 1989. "Developing Leaders for the Global Enterprise." *Training and Development Journal* April.

Rinke, W. J. 1985. "Holistic Education: An Answer." *Training and Development Journal* August.

Roback, T. H. 1989. "Personnel Research Perspectives on Human Resource Management and Development." *Public Personnel Management* Summer.

Robinson, D. G., and Robinson, J. C. 1989. *Training for Impact*. San Francisco: Jossey-Bass.

Rothman, J., and Jones, W. 1971. *A New Look at Field Instruction: Education for Application of Practice Skills in Community Organization and Social Planning*. New York: Association Press.

Rutman, L., ed. 1977. *Evaluation Research Methods: A Basic Guide*. Beverly Hills, CA: Sage.

———. 1980. *Planning Useful Evaluations*. Beverly Hills, CA: Sage.

Saari, L., Johnson, T., McLaughlin, S., and Zimmerle, D. 1988. "A Survey of Management Training and Education Practices in U.S. Companies." *Personnel Psychology* 41.

Sacks, O. 1990. "Neurology and the Soul." *The New York Review of Books*, November 22.

Sashkin, M. 1986. "True Vision in Leadership." *Training and Development Journal* May.

Safire, W. 1989. "How 'Managing' Is Managing." *New York Times Magazine*, February 19.

Sampson, R. 1953. "Train Executives While They Work." *Harvard Business Review* November–December.

Saint, A. M. 1980. "Bringing Training-Learning Concepts into the Classroom." *Training and Development Journal* December.

Saunders, W. J. 1988. "Establishing a Centralized Training Facility." In *The Practice of Management Development*. Edited by S. Mailick, S. Hoberman, and S. Wall. New York: Praeger.

Saxe, S. 1988. "Peer Influence and Learning." *Training and Development Journal* June.

Schein, E. H. *Organizational Culture and Leadership* 1985. San Francisco: Jossey-Bass.

———. 1986. "What You Need to Know About Organizational Culture." *Training and Development Journal* January.

Schein, E. H., and Bennis, W. G. 1965. *Personal and Organizational Change Through Group Methods*. New York: Wiley.

Scribner, S. 1984. "Studying Working Intelligence." In *Everyday Cognition: Its Development in Social Context*. Edited by B. Rogoff and J. Lave. Cambridge, MA: Harvard University Press.

Seaman, D. F. 1977. *Adult Education Teaching Techniques*. Information Series no. 110. Columbus: National Center for Research in Vocational Education, Ohio State University.

Settle, Mary E. 1988. "Developing Tomorrow's Managers." *Training and Development Journal* April.

Shannon, L. R. 1990. "Peripherals." *New York Times*, March 27.

Shangraw, R. F., and Crow, M. M. 1989. "Public Administration as a Design Science." *Public Administration Review* March/April.

Schneier, C. 1986. "How to Construct a Successful Performance Appraisal System," *Training and Development Journal* April.

Silverman, D. 1971. *The Theory of Organizations*. New York: Basic Books.

Simon, H. 1947. "A Comment on 'The Science of Public Administration'." *Public Administration Review* Summer.

———. 1957. *Administrative Behavior*. 2nd ed. New York: The Free Press.
———. 1969. *Sciences of the Artificial*. Cambridge, MA: M.I.T. Press.
———. 1973. "Applying Information Technology to Organization Design." *Public Administration Review* May–June.
Simpson, J. 1990. "Visioning: More Than Meets the Eye." *Training and Development Journal* September.
Skinner, B. F. 1948. *Walden Two*. New York: MacMillan.
———. 1971. *Beyond Freedom and Dignity*. New York: Knopf.
Slavenski, L. 1987. "Career Development: A Systems Approach." *Training and Development Journal* February.
Sleezer, C. M., ed. 1989. *Improving HRD Through Measurement*. Baltimore: ASTD Publishing Service.
Smith, P. J., and Peterson, M. F. 1988. *Leadership, Organizations, and Culture*. London: Sage.
Smith, R. 1982. *Learning How to Learn: Applied Theory for Adults*. Chicago: Follett.
Smythe, O. 1990. "Practical Experience and the Liberal Arts: A Philosophical Perspective." In J. C. Kendall and Associates, *Combining Service and Learning*. Raleigh, NC: National Society for Internships and Experiential Education.
Sorcher, M. 1985. *Predicting Executive Success: What It Takes to Make It into Senior Management*. New York: Wiley.
Spiro, J. D. 1979. "Evaluation of the Modular Preceptor Training Method as in NYU's Doctoral Program in Mental Health Policy and Administration." Master's thesis, New York University.
Stowell, S. J. 1988. "Coaching: A Commitment to Leadership." *Training and Development Journal* June.
Stroul, N. A., and Schuman, G. 1983. "Action Planning for Workshops." *Training and Development Journal* July.
Struening, E. L., and Guttentag, M. 1979. *Handbook of Evaluation Research*. Beverly Hills, CA: Sage.
Suchman, E. A. 1967. *Evaluative Research*. New York: Russell Sage Foundation.
Sutton, E. E., and McQuigg-Martinez, B. 1990. "The Development Partnership: Managing Skills for the Future." *Training and Development Journal* April.
Szasz, T. S. 1961. *The Myth of Mental Illness*. New York: Harper & Row.
Tapuach, P. 1980. "An Evaluation of Israel's Staff College." Masters's thesis, Graduate School of Public Administration, New York University.
Taylor, M. S., Giannantonio, C. M., and Brown, J. S. 1989. "Participants' Reactions to Special Assignment Programs: Favorability and Predictors." *Public Personnel Management* Winter.
This, L. E., and Lippitt, G. 1979. "Learning Theories and Training." *Training and Development Journal* June.
Thompson, J. D. 1967. *Organizations in Action*. New York: McGraw-Hill.
Thompson, J. T. 1981. "Helping Line Managers to Be Change Agents." *Training and Development Journal* April.
Thompson, M. Z. 1981. *An Evaluation of Management Development Programs*. Rock Island, IL: U.S. Army Engineering Training Activity.
Thomson, R. 1959. *The Psychology of Thinking*. Baltimore: Penguin Books.
Thorne, B. 1973. "Professional Education in Medicine." In E. C. Hughes et al.,

Education for the Professions of Medicine, Law, Theology and Social Work. New York: McGraw-Hill.

Thurow, L. C., ed. 1985. *The Management Challenge: Japanese Views*. Cambridge, MA: M.I.T. Press.

Tocqueville, A. de. 1945. *Democracy in America*. Edited and translated by George Lawrence. Vols. 1 and 2. New York: Knopf.

Toppins, A. D. 1989. "Research of HRD Research." *Training and Development Journal* October.

Tragash, H. J. 1988. "Reinforcing Learning on the Job: The Role of the Manager." In *The Practice of Management Development*. Edited by S. Mailick, S. Hoberman, and S. Wall. New York: Praeger.

Tregoe, B. B. and Zimmerman, J. W. 1980. *Top Management Strategy*. New York: Simon and Schuster.

United Nations, Department of Economic and Social Affairs, Public Administration Division. 1969. *Appraising Administrative Capability for Development*. New York: United Nations.

Useem, M. 1989. *Liberal Education and the Corporation: The Hiring and Advancement of College Graduates*. Hawthorne, NY: Walter De Gruyter.

Vancil, R. 1988. "Passing the Baton." *New York Times*, March 3.

VanGrundy, A. B. 1987. *Creative Problem Solving: A Guide for Trainers and Management*. Westport, CT: Quorum Books.

Veltrop, B., and Harrington, K. 1988. "Roadmap to New Organizational Territory." *Training and Development Journal* June.

Verlander, E. G. 1988. "Executive Transformation Programs." *Training and Development Journal* December.

Vertz, L. 1985. "Women, Occupational Advancement, and Mentoring: An Analysis of One Public Organization." *Public Administration Review* May/June.

Vroom, V. H. 1964. *Work and Motivation*. New York: Wiley.

Wall, S. J., and Ondrasik, A. L. 1988. "Determining Managerial Training and Development Needs." In *The Practice of Management Development*. Edited by S. Mailick, S. Hoberman, and S. Wall. New York: Praeger.

Wallach, E. J. 1983. "Individuals and Organizations." *Training and Development Journal* February.

Walle, A. 1968. Unpublished paper prepared for workshop "The Learning Process and Teaching Methods." Egelund, Denmark, June 16–19.

Weick, K. E. 1969. *The Social Psychology of Organizing*. Reading, MA: Addison-Wesley.

Wexley, K. N., and Baldwin, T. T. 1986. "Post-training Strategies for Facilitating Positive Transfer: An Empirical Exploration." *Academy of Management Journal* September.

Wexley, K. N., and Latham, G. P. 1981. *Developing and Training Human Resources in Organizations*. Glenview, IL: Scott, Foresman.

Whitehead, A. N. 1953. *Science and the Modern World*. New York: New American Library.

Whitehead, A. N. 1955. *The Aims of Education and Other Essays*. New York: New American Library.

———. 1958. *An Introduction to Mathematics*. New York: Oxford University Press.

Wholey, J. S. 1979. *Evaluation: Promise and Performance*. Washington, DC: Urban Institute.

Wilbur, J. 1986. *Mentoring and Achievement Motivation as Predictors of Career Success*. Downers Grove, IL: Service Master Industries.

Wilkinson, H. E., and Orth, C. D. 1986. "Toning the Soft Side." *Training and Development Journal* March.

Will, G. F. 1990. *Men at Work: The Craft of Baseball*. New York: Macmillan.

Wilson, W. 1941. "The Study of Administration." *Political Science Quarterly* December.

Witherell, C. S., and Erickson, V. L. "Teacher Education as Adult Education." *Theory into Practice* 17(3).

Wolf, J. F., and Sherwood, F. P. 1981. "Coaching: Supporting Public Executives on the Job." *Public Administration Review* January/February.

Wolking, W. 1971. "Management Training: Where Has It Gone Wrong?" *Training and Development Journal* December.

Wynia, B. L. 1972. "Executive Development in the Federal Government." *Public Administration Review* July/August.

Zawacki, R. A., and Warrick, D. D. 1977. *Organization Development: Managing Change in the Public Sector*. International Personnel Management Association.

Zey, M. 1984. *The Mentor Connection*. Homewood, IL: Dow Jones-Irwin.

INDEX

ABOUT THE AUTHORS

SOLOMON HOBERMAN is a management consultant and a former Personnel Director, Chairman of Civil Service Commission, Director of Training for New York City. His clients include public (all levels), non-profit, and private sector organizations. He has conducted training and research as well as published papers in mathematics, training and development, human resources, organizational theory, and experiential education.

SIDNEY MAILICK is Professor of Public Administration at the Robert F. Wagner Graduate School of Public Service of New York University, where he served as the director of the doctoral program in mental health policy and administration. Mailick has also directed executive development programs at the University of Chicago and New York University. Founder and director of Israel's Administrative Staff College, he has served as a consultant on training and development for numerous organizations, including the U.S. Department of State and the United Nations.

WITHDRAWN
From Library Collection